C000144205

THE LIFE AND DEATH OF
INTERNATIONAL TREATIES

The Life and Death of International Treaties

Double-Edged Diplomacy and the Politics of Ratification in Comparative Perspective

JEFFREY S. LANTIS

OXFORD
UNIVERSITY PRESS

OXFORD
UNIVERSITY PRESS

Great Clarendon Street, Oxford, OX2 6DP,
United Kingdom

Oxford University Press is a department of the University of Oxford.
It furthers the University's objective of excellence in research, scholarship,
and education by publishing worldwide. Oxford is a registered trade mark of
Oxford University Press in the UK and in certain other countries

© Jeffrey Lantis 2009

The moral rights of the authors have been asserted

First Edition published in 2009

All rights reserved. No part of this publication may be reproduced, stored in
a retrieval system, or transmitted, in any form or by any means, without the
prior permission in writing of Oxford University Press, or as expressly permitted
by law, by licence or under terms agreed with the appropriate reprographics
rights organization. Enquiries concerning reproduction outside the scope of the
above should be sent to the Rights Department, Oxford University Press, at the
address above

You must not circulate this work in any other form
and you must impose this same condition on any acquirer

Published in the United States of America by Oxford University Press
198 Madison Avenue, New York, NY 10016, United States of America

British Library Cataloguing in Publication Data
Data available

Library of Congress Control Number: 2008027740

ISBN 978–0–19–953501–9

For Joshua and Megan

Contents

Preface and Acknowledgments

International treaties were a mainstay of international cooperation during much of the twentieth century. Great powers employed treaties to institutionalize commitments in both good times and bad. Treaties became especially important diplomatic instruments to help draw the superpowers back from the brink during the Cold War.

Treaty negotiations, ratification, and implementation have never been easy, but the post-commitment political process appears more controversial than ever in the twenty-first century. Multilateral treaty negotiations such as the World Trade Organization's Doha Round illustrate the incredible challenge of finding common ground for hundreds of state actors. The Doha Round was initiated in 2001 as a way to focus on economic development. As of this writing, however, governments appear no closer to an agreement to lower tariff barriers to trade due, in part, to sharp constraints on their behavior originating in the domestic arena. These concerns are not isolated to trade negotiations. A similar dynamic has prevented some countries from ratifying and implementing recent treaties such as the Lisbon Treaty on European Integration, the Convention on the Elimination of All Forms of Discrimination Against Women (CEDAW), the United Nations Convention on the Law of the Sea, and the Framework Convention on Tobacco Control. Domestic constraints are also limiting progress in discussions underway on treaties to cut off production of fissile materials, extend the Kyoto agreement to lower greenhouse gas emissions, and define the rights of environmental refugees.

This investigation began with a simple premise: the ratification phase for international treaties represents the true legislative phase of world politics and can profoundly impact prospects for cooperation. Since ratification processes in advanced industrialized democracies have become the most standardized and transparent, they were a logical point of focus for the study. What I quickly learned was that there are hundreds, perhaps thousands, of cases where the success or failure of international cooperation has hinged on the outcome of dramas playing out in the post-commitment political phases in democracies. There are many more near-failures of international treaties than one might imagine, and these struggles can change the political climate and shape subsequent treaty negotiations. Yet it is only the final outcomes of ratification processes that are typically reported (if at all). This book sheds light on these dilemmas of "double-edged diplomacy" by examining international treaty ratification in comparative perspective.

This study is the product of more than eight years of research, and I am indebted to a number of institutions and individuals for their support. First, I thank colleagues at The College of Wooster for their encouragement and interest in my project. I received three separate research leaves from the College that provided me valuable time to complete the book. I am also indebted to the College's Henry Luce III Scholarship Fund for support of my field research in Bonn, Germany, and Ottawa, Canada. In addition, I would like to acknowledge valuable research assistance from Kimberly Chin-See, Lois Ribich, Steven Schott, Lauren Schreur, and Lara Pfaff. These talented students helped me to gather data on ratification struggles and offered their own perspectives on the dynamics at work.

I am honored to have received a J. William Fulbright Senior Scholar Award to conduct a final round of research in Australia in 2007. I served as a Fulbright Visiting Fellow with joint appointments in the Department of International Relations in the Research School of Pacific and Asian Studies at the Australian National University and the School of Social Sciences and International Studies at the University of New South Wales. I am indebted to Christian Reus-Smit, Chair of the Department of International Relations at ANU, for his helpful comments and the opportunity to interact with many fine colleagues in the department. I also thank members of the Politics and International Relations programs at UNSW, including Shirley Scott, Anthony Burke, and Marc Williams, for their friendship and insights. Colleagues in the School of Political Science at the University of Melbourne, especially Ann Capling and Robyn Eckersley, offered many helpful suggestions that enriched this study. Finally, the Fulbright Commission staff, including Mark Darby and Lyndell Wilson, were terrific sponsors. I am truly impressed by their dedication to the promotion of international educational and cultural exchange.

My work as a Visiting Scholar at the Deutsche Gesellschaft für Auswärtige Politik (German Council on Foreign Relations) was a formative experience, and I appreciate the support of past directors Karl Kaiser and Hanns Maull. I also served as Visiting Scholar at the Norman Paterson School of International Affairs (NPSIA) at Carleton University in Ottawa. There I received helpful suggestions from Maureen Appel-Molot, Fen Osler Hampson, Bruce Doern, Brian Tomlin, and many others. Overall, the field experiences afforded me the opportunity to speak with dozens of policymakers, experts, and observers of treaty-ratification struggles. While most of my subjects spoke on background, I have nevertheless endeavored to bring their perspectives to the case studies.

In addition, I would like to express my gratitude to many colleagues and friends who have offered suggestions on the study. They include Julie Kaarbo, Charles Hermann, Kent Kille, Matt Krain, Karen Beckwith, Steven Bernstein, Madelaine Chiam, Loren Cass, James McCormick, Dan Caldwell,

Lisa Martin, Christian Reus-Smit, Steve Hook, David Auerswald, James Scott, Darryl Howlett, Kerry Kartchner, Chris Twomey, Ralph Carter, and many others.

My editor, Dominic Byatt, has been supportive of the project from the start, and I have enjoyed working with the fine editorial staff at Oxford University Press. I also appreciate helpful comments from anonymous reviewers who guided me toward refinement of the arguments in the book. Needless to say, any errors in the manuscript remain my own.

Finally, I would like to thank my family. My parents, Paul and Patricia Lantis, have provided steadfast support for my work for more than forty years. John and Linda Crouch also have devoted a great deal of their time and energy to support our family. My children, Joshua and Megan Lantis, inspire me everyday. I dedicate this book to them. Finally, I am eternally grateful to Holly Lantis for her constant encouragement, love, and support.

June 2007 Jeffrey Lantis
Sydney, Australia

1

The Life and Death of International Treaties

I. INTRODUCTION

In the spring of 2005, voters in France and the Netherlands went to the polls and rejected the European Constitution. Government officials from European Union (EU) member states had spent years negotiating the agreement, which was designed to centralize power and improve the organizational structure of the institution. After the treaty progressed smoothly through nine European capitals, however, French voters struck it down on May 29, 2005. Three days later, voters in the Netherlands said "no" by an even stronger margin. These votes effectively killed the momentum toward intensified European integration and prompted a divisive and reflective period for the EU.

Ratification processes for international treaties appear to have become increasingly politicized in advanced industrial democracies.[1] In a number of recent cases, prime ministers and presidents have watched their struggle for ratification end in breakdowns, or near-breakdowns, of international cooperation. In the 1990s, for example, Germany was one of the primary sponsors of the Maastricht Treaty on European Union (TEU) but the last nation to ratify it because of domestic opposition. U.S. President Bill Clinton chose not to support the International Convention to Ban Landmines and the Convention on the Elimination of All Forms of Discrimination Against Women, and he witnessed the Senate rejection of the Comprehensive Nuclear Test-Ban Treaty. In 2001, President George W. Bush announced that the U.S. government would not support the Kyoto Protocol to lower greenhouse gas emissions, even though it had been ratified by more than 100 other nations. In 2004, the Australian government faced an unprecedented fight over ratification of a free trade agreement with the United States.

While the absence of any one country's support for a treaty need not mean its "death," episodes of ratification failure are often watershed events in foreign policy development. The question of why governments succeed or fail in ratifying treaties is of crucial importance. If governments cannot ratify their international commitments, a serious obstacle exists to the development of international cooperation and legal governance.

Cases examined in this book explore debates over a select number of treaties on trade cooperation, the environment, the future of the European Union, and the nuclear nonproliferation regime. A study of the politicization of international agreements also addresses an important gap in the scholarship. There are very few studies of ratification struggles that truly define the success or failure of international commitments; fewer still have studied the dynamics of ratification struggles in comparative perspective. This study sets out to investigate the role that political actors and conditions play in this crucial stage of international cooperation.[2] Finally, cases where international treaties barely attained necessary political support or were actually blocked at the ratification stage raise important research questions, including: How do the political requirements for ratification of an international agreement compare across democratic systems? What conditions influence the likelihood of ratification success? What conditions lead to failure? Why would treaty ratification processes ever fail if the chief negotiators are fully aware of domestic political constraints?

II. A SHORT HISTORY OF RATIFICATION

International treaties are public, legal mechanisms by which states demonstrate their commitment to address common problems. Treaties can be bilateral (completed between two states) or multilateral (between three or more states). Scholars typically identify four, crucial stages of treaty development: the negotiation process, signature and accession, ratification, and compliance. For the purposes of this study, ratification is defined as the final, legal confirmation by a government for a treaty and "an expression of consent whereby the state assumes the rights and duties imposed by the instrument ratified."[3] Treaties typically enter into force, with the backing of international legal foundation, once they have achieved a required number of signatories and ratifications.[4]

The earliest forms of ratification of international agreements entailed the exchange of hostages or oaths, but the process became more formal in ancient Greece and the Roman Empire. In Rome, for example, "treaties usually contained the proviso subject to the ratification of the people" and were submitted to the deliberation of the Senate or to a plebiscite.[5] This tradition of gathering domestic support for treaties continued in various forms to the foundation of modern democracy. In 1789, U.S. President George Washington said that treaty ratification represented a significant "check on the mistakes and indiscretions of ministers or commissioners."[6] A century later, Woodrow Wilson, a young doctoral candidate in political economy at Johns Hopkins University, said: "[T]he greatest consultative privilege of the Senate—the greatest in dignity—is its right to a ruling voice in the ratification of treaties with foreign powers."[7] Later, President Wilson would face the power of this privilege as he struggled in vain to win Senate ratification of the Treaty of Versailles.

Most democratic states had established mechanisms for the ratification of international treaties by the twentieth century. In presidential systems such as the United States, the ratification process requires the president to submit a treaty for consideration by the Senate and a two-thirds vote in favor of the treaty. This process was modified for trade agreements through special provisions of the Trade Act of 1974, allowing treaties to also be negotiated by the executive branch and passed by a simple majority vote in both houses of Congress. Some parliamentary governments require the ratification of international agreements through votes by the legislature or popular referendums. In the few parliamentary systems where the legislature does not have a constitutional role in ratification (such as Canada and Australia), there are still requirements for implementing legislation whereby international agreements are converted into domestic laws. Prime ministers also have made political commitments to seek parliamentary endorsement of the agreements.

While there are institutional differences in ratification in democratic states, this book identifies surprisingly similar dynamics in the *political process* of treaty ratification in comparative perspective. Democratic leaders are aware that, regardless of the political system, international agreements are greatly facilitated by negotiations at home and abroad. Regional integration and intergovernmental negotiations also have fostered a sense of "oneness" in ratification processes. Today, democratic leaders recognize all too well the need for popular legitimacy in international agreements and the dangers of overcommitment. Even leaders of majoritarian parliamentary democracies have made concerted efforts to increase the role of the legislature, interest groups, and concerned citizens in the treaty process. In many ways, similarities in the ratification process have grown in accord with the increasing complexity of international agreements and intermestic issues.[8]

III. THE RATIFICATION GAME

Two-level game theory offers a valuable perspective on the complex political process of ratification. This interdisciplinary approach draws on ideas from economics, psychology, mathematics, and political science. Robert Putnam's work on two-level game theory and subsequent scholarship on double-edged diplomacy offers promise for a systematic study of treaty ratification processes in comparative perspective. Two-level games help explain the dynamics involved in international negotiations, and they challenge the realist treatment of the state as a unitary rational actor. Putnam argues that many studies of the international negotiation process focus solely on the preferences of the negotiators and their bargaining with others (at Level I), but the chief of government must also be certain that any agreement will receive the support of domestic actors (at Level II).

Putnam contends that leaders must simultaneously manage conditions at both levels of negotiation. Specifically, he suggests that success or failure of agreements is dependent upon the size of the win-set, or "the set of all possible Level I agreements that would win by gaining the necessary majority among the constituents when simply voted up or down."[9] In subsequent studies of double-edged diplomacy, scholars have developed case studies of various win-set structures in order to understand how leaders tend to act in relation to constituent pressures.[10] Win-sets may be narrow when agreements have deep costs for domestic constituents, but leaders also have the ability to manipulate the size of win-sets through sophisticated strategies at both levels of negotiation.

These studies direct needed attention to the interaction between external and internal conditions on international negotiating behavior, but important process questions remain open. Putnam and others have not systematically explained how voluntary and involuntary defections from agreements may occur, for example. The two-level game model suggests that a rational leader would not sign a treaty and subject it to ratification if he or she did not believe the agreement would receive political support back home. Indeed, Milner notes that the whole idea of "bringing home an unratifiable agreement is likely to be costly both domestically and internationally."[11] Yet, critics contend, leaders often misjudge what may be ratifiable at home. Involuntary defections can be the product of pressure from "awakened" and mobilized domestic constituencies.[12] For example, the French rejection of the European Constitution was the product of a highly mobilized opposition campaign following Chirac's call for a referendum. Conversely, leaders may oppose major international agreements in spite of overwhelming popular support. In Australia, for example, Prime Minister John Howard announced in 2001 that his government would not ratify the Kyoto Protocol in spite of the fact that more than 80 per cent of Australians supported the treaty.[13]

In addition to an absence of dimensionality in these studies, scholars have not categorically identified key actors in the ratification process or the conditions in which they may influence foreign policy decisions about cooperation. While some early works on two-level game theory frameworks acknowledge the potential latitude granted to leaders regarding the strategic use of side payments, there has been little systematic attention devoted to this theme. In addition, studies have begun to explore the democratization of the treaty process in select countries, but much of the work on domestic–international linkages proceeds inductively and fails to develop middle-range theory identifying scope conditions of cooperation. For this approach to become more refined theoretically, the specification of domestic politics (the nature of the win-sets and the study of statesman's preferences) is essential.[14]

A Conceptual Framework for the Study of Treaty Ratification

This study is founded on the assumption that cooperation is the product of a *sequential policy process* in liberal democracies—not a simultaneous alignment of domestic and international conditions, as Putnam argues. By studying the "long term outcome of individual policies at the national level," scholars can provide a useful bridge between international relations and comparative politics. For example, Jordan contends that a study of the "post-decisional" phase of European integration initiatives raises "fresh questions and interesting puzzles that have not generally been addressed by scholars of international relations."[15] In the context of this study, a leader's initial commitment to cooperate with other states (regardless of issue area) often mobilizes domestic political actors and conditions in liberal democracy and marks the beginning of the post-commitment phase. While Putnam chose to interpret two-level games as simultaneous, subsequent scholarship on double-edged diplomacy has acknowledged that the ratification of international agreements involves a longitudinal process during which leaders' strategies for ratification may evolve to reflect changing domestic and international circumstances.[16]

In the post-commitment politics phase, actors mobilize for or against elements of the agreement in relation to their particular roles, interests, and identities. These perspectives are highly significant. According to Raustiala, "the anticipated 'refraction' of common external commitments by domestic institutions helps to determine the impact of international commitments on domestic actors and politics, and political incentives structure the political costs and benefits associated with these regime impacts." During the post-commitment phase, Raustiala asserts, "what matters most are the likely effects of the political solution, not the impact of the underlying [subject of the treaty]."[17] Indeed, ratification processes in the post-commitment phase may require as much or even more time than the negotiation of the agreement itself.

This study focuses on six conditions that may influence the ratifiability of a treaty in democratic states. At the international level, considerations of the maximization of state power and normative commitments may shape ratification decisions. At the domestic level, significant conditions include executive strategies for ratification (developed by a president or prime minister), the type of electoral system (which conditions executive–legislative relations), interest group pressure, and public support. While certainly not an exclusive list, these conditions have been advanced in the scholarship on foreign policy analysis as potentially most salient and worthy of further attention. Each of these conditions may be causally linked through exploratory propositions to the dependent variable of the study, the likelihood that an international agreement will be ratified. What follows is a set of derived propositions for this study.

Proposition 1

Once a treaty has been signed, the greater the benefits in terms of national interests and maximization of state power, ceteris paribus, the more likely it is that the government will successfully ratify the treaty.

International treaties often represent both opportunities and dilemmas for conscientious government leaders. Regardless of issue area, international commitments touch on a wide range of state concerns including sovereignty, reciprocity, and the distribution of costs and benefits. The first proposition for this study reflects a structural realist (or neorealist) perspective. Some neorealists would contend that international treaties themselves are rare instruments of international cooperation. Kenneth Waltz argues, for example, that "international politics is the realm of power, struggle, and accommodation," while domestic politics "is the realm of authority, of administration, and of law."[18] Assuming that a linkage is nevertheless possible, a longitudinal analysis focused on ratification would find neorealists attending to calculations of expected costs and benefits from an agreement. National interest calculation might thus be seen as a continuous process, and decisions in the post-commitment phase would reflect interpretations of gains versus vulnerability.[19]

Two-level game theory helps to bridge the gap between international and domestic pressures relative to ratification. For example, Putnam acknowledges a role for international pressures in determining the outcome of negotiations but devotes scant attention to national interest definition in the post-commitment phase.[20] Other scholars have taken up this challenge. In a popular study of arms control treaties in the 1980s, for example, Krepon argues that the first key to understanding ratification success is gauging the extent to which an agreement provides "tangible benefits to the nation's security."[21] For this study, international cooperation is viewed as the product of absolute versus relative gains. Ratification, as a form of cooperation, may be more likely to occur in situations where the benefits to the state are perceived to outweigh the costs (i.e., situations that represent a maximization of national interests). Conversely, one would expect that more costly agreements perceived as less likely to benefit national interests, if signed at all, would not likely be ratified.

Proposition 2

The greater the level of normative pressure to cooperate, the more likely it is that the government will successfully ratify the treaty.

Constructivist international relations theory provides a very different lens through which to interpret the likelihood of treaty ratification. Beyond material constraints, constructivists argue that state identities and interests should be seen as "socially constructed by knowledgeable practice."[22] Finnemore characterizes norms as "shared expectations about appropriate behavior held by a community."[23] Scholars believe that it is important to explore the pressure on states to maintain a reputation of belonging "to a normative community of nations."[24] Constructivists also draw inspiration from international law regarding the normative basis of compliance. Where international norms overlap with international legal structures, scholars argue, there is even greater pressure for compliance. Deriving arguments from this literature vis-à-vis treaty ratification, one can posit that states are subject to varying degrees of international pressure to cooperate and that the intersubjective nature of normative pressure means that social identities influence their likelihood of cooperation.[25] Through process tracing, this study investigates how international norms and institutions may create pressure to ratify treaties.

Proposition 3

The more active and sophisticated the executive strategy for generating domestic support for an international agreement in the post-commitment phase, the more likely it is that the government will successfully ratify the treaty.

Putnam acknowledged that the chief of government could influence negotiation outcomes, yet two-level game theory has not systematically examined the role of elites in the process of international cooperation. This study posits that the ratification of international treaties often relies upon sophisticated executive strategies to gain domestic support. Given political and constitutional requirements for ratification in democratic states, executives must consider domestic political factors when formulating treaties at the Level I negotiating table. Throughout the ratification process, executives must continue to try to manage conditions at both levels—striving to maintain the state's credibility of commitments as precedent for future exchange and mutual gain, while at the same time minding the internal political situation.[26]

Scholars have suggested that at least three different executive strategies may be employed to overcome domestic ratification obstacles. First, side payments represent the most traditional strategy. Side payments have been defined as "granting compensation—through direct monetary payments or material concessions on other issues—in an attempt to encourage concessions on a given issue."[27] Second, "synergistic issue linkage" involves striking an international deal that creates a policy option that was previously beyond domestic control. This strategy works by providing domestic constituents who are initially opposed to the international agreement with a domestic level policy linked to, or resulting from, the international agreement, which they prefer. Third, "issue redefinition" occurs when international agreements are defined as vital to the country's national security. This approach essentially portrays decisions to ratify an agreement as a cost–benefit calculation where domestic benefits will always outweigh international gains.

In theory, the most active and sophisticated elite strategies for ratification would employ all three strategies—side payments, synergistic issue linkages, and issue redefinition—as necessary to secure domestic support. Leaders who face ratification struggles and choose to explore all options, such as making synergistic issue linkages by reopening international negotiations on contentious matters and offering side payments to reluctant legislators, demonstrate a great deal of commitment to the ratification process. Executives who employ only one of these strategies, such as trying to force a deal through last-minute side payments, would exhibit a lower level of commitment to ratification. Leaders who fail to employ such options may face a greater risk of ratification failures.

Proposition 4

The more centralized the power is within an electoral system, the more likely it is that the government will successfully ratify the treaty.

This proposition derives from a lively scholarly debate about whether institutional differences between presidential and parliamentary systems affect the likelihood of international cooperation.[28] It is often assumed, for example, that prime ministers in majoritarian parliamentary systems have an institutional advantage over leaders of other democracies in terms of potential to generate support for preferred policies. The majoritarian (Westminster) model operates on a principle of "first-past-the-post" plurality victory for a party, and votes are translated into a disproportionate advantage of seats in the legislature. However, others contend that governments with more diffusion of power are more likely to cooperate on issues such as liberalizing international trade.[29] Some studies even suggest that parliaments around the world are becoming increasingly more active (more "Congress-like") in shaping policy outcomes.[30] Parliamentary systems based on proportional representation definitely allow for a wider array of political parties to be represented in government. Finally, presidential systems based on the principle of separation-of-powers mean that while the executive branch often sets the agenda on issues like trade and the environment, policy outcomes are shaped by Congressional oversight and approval. Recent studies show a steep increase in partisanship in presidential systems and a decrease in the frequency with which countries like the United States enter into international agreements.[31]

Proposition 5

The less organized interest group opposition is to an international treaty, the more likely it is that the government will successfully ratify the treaty.

Scholars contend that the larger the number of competing groups, the more likely it is that policymaking processes will entail bargaining and coalition-building. Studies of interest group behavior have also shown that there is often a lag between the time that an issue is placed on the agenda and the time groups become mobilized. Because domestic actors are familiar with the policy process and are often preoccupied with the crisis of the moment, the most efficient use of their collective energy is in lobbying the government related to expected domestic distributional effects only when an issue has mobilized government, private, individual, and media resources. Evans summarizes this phenomenon as an "awakening"—whereby the mobilization of constituencies could eventually have the "potential of undercutting the attempted agreement."[32] For this study, it is assumed that the less organized the opposition to a treaty presented by interest groups, the greater is the likelihood of successful ratification. Leaders of democratic states will have more difficulty achieving ratification if large and vocal interest groups are mobilized to challenge Level I agreements.

Proposition 6

The greater the level of public support for an international treaty, the more likely it is that the government will successfully ratify the treaty.

Scholars disagree over whether public attitudes can shape international outcomes. Some contend that the public can be very knowledgeable about specific
issues and that their views constrain policymaking in democratic countries.
Others suggest that leaders need only a "permissive consensus" to pursue
major international agreements in key issue areas.[33] Several double-edged
diplomacy studies focus on the ability of the leaders to shape the contours
of public opinion in ways favorable to international agreements.

As noted earlier, mainstream studies of international trade cooperation suggest the importance of democratic institutional arrangements. Other scholars argue that while direct ratification power is comparatively rare, indirect
power to ratify an international agreement is far more common. Nincic and
Hinckley suggest that elections serve as a powerful, indirect influence on
treaty ratification, and they contended that the conduct of foreign policy and
foreign policy issues figures prominently in voters' evaluations of presidential
candidates.[34] For this study, it is assumed that public support for an international agreement will increase the likelihood of ratification success. Public
support may be demonstrated through opinion polls in which a majority of
respondents favor ratification and compliance with an international treaty.
Conversely, if public attitudes are strongly against an international treaty,
there is a greater chance that opponents will undermine the deal and prevent
ratification.

In summary, this study recognizes two scope conditions at Level I and
four scope conditions embedded in Level II that may influence ratification
success or failure. These propositions regarding post-commitment politics are
explored through the cases in this book.[35]

IV. WHO NEEDS TREATIES?

A Theoretical and Empirical Preview

This chapter has argued that international treaties are generating serious
controversies in advanced industrialized democracies and that domestic constraints may limit the degree of state cooperation with agreements. Indeed,
treaty non-ratifications may be surprisingly common; they also appear to
be on the rise.[36] In the United States alone, there have been more than 500
instances of presidential endorsement that did not lead to Congressional
ratification.[37] Treaties have come under intensified scrutiny by Congress, and
partisanship seems to have crept into the discourse on U.S. commitments to

the global community. The referendum system has fostered a sense of turbulence in treaty ratification processes across Europe. And in other democracies, including Canada and Australia, some leaders are advocating for a shift in constitutional authority away from the executive to the parliament for treaty negotiation and ratification.

To some degree, this trend might be expected with the rise of complex intermestic issues related to the environment and trade. However, there are surprising developments in recent ratification struggles. For example, there appear to be growing controversies over arms control and security agreements in many democracies, once considered "above the political fray." It is also noteworthy that ratification has become politicized in parliamentary regimes where such controversies tended not to arise in the past. Prime ministers in majoritarian parliamentary systems seem to be facing more serious pressure to engage with domestic constituencies in the formulation of international agreements. The governments of Canada and Australia have responded with significant overtures including open public hearings on international treaties. Interpretation of international law may be on the rise, but it is also generating significant political controversy.[38] Meanwhile, European governments are grappling with the complexity of integration. A trend of popular resistance that began with controversy over the Single European Act in the 1980s and extended to the European Constitution is a warning to elites of the power of domestic constraints in ratification of international agreements. In this context, French President Jacques Chirac's decision to submit the Constitution to a referendum in his country can be interpreted as a tragic misstep. One should not underestimate the extent to which the 2005 failure of the European Constitution signals popular opposition to deepening integration in key member states.

The argument of this book, in its most basic form, is that it is possible to develop a comparative framework for the study of treaty ratification that acknowledges both distinct and more generalizable sets of conditions shaping ratification around the globe. More careful scrutiny of successes, failures, and near-failures of agreements can yield insights into what it takes to manage the ratification process effectively. A study of treaty failures is of crucial importance for understanding the potential for international legal governance and the fate of international institutions. Cases examined in this book show that a central assumption of two-level game theory—that the executive can anticipate the preferences of domestic actors and, therefore, only develops agreements that are ratifiable—does not hold. Instead, treaty ratification is a process that requires an incredible investment of time and energy by committed leaders.

Case Study Insights

The book tests its propositions against the histories of ratification processes related to six major international treaties. Three of the treaties can be characterized as broadly successful: the North American Free Trade Agreement (NAFTA), the Maastricht TEU, and the Australia–United States Free Trade Agreement (AUSFTA). For this study, success is measured as not only the attainment of ratification by the required number of signatories for a convention to become legally binding but also the achievement of de facto normative status. The other three—the Kyoto Protocol, the Comprehensive Nuclear Test Ban Treaty (CTBT), and the European Constitution—were less successful. To date they have failed to receive sufficient support to guarantee implementation by major powers and failed to legitimize a new normative arrangement. The treaties may "live on," and even gain ratification by the required number of signatories to come into effect, but their potential impact is significantly handicapped by the absence of participation by key countries. Probing the roots of these successes and failures in government debates yields insight into the potential for major agreements in the twenty-first century.[39]

Cases developed for this book are based on intensive field research, including exploration of government archives and interviews with dozens of high-ranking current and former government officials in Australia, Canada, the Federal Republic of Germany, and the United States. Case work represents a synthesis of these original perspectives with primary and secondary accounts available only in the host countries. While certainly not representative of the universe of possible cases, this study yields fascinating insights, including:

- The 1993 NAFTA nearly collapsed during the ratification struggle in the United States. President Clinton, who had campaigned in 1992 against several key clauses of the treaty, became its most vocal champion in 1993. He lent his own political capital to the campaign for NAFTA ratification, selling the agreement as a bipartisan, win–win situation. He used synergistic issue linkages to open negotiations with a reluctant Canada and Mexico for supplemental agreements on labor and the environment, and employed targeted side payments in Congress to win the necessary votes. While the NAFTA debate in Canada was much more muted, this was only true because Canadian parliamentarians had struggled mightily with the preceding agreement, the Canada–United States Free Trade Agreement in the late 1980s.

- The Maastricht TEU was ratified by a number of countries in 1992, but its primary supporters, Germany and France, were the last to confirm the treaty. German Chancellor Helmut Kohl worked hard to gain domestic support including the use of synergistic issue linkage through deliberations on convergence criteria and side payments to secure necessary support from state governments. French President François Mitterand took the treaty directly to the people through a referendum—a tactical mistake that almost led to its defeat. The referendum passed by only a 51 per cent majority in September 1992; after a series of currency crises and doubts about European integration, Mitterand's Socialists were washed out of power in the French parliament six months after the referendum.

- Canadian Prime Minister Chrétien's approach to ratification of the Kyoto Protocol may represent a perfect example of what *not* to do for leaders who believe in treaties. Chrétien chose not to devote political capital to ratification of the treaty or to go on the offensive to counter the growing opposition to the treaty by provincial leaders. Five years after signing the treaty the prime minister attempted to jump-start the process by announcing his plan to ratify it within four months. Some provincial leaders fought the ratification plan bitterly, even making veiled threats to secede from the union. While the government did vote to ratify the treaty in December 2002, key elements of implementing legislation have never been completed.

- The AUSFTA of 2004 offered the promise of liberalized trade between two friendly nations. The deal sailed through the U.S. Congress, but it provoked resentment in some Australian political circles. Facing the potential that the Senate would reject the legislation implementing the treaty, Prime Minister John Howard's government allowed amendments to the treaty sponsored by the opposition. The deal was saved, but at the cost of some degree of executive autonomy in the treaty process.

- Finally, struggles over the European Constitution led to its ultimate downfall in 2005. A referendum in France failed in May, even with the full support of the center-right government of President Jacques Chirac. Opponents of the treaty, including farm groups, labor unions, and grassroots organizations, lobbied strongly to kill the treaty. Days later, voters in the Netherlands also rejected the treaty and the British government announced that it would suspend its own plans for a referendum.

The book is organized as follows. Chapter 2 examines the similarities and differences in ratification processes across political systems to set the foundation for broader comparison. The chapter explores the constitutional foundations of ratification processes and identifies the major actors involved in contemporary treaty debates. It also outlines the method of structured, focused comparison of cases that is employed in the project. Chapters 3 through 8 present case studies of eighteen "rounds" of treaty negotiations and ratification struggles related to the NAFTA, the Maastricht TEU, the Kyoto Protocol, the CTBT, the AUSFTA, and the European Constitution. Finally, Chapter 9 summarizes the findings of the study and explores implications for international relations theory and policy development.

NOTES

1. Trone and Duchacek contend that treaties are generating more serious disputes over federal versus state interests in an era of globalization. Martin asserts that the credibility of international commitments is a serious concern in contemporary global politics; see John Trone, *Federal Constitutions and International Relations* (St. Lucia, Queensland: University of Queensland Press, 2001); Ivo Duchacek, "Perforated Sovereignties: Towards a Typology of New Actors in International Relations," in Hans J. Michelmann and Panayotis Soldatos, eds., *Federalism and International Relations* (Oxford: Clarendon Press, 1990), pp. 1–33; Lisa Martin, *Democratic Commitments* (Princeton, NJ: Princeton University Press, 2000).
2. While there are no data available on the number of treaty contestations around the world, case evidence points strongly to this pattern in many advanced industrialized countries.
3. This definition is derived from Francis O. Wilcox, *The Ratification of International Conventions: A Study of the Relationship of the Ratification Process to the Development of International Legislation* (London: Allen & Unwin, 1935), pp. 32–3; related works on ratification include Harold Koh, "The President Versus the Senate in Treaty Interpretation," *Yale Journal of International Law*, vol. 15 (Summer 1990), pp. 331–44; Philip Trimble and Alexander Koff, "All Fall Down: The Treaty Power in the Clinton Administration," *Berkeley Journal of International Law*, vol. 16, no. 1 (1998), pp. 55–70; Michael Glennon, "The Constitutional Power of the United States Senate to Condition Its Consent to Treaties," *Chicago-Kent Law Review*, vol. 67 (1991), pp. 530–42.
4. For more on the international legal dynamics of treaties, see Hilary Charlesworth, Madelaine Chiam, Devika Hovell, and George Williams, *No Country Is an Island: Australia and International Law* (Sydney: University of New South Wales Press, 2006).
5. Wilcox reports that one of the first political debates over an international agreement occurred when Romans refused to ratify the treaty to end the first Punic War in 242 BC, and citizens only agreed to the deal when punishments for the defeated enemy were intensified; *The Ratification of International Conventions*, p. 28.

6. Ibid., p. 30.

7. Robert D. Putnam and Nicholas Bayne, *Hanging Together* (Cambridge, MA: Harvard University Press, 1987), p. 14.

8. This book examines one dimension of the increased complexity and politicization of international agreements. Other works address how globalization has come to challenge state sovereignty. For example, Michelmann and Soldatos explore ways that the international system has become victim of "perforated sovereignty" in which states and provinces are now practicing their own forms of "para-diplomacy"; Michelmann and Soldatos, eds., *Federalism and International Relations*, pp. 1–22.

9. Robert D. Putnam, "Diplomacy and Domestic Politics: The Logic of Two-Level Games," *International Organization*, vol. 42, no. 3 (1988), p. 437.

10. Studies of double-edged diplomacy include: Peter B. Evans, Harold K. Jacobson, and Robert D. Putnam, eds., *Double Edged Diplomacy: International Bargaining and Domestic Politics* (Berkeley: University of California Press, 1993); Helen V. Milner, *Interests, Institutions, and Information: Domestic Politics and International Relations* (Princeton, NJ: Princeton University Press, 1997); Frederick W. Mayer, *Interpreting NAFTA: The Science and Art of Political Analysis* (New York: Columbia University Press, 1998); Maxwell Cameron and Brian W. Tomlin, *The Making of NAFTA: How the Deal Was Done* (London: Cornell University Press, 2000); Pierre Marc Johnson and Andre Beaulieu, *The Environment and NAFTA: Understanding and Implementing Continental Law* (Washington, DC: Island Press, 1996); Robert Pahre and Paul A. Papayoanou, "New Games: Modeling Domestic-International Linkages," Special Issue of the *Journal of Conflict Resolution*, vol. 41, no. 1 (1997); George Tsebelis, *Nested Games: Rational Choice in Comparative Politics* (Berkeley: University of California Press, 1990); Neal G. Jesse, Uk Heo, and Karl DeRouen, Jr., "A Nested Game Approach to Political and Economic Liberalization in Democratizing States: The Case of South Korea," *International Studies Quarterly*, vol. 46, no. 3 (2002), pp. 401–22.

11. Milner, *Interests, Institutions, and Information*, p. 73.

12. Evans, "Building an Integrative Approach to International Domestic Politics: Reflections and Projections," *Double Edged Diplomacy*, p. 400.

13. Clive Hamilton, *Running from the Storm: The Development of Climate Change Policy in Australia* (Sydney: University of New South Wales Press, 2001), p. 41; see also Ching-Cheng Chang, Robert Mendelsohn, and Daigee Shaw, *Global Warming and the Asian Pacific* (Cheltenham, UK: Edward Elgar, 2003).

14. Andrew Moravcsik, "Integrating International and Domestic Theories of International Bargaining," *Double Edged Diplomacy*, p. 23.

15. Jordan develops the concept of post-decisional politics to examine policy implementation in the European Union, with special attention to the utility of the approach as an alternative to intergovernmentalism and neofunctionalism; Andrew Jordan, "Overcoming the Divide Between Comparative Politics and International Relations Approaches to the EC: What Role for 'Post-Decisional Politics,'?" *West European Politics*, vol. 20, no. 4 (October 1997), pp. 43–70.

16. See, for example, Richard C. Eichenberg, "Dual Track and Double Trouble: The Two-Level Politics of INF," *Double Edged Diplomacy*, pp. 45–76; Peter B. Evans, "Building an Integrative Approach to International and Domestic Politics: Reflections and Projections," *Double Edged Diplomacy*, pp. 397–430.

17. Kal Raustiala, "Domestic Institutions and International Regulatory Cooperation: Comparative Responses to the Convention on Biological Diversity," *World Politics*, vol. 49, no. 4 (1997), p. 487; see also Detlef Sprinz and Tapani Vaahtoranta, "The Interest-Based Explanation of International Environmental Policy," *International Organization*, vol. 48, no. 1 (Winter 1994), pp. 77–106.

18. Kenneth N. Waltz, *Theory of International Politics* (Reading, MA: Addison-Wesley, 1979), p. 113; see also Joseph Grieco, "Anarchy and the Limits of Cooperation: A Realist Critique of the Newest Liberal Institutionalism," *International Organization*, vol. 43, no. 3, pp. 485–507.

19. This is a simplification for the purposes of the study. Waltz draws an important distinction between structural realism and theories of foreign policy; see Waltz, *Theory of International Politics*, p. 72; Sprinz and Vaahtoranta, "The Interest-Based Explanation of International Environmental Policy," pp. 77–106; Arild Underdal, "Modeling the International Climate Change Negotiations: A Non-Technical Outline of Model Architecture," *CICERO Working Paper*, no. 8 (1997), p. 3.

20. One exception to this argument can be found in Harold K. Jacobson, "Climate Change, Unilateralism, Realism, and Two-Level Games," in Shepard Forman and Stewart Patrick, eds., *Multilateralism and U.S. Foreign Policy; Ambivalent Engagement* (Boulder, CO: Lynne Rienner 2002), pp. 424–36.

21. Michael Krepon, "Conclusions," in Krepon and Dan Caldwell, eds., *The Politics of Arms Control Treaty Ratification* (New York: St. Martin's Press, 1991), pp. 399–416.

22. Alexander Wendt, "Anarchy Is What States Make of It: The Social Construction of Power Politics," *International Organization* 46, no. 2, Spring 1992, p. 392. For more detailed studies of norms in world politics, see Alexander Wendt, "Collective Identity Formation and the International State System," *American Political Science Review* 88, no. 2 (1994): 384–96; Martha Finnemore and Kathryn Sikkink, "International Norm Dynamics and Political Change," *International Organization* 52, no. 4 (1998), pp. 887–917; Jeffrey Checkel, "Norms, Institutions and National Identity in Contemporary Europe," Arena Working Paper 98/16 (Oslo: Advanced Research on the Europeanisation of the Nation-State, University of Oslo, 1998); Ronald Jepperson, Alexander Wendt, and Peter J. Katzenstein, "Norms, Identity and Culture in National Security," in Peter J. Katzenstein, ed., *The Culture of National Security: Norms and Identity in World Politics* (New York: Columbia University Press, 1996), pp. 33–75.

23. Martha Finnemore, "Norms, Culture, and World Politics: Insights from Sociology's Institutionalism," *International Organization*, vol. 50, no. 2 (1996), p. 326.

24. Margaret Keck and Kathryn Sikkink, *Activists Beyond Borders: Advocacy Networks in International Politics* (Ithaca, NY: Cornell University Press, 1998), p. 20; see also Beth A. Simmons and Daniel J. Hopkins, "The Constraining Power of International Treaties: Theory and Methods," *American Political Science Review*, vol. 99, no. 4 (2005), p. 623; see also Oran Young, *International Governance: Protecting the Environment in a Stateless Society* (Ithaca, NY: Cornell University Press 1994); Ted Hopf, "The Promise of Constructivism in International Relations Theory," *International Security* vol. 23, no. 2 (1998), pp. 171–200; Kal Raustiala and Anne-Marie Slaughter, "International Law, International Relations, and Compliance," *Handbook of International Relations* (Princeton, NJ: Princeton University Press, 2002); see also Friedrich V. Kratochwil, *Rules, Norms, and Decisions: On the Conditions of Practical and Legal Reasoning in International Relations and Domestic Affairs* (Cambridge: Cambridge University Press, 1989).

25. Thomas Risee-Kappen, "Ideas Do Not Float Freely: Transnational Coalitions, Domestic Structures and the End of the Cold War," *International Organization*, vol. 48, no. 2 (1994), pp. 185–214; Jeffrey T. Checkel, "Norms, Institutions, and National Identity in Contemporary Europe," *International Studies Quarterly*, vol. 43, no. 1 (1999), pp. 83–114; Christian Reus-Smit, *The Politics of International Law*, p. 21.

26. This is supported not only by a range of studies of leadership, but also by traditional studies of institutions; see R. Kent Weaver and Bert A. Rockman, "When and How Do Institutions Matter?" in Weaver and Rockman, eds., *Do Institutions Matter? Government Capabilities in the United States and Abroad* (Washington DC: Brookings Institution, 1993), pp. 445–61.

27. H. Richard Friman, "Side-Payments Versus Security Cards: Domestic Bargaining Tactics in International Economic Negotiations," *International Organization*, vol. 47, no. 3 (1993), p. 388; William H. Riker, *The Theory of Political Coalitions* (New Haven, CT: Yale University Press, 1962).

28. Alberto Alesina and Howard Rosenthal, *Partisan Politics, Divided Government, and the Economy* (New York: Cambridge University Press, 1995); Michael Bailey, Judith Goldstein, and Barry R. Weingast, "The Institutional Roots of American Trade Policy: Politics, Coalitions, and International Trade," *World Politics*, vol. 49 (1997), pp. 309–38; see also David R. Mayhew, *Divided We Govern: Party Control, Lawmaking, and Investigations, 1946–1990* (New Haven, CT: Yale University Press, 1991); Sharyn O'Halloran, *Politics, Process, and American Trade Policy* (Ann Arbor, MI: University of Michigan Press, 1994); Helen V. Milner and B. Peter Rosendorff, "Democratic Politics and International Trade Negotiations: Elections and Divided Government as Constraints on Trade Liberalization," *Journal of Conflict Resolution*, vol. 41, no. 1 (1997), pp. 117–46; Edward D. Mansfield, Helen V. Milner, and B. Peter Rosendorff, "Why Democracies Cooperate More: Electoral Control and International Trade Agreements," *International Organization*, vol. 56, no. 3 (2002); James D. Fearon, "Domestic Political Audiences and the Escalation of International Disputes," *American*

Political Science Review, vol. 88, no. 1 (1994), pp. 577–92; Lisa L. Martin, *Democratic Commitments*; William R. Keech and Kyoungsan Pak, "Partisanship, Institutions, and Change in American Trade Politics," *Journal of Politics*, vol. 57, no. 4 (1995), pp. 1130–42.

29. Mansfield, Milner, and Rosendorff, "Why Democracies Cooperate More: Electoral Control and International Trade Agreements"; see also Elizabeth McLeay and John Uhr, "The Australian and New Zealand Parliaments: Context, Response and Capacity," *Australian Journal of Political Science*, vol. 41, no. 2 (June 2006), pp. 257–72.

30. Martin, *Democratic Commitments*; see also John Uhr, "Bicameralism," in R.A.W. Rhodes, Sarah A. Binder, and Bert A. Rockman, eds., *The Oxford Handbook of Political Institutions* (Oxford: Oxford University Press, 2006), pp. 474–94.

31. DeLaet, Rowling, and Scott, "Politics Past the Edge: Partisanship and Arms Control Treaties in the U.S. Senate"; Eugene R. Wittkopf and James M. McCormick, "Congress, the President, and the End of the Cold War," *Journal of Conflict Resolution*, vol. 42, no. 4 (1998), pp. 440–67; Ralph G. Carter, "Congress and Post-Cold War U.S. Foreign Policy," in James M. Scott, ed., *After the End: Making U.S. Foreign Policy in the Post-Cold War World* (Durham, NC: Duke University Press, 1998), pp. 108–37.

32. Evans, "Building an Integrative Approach to International Domestic Politics," *Double-Edged Diplomacy*, p. 411; see also Sebastian Oberthuer and Hermann E. Ott, *The Kyoto Protocol* (New York: Springer Verlag, 1999), p. 18.

33. Leon N. Lindberg and Stuart A. Scheingold, *Europe's Would-Be Polity: Patterns of Change in the European Community* (Englewood Cliffs, NJ: Prentice-Hall, 1970); see also V. O. Key, Jr., *Public Opinion and American Democracy* (New York: Alfred J. Knopf, 1961).

34. See Miroslav Nincic and Barbara Hinckley, "Foreign Policy and the Evaluation of Presidential Candidates," *Journal of Conflict Resolution*, vol. 35, no. 1 (1991), pp. 333–55.

35. While examined as distinct propositions, it is also possible that variables identified here may have mediating effects upon one another.

36. While there are very few studies of ratification patterns over time, recent analyses appear to bolster this claim. For example, Robyn Eckersly identifies an increase in the proportion of environmental treaties that have not been ratified by the U.S. government from the 1970s to the present; Robyn Eckersley, "The Environment," in Michael Cox and Douglas Stokes, eds., *American Foreign Policy* (Oxford: Oxford University Press, 2008); Matthew Zierler, "Failing to Commit: The Politics of Treaty Nonratification," Ph.D. Dissertation, The University of Wisconsin-Madison (unpublished, 2003), p. 2.

37. Zierler, "Failing to Commit," p. 2.

38. While relevant, a full analysis of this question is beyond the scope of this research project; see Hilary Charlesworth, Madelaine Chiam, Devika Hovell, and George Williams, "Deep Anxieties: Australia and the International Legal Order," *Sydney Law Review*, vol. 25, no. 4 (December 2003), pp. 424–65; Brian

Opeskin and Rothwell, *International Law and Australian Federalism* (Sydney: University of New South Wales Press, 1997).

39. This study focuses on a select number of treaties that, despite their differences, cannot be representative of the vast number and complexity of treaties negotiated each year. In addition, it is important to recognize that the current stance of the United States or other great powers may not determine the final outcome of the treaty. Indeed, the Kyoto Protocol came into effect in February 2005 without the support of two key advanced industrialized countries, Australia and the United States.

2

Ratification Processes in Comparative Perspective

I. RESEARCH DESIGN

This book tests propositions against case histories of ratification processes related to six major international treaties. The study employs the comparative case study method to explore episodes of treaty ratification struggles, including breakdowns and near-breakdowns of international cooperation. Table 2.1 illustrates the case studies to be examined. Each treaty ratification effort for countries examined is referred to as a "round" of consideration in the larger study. Of the eighteen rounds examined here, eleven entailed challenging processes of political deliberation (coded as "moderate" or "high" intensity struggles).

Table 2.1 indicates first whether the country has signed and ratified the treaty according to their constitutional requirements. Second, I code the degree of intensity in domestic political debates in the ratification process. Those processes that generated little to no debate were coded as "low" intensity. Those which generated some political differences that resulted in delays in ratification and public debates were coded as "moderate." "High" intensity ratification struggles were those that generated heated political debate, extensive delay in treaty consideration, intense demands for side payment or opt-out arrangements, and (sometimes) resulted in government rejections of treaties.

Case Studies

Selection of the types of case studies to examine is based upon several criteria, including their fit to the relevant variables in the study and representation of contemporary debates on treaty ratification. Cases represent a range of democratic political systems, in three distinct regions of the world, with key institutional differences in ratification processes. As illustrated in Table 2.2, Australia and Canada are constitutional monarchies with parliamentary governments. Each represents a majoritarian system in which parties that receive

Table 2.1. Summary of ratification outcomes/struggles

	Kyoto Protocol	CTBT	NAFTA	TEU	AUSFTA	European Constitution
Canada	Yes/moderate	Yes/low	Yes/low	NA	NA	NA
USA	No/high	No/high	Yes/high	NA	Yes/low	NA
France	Yes/low	Yes/high	NA	Yes/high	NA	No/high
Germany	Yes/low	Yes/low	NA	Yes/moderate	NA	Yes/moderate
Australia	No/high	Yes/low	NA	NA	Yes/high	NA

the most votes win a governing majority in the lower house of parliament. The prime minister is the elected head of government. The Federal Republic of Germany is a parliamentary democracy based on a modified system of proportional representation. Fifth Republic France represents a hybrid system in that both the president and the parliament are granted a share of governing authority. The French president is vested with significant powers, but in some cases the prime minister and parliament are able to influence the direction of government policy. Finally, the United States of America is a presidential system in which there is a separation of powers between the three branches of government: executive, legislative, and judicial. Congressional representatives are elected to represent single-member districts.

This study examines similarities and differences in political systems and their implications for ratification success. While this is not a comparative examination of ratification methods per se, the study does address factors including the relationship between elite strategies for ratification (and thereby, choice of method) and likelihood of success; the relationship between the degree of the fusion of power between executive and legislature and the likelihood of success; institutional opportunities for access by interest groups

Table 2.2. Comparative political institutions

Australia	Canada	Germany	France	United States
Political system				
Parliamentary (constitutional monarchy)	Parliamentary (constitutional monarchy)	Parliamentary	Mixed: presidential and parliamentary	Presidential (separation of powers)
Electoral system (Lower House)				
Majoritarian	Majoritarian	Modified proportional representation	Proportional representation	Single-member districts: plurality

and success; and the degree of democratic openness in the treaty ratification process and the likelihood of success.[1]

Cases were also selected for this study to represent different international agreements across a range of issue areas. Issues like climate change, international trade, integration, and security represent common challenges and opportunities, yet states vary significantly in their response to these issues. Rounds of treaty debate provide a window into the role that actors and institutions play in the process, and they also may yield evidence of the evolution of the nature of ratification struggles over time.

Finally, cases were chosen as representative of contemporary debates in international politics. Each of these issues remains high on the agenda for advanced industrialized democracies in an era of globalization. In 2007 alone, the United States and Australian governments rejected international pressure to ratify the Kyoto Protocol and presented an alternative plan to encourage developing countries to join a new climate change program. France elected a new president, Nicholas Sarkozy, who promised renewed efforts to building stronger European institutions and to revive some elements of the European Constitution. The German economy gained ground after years of stagnation, changing the tone of debates about the benefits of regional integration. The Canadian and U.S. governments conducted negotiations with countries in South America regarding the creation of a Free Trade Area of the Americas (FTAA). And the Australian government openly debated a change in its nuclear posture. A survey of recent historical cases in this book should yield valuable insights into contemporary treaty ratification processes in comparative perspective.

Methodology

The structured, focused comparison method is primarily qualitative, involving the selection of a limited number of case studies and systematic assessment of the values of variables. The method applies a set of theoretically relevant, standard questions to the hypotheses of study.[2] This approach lends itself to a phased process analysis, viewing the development of international agreements as a process over time, including ratification as a distinct phase.[3] Elite interviews and archival evidence of the importance of domestic political conditions behind foreign policy decisions provide critical information for these valuations. In sum, the case method is appropriate for exploring the conditions that affect the foreign-policy decision-making process over time and allows for a mixture of richness and rigor in a study of political behavior.

Cases developed for this book are based on intensive field research, including work in Australia, Europe, and North America. Interviews with dozens of current and former policymakers and experts on international treaty debates provide valuable perspective. I also drew on government documents, political party archives, media records, and critical analyses by country specialists. In sum, cases represent a synthesis of original research, primary accounts available only in foreign capitals, and secondary materials.

II. RATIFICATION PROCESSES IN COMPARATIVE PERSPECTIVE

The Commonwealth of Australia

The Commonwealth of Australia is a constitutional monarchy with a Westminster-style parliamentary system. Reflecting its colonial history, the Queen of England is head of state, represented by the governor-general in Australia. Indeed, the original constitution of the Commonwealth includes only vague references to foreign policy authority, with the expectation at the time that British Crown authority would dictate Australia's external affairs.[4] While Australia celebrated its independence in 1901, the gradual devolution of foreign policy powers from the British Empire took decades, and it was not until World War II that Australia began to articulate what scholar D.P. O'Connell has called its own "international personality."[5]

Today, Australian foreign policy is dominated by the prime minister as the elected head of the majority party (or coalition of parties) in the lower house of parliament (the House of Representatives).[6] The prime minister works closely with the cabinet and his majority party to shepherd policy initiatives through the lower house of the legislature. House members (or Members of Parliament, MPs) represent single-member electoral districts that are strongly influenced by party politics.[7] The Australian Senate is elected through proportional representation, a system that enables opposition parties to gain control of the body periodically. The constitution grants parliament the power to legislate on matters of foreign affairs (Section 51), but in practice these powers have been circumscribed.[8]

According to the Australian constitution, treaty ratification is an executive act. Section 61 grants the executive the, "authority to initiate, sign and ratify international treaties, which are formally approved by the Governor-General."[9] However, most major treaties require the passage of implementing (or enabling) legislation through parliament. This provides the legislature with de facto influence on the ratification process. Prime ministers traditionally have sponsored implementing legislation through parliament before officially declaring treaties ratified.

Prime ministers traditionally have had little difficulty generating support for treaties.[10] But political winds began to change in the 1990s. Australia experienced a period of debate about a "democratic deficit" in treaty development. In response to grassroots pressure for reforms, the Senate Legal and Constitutional References Committee conducted a review of the treaty process in the mid-1990s that resulted in publication of an influential report, entitled "Trick or Treaty? Commonwealth Power to Make and Implement Treaties." The report recommended a number of reforms of the treaty-making process that were quickly embraced by the newly elected Howard government in 1996. Treaties would now be tabled in parliament for at least fifteen sitting days, providing legislators a longer period for consideration of the issues at hand. The government would produce treaty impact statements (termed National Interest Analyses) that surveyed potential costs and benefits of the commitment. The most significant reform, however, was the creation of a new Joint Standing Committee on Treaties (JSCOT), empowered to conduct inquiries on international treaties negotiated by the executive and to hold public hearings.[11] This restructured treaty review process was in force throughout the period examined in this study.

Canada

Canada is also a constitutional monarchy and a former colony of the United Kingdom. The Queen of England is head of state and is represented by the governor-general in Ottawa. The prime minister is the head of government in what is a distinct Westminster-style parliamentary democracy. Canada's foreign policy profile began to develop independent of the United Kingdom through the Canada's 1867 Constitution Act (derived from the British North America Act), but ties remain strong between the two political systems even today.

Canada's majoritarian system is highly centralized. The constitution grants the prime minister near absolute authority. While the statutory authority to make foreign policy rests with the Crown, the real actors that manage Canadian foreign policy are prime ministers and their cabinets. According to Nossal: "[T]he prime minister occupies a central and commanding position in Canadian politics...within these parameters, a prime minister's prerogative is sweeping....The prime minister is the head of government, its chief spokesperson, in and outside Parliament; the chair of cabinet; and head of parliamentary caucus."[12] Another expert contends that Canadian parliamentary democracy "places more power in the hands of the prime minister than does any other democracy, far more than the U.S. president wields."[13]

While most legislation is initiated within the executive branch, the parliament is an important venue for policy debate under certain conditions. The majority party in the House of Commons works closely with the prime minister and key executive agencies in drafting legislation. Consideration of matters in parliament is influenced by party discipline; party leaders enforce this system to maintain majority support for policies and suppress public airing of disagreements. At the same time, opposition parties have an opportunity to vocalize concerns about legislation through parliamentary committee mechanisms, floor debate, and question time.

Treaty ratification in Canada operates on two planes. As in the Australian system, bylaw ratification is carried out by the executive with the blessing of the governor-general. The prime minister proclaims a treaty ratified, establishing Canada's formal commitment to the international community. However, ratification of most major agreements requires accompanying implementing (or enabling) legislation to come into force, requiring participation by parliament in a broader dialogue about the implications of international agreements. Finally, it is important to note that Canadian prime ministers have sought to build a broader base of support for international treaties by bringing them to parliament for endorsement. These and other changes in the ratification process over time suggest a strong de facto role for parliament.

The French Republic

The government of modern France represents a hybrid of presidential and parliamentary systems. Established by Charles De Gaulle in 1958, this system includes independent elections for the president and parliament.[14] De Gaulle orchestrated the Constitution of the Fifth Republic to ensure significant influence for the president and a much more constrained role for the parliament. He believed in the need for a more powerful president to stand above, and separate from, the fractious politics of the parliament. The president would be both executive and mediator, providing the French government greater stability and cohesion.[15] When the president has a majority in the National Assembly, he or she enjoys tremendous power. When an election shifts control of the legislature to the opposition, however, the prime minister and the president enter into a period of "cohabitation" that empowers the prime minister.

The Constitution grants the president authority to appoint the prime minister, to dissolve the National Assembly, to order elections, and to call plebiscites (or referendums) to determine popular will on major issues. Referendums can be effective tools for the legitimation of preferred policies, and they allow the president to sidestep parliament on major issues.[16] According to Uleri and Gallagher, France has tended to have referendums "clustered within several specific periods corresponding to phases of political transformation, crisis, or authoritarian regimes."[17] Finally, presidential authority is further strengthened by the power of government agencies to guide French policies over time.

France has a bicameral legislature. Members of the National Assembly are directly elected through a double-ballot method for single-member districts; the two candidates that receive the most support in the first round of elections have the opportunity for a runoff to determine who will occupy the parliamentary seat. This system has traditionally supported major center-right and center-left political parties. The prime minister is the elected head of the majority party in the legislature, or a governing coalition, who has limited authority to pass legislation. In multiparty systems such as the French legislature, this can lead to significant instability and fragmentation of governance.

Treaty ratification can take one of several forms in the Fifth Republic. As head of state, the president can proclaim the treaty ratified and confirm French implementation through a simple majority vote in the National Assembly. But the executive's role as guardian of the constitution also means that they must ensure that its implementation would not represent a challenge to prevailing French law. In cases of uncertainty, Article 54 of the constitution calls on the president to request that the French Constitutional Council to review the agreement. This body may rule that international agreements challenge French sovereignty and require constitutional amendments.[18] When this occurs, the president has two routes to pursue a constitutional amendment. The president can request that the National Assembly and the Senate vote on an identically worded constitutional revision, which would then be subject to a public referendum. Or, the president can call for the two houses of parliament to meet as one (termed a *Congrés du Parlement*) where a three-fifths majority vote would be required to pass an amendment.[19] Given the tradition of majority control of the legislature, presidents have typically opted to call a *Congrés*, opting for referendums only in rare instances.

The Federal Republic of Germany

The Federal Republic of Germany was established in 1949 as a parliamentary democracy. The new system was designed to provide transparency and stability, and it represented a radical departure from the era of National Socialist Party (Nazi) control. The new arrangement called for a modified proportional representation system in which half of the members of the *Bundestag*, or lower house, would be elected directly in single-member districts, and the remainder of seats allocated based on proportional representation of political parties. The chancellor is the elected head of the majority party (or coalition of parties). Most importantly, the new system emphasized the principles of consensus and coalition-building.

Germany's Basic Law provides the legal authority for the chancellor to determine foreign and domestic policy, but most have interpreted this authority as a responsibility for management of the policy process. Cabinet meetings serve as an important forum for policy formulation. According to established rules of procedure, the cabinet must engage with "all matters of general domestic, foreign economic, social, financial or cultural importance."[20] Furthermore, cabinet deliberations represent a microcosm of government-wide consensus practices. Meetings operate on the principle of "collegiality" and, as stipulated in the Basic Law, the right of concurrence (*Mitzeich-nungsrecht*).[21] The chancellor cannot work alone.

This emphasis on consensus extends, to some degree, to the dynamic relationship between the executive and the legislature. The *Bundestag* includes traditional mechanisms for policymaking through its committee structure and voting procedures. The chancellor works with their governing coalition to sponsor legislation that is then reviewed by both houses of parliament. Given the potential for the upper house (the *Bundesrat*) to be controlled by opposition parties and/or to represent contentious *Länder* (or state) interests, governance often involves a delicate balancing act.

Germany's proportional representation system has generated a ruling coalition of parties throughout its postwar history. Indeed, political parties play a very important role in the German policy process.[22] Major party organizations have deep roots in civil society, and they tend to dictate the direction of politics in any given period. Parties have influence over the process within the broader societal context, representing a bridge between the electorate and government. Yet party structures are also traditionally hierarchical, with significant distance between elected leaders and average citizens.[23]

The treaty ratification process in Germany involves executive branch negotiations and legislative approval. Traditionally, the executive branch negotiates and signs international agreements, then seeks approval by a simple majority in both houses of the legislature. There is no constitutional foundation for national referendums on treaties. However, international agreements that have implications for the constitution may be interpreted as amendments to the Basic Law (requiring a two-thirds majority vote in both houses of parliament).[24] All major initiatives related to the European Union, especially treaties and amendments to treaties, require consultation with the *Bundestag* and two-third majority votes in both houses of the parliament. Given that opposition parties can sometimes control a majority of seats in the *Bundesrat* and that *Länder* concerns dominate discourse in the chamber, amendments may be difficult to achieve in some circumstances.

The United States of America

The United States was founded as a federal republic through its Constitution of 1787. The system provides for a separation of powers among the executive, legislative, and judicial branches of government. The president is directly elected by the voters, and the bicameral legislature is elected to represent single-member districts.

Article II of the Constitution gives the president authority to execute all laws as well as negotiate treaties and serve as commander-in-chief of the armed forces.[25] However, governance in the United States is a permanent balancing act, and the president must share powers with the Congress in matters of domestic and foreign policy.[26] The separation of powers system, and with it the possibility of divided government, often creates a competitive dynamic between the legislature and the executive. In a number of instances, the president's political party may not reflect the majority in control of one or both houses of the legislature. In divided government, there is an increased potential for differences over issues ranging from domestic disputes to international treaty commitments.[27]

The U.S. ratification process for international treaties reflects this competitive dynamic. The traditional ratification process entails presidential negotiation and signature of an international treaty and then review by the Senate. The Senate is empowered by the Constitution to provide its "advice and consent" on international agreements. Treaties require a supermajority of support in the Senate (two-thirds, or sixty-seven votes) for passage. The Senate may also attach reservations to the legislation for treaty ratification.[28]

The treaty ratification process has been modified over time in the United States. In the Trade Act of 1974, Congress established a system whereby the president may be granted "fast-track" authority for negotiation of international agreements. The fast-track process allows the president to negotiate a trade deal that his administration considers in the best interest of the nation. The treaty is then submitted to Congress for an up-or-down vote, with no amendments, within a fixed time period. Destler describes this process as a "pressure-diverting policy management system" in that Congress provides negotiating authority to the president with the expectation that the executive will search for ways to mediate the effects of an international agreement on the country.[29]

Finally, it is important to note that the president may use executive agreements for dealings with other countries. Executive agreements do not require Senate ratification. The number of executive agreements increased dramatically in the twentieth century—constituting some 90 per cent of all U.S. diplomatic agreements with foreign countries. However, most executive agreements involve routine matters of international transactions and do not typically encroach upon issue areas addressed through multilateral treaty negotiations.[30]

Conclusion

This chapter has begun to explore the similarities and differences in the ratification processes of the democracies under review. Adopting a broad view, ratification in all five countries requires the consent of the governed. Treaty commitments involve a pledge to the international community coupled with the exchange of government resources at home. Contemporary cases suggest that ratification may be becoming more complicated in the twenty-first century, however, with trends toward greater transparency and democratization of the treaty process. These fascinating dynamics are examined in greater depth in the chapters that follow.

NOTES

1. This study does not provide a comprehensive study of the propositions given the small number of cases. Rather, I seek to evaluate the plausibility of the propositions for explaining these specific cases—with the assumption that this has potential for assessment of related case studies of ratification struggles in

advanced industrial democracies. Scope conditions that characterize relative influence are also identified through the study.

2. See Alexander L. George, "Case Studies and Theory Development: the Method of Structured, Focused Comparison," in Paul Gordon Lauren, ed., *Diplomatic History: New Approaches* (New York: Free Press, 1979); Harry Eckstein, "Case Studies and Theory in Political Science," in Fred Greenstein and Nelson Polsby, eds., *Handbook of Political Science*, vol. 7 (Reading, MA: Addison-Wesley, 1975), pp. 79–138; Arend Lijphart, "Comparative Politics and the Comparative Method," *American Political Science Review*, vol. 65 (September 1971), pp. 682–93; Alexander L. George and Andrew Bennett, *Case Studies and Theory Development in the Social Sciences* (Cambridge, MA: MIT Press, 2004).

3. Phases are isolated here for analytical purposes. In reality, they may tend to overlap.

4. John Ravenhill, "Australia," in Hans J. Michelmann and Panayotis Soldatos, eds., *Federalism and International Relations* (Oxford: Clarendon Press, 1990), pp. 79–80.

5. D.P. O'Connell, "The Evolution of Australia's International Personality," in D.P. O'Connell, ed., *International Law in Australia* (Sydney: Law Book Co., 1965), pp. 1–33; see also Hugh Collins, "Political Factors," in Paul Dibb, ed., *Australia's External Relations in the 1980s: The Interaction of Economic, Political and Strategic Factors* (Canberra: Croom Helm, 1983), p. 216.

6. A.H. Body, "Australian Treaty Making Practice and Procedure," in D.P. O'Connell, ed., *International Law in Australia*; see also Anne Twomey, "International Law and the Executive," in Brian Opeskin and Don Rothwell, eds., *International Law and Australian Federalism* (Melbourne: Melbourne University Press, 1997), pp. 69–76.

7. Government of the Commonwealth of Australia, Senate Legal and Constitutional References Committee, Parliament of Australia, "Trick or Treaty? Commonwealth Power to Make and Implement Treaties" (Canberra: Government Printing Office, 1995).

8. See Greg Craven, "Federal Constitutions and External Relations," in Brian Hocking, ed., *Foreign Relations and Federal States* (New York: Leicester University Press, 1993).

9. Ann Capling, "Can the Democratic Deficit in Treaty-Making Be Overcome? Parliament and the Australia-United States Free Trade Agreement," in Hilary Charlesworth, Madelaine Chiam, Devika Hovell, and George Williams, eds., *The Fluid State: International Law and National Legal Systems* (Sydney: Federation Press, 2005), p. 72.

10. See Philip Alston and Madelaine Chiam, *Treaty-Making and Australia: Globalisation Versus Sovereignty* (Canberra: Federation Press, 1995).

11. Parliament of the Commonwealth of Australia, Joint Standing Committee on Treaties, *Treaty Scrutiny: A Ten Year Review*, Report #78 (Canberra: Government Printing Office, 2006).

12. Kim Richard Nossal, *The Politics of Canadian Foreign Policy*, Third Edition (Scarborough, Ontario: Prentice Hall Canada, 1997), p. 11.
13. Jeffrey Simpson, *The Friendly Dictatorship* (Toronto: McClelland & Stewart 2001), p. xi.
14. William G. Andrews, *Presidential Government in Gaullist France* (Albany: SUNY Press, 1982).
15. John T.S. Keeler and Martin A. Schain, *Chirac's Challenge: Liberalization, Europeanization, and Malaise in France* (New York: St. Martin's Press, 1996).
16. Henry Ehrmann and Martin A. Schain, *Politics in France*, 5th ed. (New York: HarperCollins, 1992); see also Vincent Wright, *The Government and Politics of France* (New York: Holmes and Meier, 1989); John T. S. Keeler, "Executive Power and Policy-Making Patterns in France: Gauging the Impact of Fifth Republic Institutions," *West European Politics*, vol. 16, no. 4 (October 1993), pp. 518–44.
17. Pier Vincenzo Uleri and Michael Gallagher, *The Referendum Experience in Europe* (New York: St Martin's Press, 1996), p. 116.
18. See Françoise de la Serre and Christian Lequesne, "France and the European Union," in Alan W. Cafruny and Glenda G. Rosenthal, eds., *The State of the European Community: The Maastricht Debates and Beyond* (New York: Longman, 1993), pp. 150–1.
19. See Philippe Keraudren and Nicolas Dubois, "France and the Ratification of the Maastricht Treaty," in Finn Laursen and Sophie Vanhoonacker, eds., *The Ratification of the Maastricht Treaty: Issues, Debates, and Future Implications* (Dordrecht: Martinus Nijhoff, 1994), pp. 147–79.
20. Judith Siwert-Probst, "Traditional Institutions of Foreign Policy," in Wolf-Dieter Eberwein and Karl Kaiser, eds., *Germany's New Foreign Policy: Decision-Making in an Interdependent World* (New York: Palgrave, 2001), p. 23.
21. For more perspective on German cabinet politics, see Paul V. Warwick and James N. Druckman, "Portfolio Salience and the Proportionality of Payoffs in Coalition Governments," *British Journal of Political Science*, vol. 31, no. 4 (October 2001), pp. 627–49.
22. Joachim Krause, "The Role of the *Bundestag* in German Foreign Policy," in Eberwein and Kaiser, eds., pp. 157–72; see also Oskar Niedermayer and Richard Stoess, eds., *Stand und Perspektiven der Parteienforschung in Deutschland* (Opladen: Westdeutscher Verlag, 1993); Oscar W. Gabriel et al., eds., *Parteiendemokratie in Deutschland* (Opladen: Wesdeutscher Verlag, 1997).
23. Dietrich Herzog, "Die Führungsgremien der Parteien: Funktionswandel und Strukturenwicklungen," in Oscar W. Gabriel et al., eds., *Parteiendemokratie in Deutschland*, pp. 301–22.
24. Rita Beuter, "Germany and the Ratification of the Maastricht Treaty," in Finn Laursen and Sophie Vanhoonacker, eds., *The Ratification of the Maastricht Treaty: Issues, Debates, and Future Implications* (London: Martinus Nijhoff, 1994), pp. 87–112.
25. Paul E. Peterson, ed., *The President, the Congress, and the Making of Foreign Policy* (Norman, OK: University of Oklahoma Press, 1994); see also James

Lindsay, *Congress and the Politics of Foreign Policy* (Baltimore, MD: Johns Hopkins University Press, 1994); Marie T. Henehan, *Foreign Policy and Congress: An International Relations Perspective* (Ann Arbor, MI: University of Michigan Press, 2000).

26. Richard Neustadt, *Presidential Power and the Modern Presidents* (New York: Free Press, 1990).

27. As noted in Chapter 1, this has contributed to a lively scholarly debate about the implications of divided government for international treaty commitments; see Richard Sherman, "Delegation, Ratification, and U.S. Trade Policy: Why Divided Government Causes Lower Tariffs," *Comparative Political Studies*, vol. 35, no. 10 (December 2002), pp. 1171–97; see also Michael A. Bailey, Judith Goldstein, and Barry R. Weingast, "The Institutional Roots of American Trade Policy: Politics, Coalitions and International Trade," *World Politics*, vol. 49, no. 2 (April 1997), pp. 309–38; David Epstein and Sharyn O'Halloran, "Administrative Procedures, Information, and Agency Discretion," *American Journal of Political Science*, vol. 38, no. 3 (1994), pp. 697–722.

28. David Auerswald, "Policymaking through Advice and Consent: Treaty Consideration by the United States Senate," Paper Presented at the Annual Meeting of the International Studies Association, New Orleans, Louisiana (March 25, 2002).

29. I.M. Destler, *American Trade Politics*, 2nd ed. (Washington DC: Institute for International Economics with the Twentieth Century Fund, 1992), p. 92.

30. See David M. O'Brien, "Presidential and Congressional Relations in Foreign Affairs: The Treaty-Making Power and the Rise of Executive Agreements," in Colton C. Campbell et al., eds., *Congress and the Politics of Foreign Policy* (Upper Saddle River, NJ: Prentice Hall, 2003); Congressional Research Service, "Treaties and Other International Agreements: The Role of the U.S. Senate" (Washington DC: Library of Congress, 2001).

3

The North American Free Trade Agreement

I. HISTORY OF THE NORTH AMERICAN FREE
TRADE AGREEMENT (NAFTA)

In the fall of 1990, U.S. President George H.W. Bush, Mexican President Carlos Salinas, and Canadian Prime Minister Brian Mulroney announced a plan to negotiate a continent-wide free trade agreement. This agreement promised greater opportunities for trade and exchange in the region, and experts argued that it would create a "rising tide to lift all boats." However, the North American Free Trade Agreement (NAFTA) garnered significant opposition in the United States and Canada. It passed Congress by only a razor-thin majority and was essentially forced through the Canadian parliament by a strong-willed Prime Minister Jean Chrétien. How did a treaty that many believed would offer great promise for North America generate such controversy?

The story of Canadian and U.S. government efforts to ratify NAFTA is actually rooted in the 1988 debate over the bilateral Canada–U.S. Free Trade Agreement (FTA). The FTA was designed to significantly reduce tariff barriers to trade between the two nations. Negotiations for the FTA were sensitive for Canada, which had a number of concerns about trade in specific sectors coupled with broader reservations that the deal would allow the United States' already strong economy to completely dominate the region.[1] The government of Conservative Prime Minister Brian Mulroney walked a fine line to balance domestic and international pressures in completing the deal. Mulroney even linked his own political future to support for the FTA during the 1998 national election campaign. His Progressive Conservative party won reelection by a narrow plurality, but Mulroney nevertheless interpreted this as an endorsement for his policies and steered the FTA through to ratification and implementation.

The 1993 North American Free Trade Agreement has been characterized as "the most comprehensive free trade pact (short of a common market) ever negotiated between trading partners, and the first reciprocal free trade pact between developing and industrial countries."[2] It expanded the free trade concept to include Mexico and required significant liberalization of member state policies. NAFTA also broadened the issues under consideration for free trade to include intellectual property rights, energy policy, transboundary investment, and transportation.

NAFTA negotiations were officially opened in June 1991 in Toronto, and hundreds of diplomats participated in the talks over a fourteen-month period. Working groups negotiated complicated deals for the reduction of tariff and nontariff barriers to trade in other sectors including agriculture, government procurement, foreign investment, telecommunications and financial services, competition policies, intellectual property rights, and investment. Particularly controversial issues during the negotiations included energy policies, labor, and environmental concerns. Rules-of-origin restrictions (which had serious ramifications for trade in textiles and automobiles) were also problematic. The final agreement, reached in August 1992, included twenty-two chapters outlining plans for reduction of tariff and nontariff barriers to trade in many different economic sectors—to be phased in over a fifteen-year period. Political leaders heralded the deal, but it could not go into effect until ratified by all three governments. This seemingly innocuous phase produced one of the most contentious debates over an international treaty in the history of the United States.

II. THE UNITED STATES AND NAFTA

From the beginning, U.S. government officials were aware that many of the issues in the international negotiations on the NAFTA would be controversial in the domestic arena. The U.S. economy was in a recession, unemployment was on the rise, and many businesses had begun to feel the effects of globalization. Therefore, any consideration of a regional free trade pact would be perceived through the lens of its potential impact on the U.S. economy. This produced a delicate balance of competing interests. Bush administration negotiators knew that labor and environmental issues would be especially controversial. While NAFTA contained references to these issues, it offered little in the way of concrete protections from heavy job losses, environmental policy noncompliance (a worry in regard to Mexico), and security against import flooding. Adding to the controversy was the fact that completion of NAFTA coincided with the presidential campaign of 1992, and Democrat Party candidate Bill Clinton expressed serious reservations about the treaty. In short, the outcome of the NAFTA treaty ratification debate in the United States was far from preordained.

International Pressure

The completion of negotiations on NAFTA in 1992 and the signature of all three government leaders marked the beginning of a key post-commitment phase. The ratification debate in the United States was delayed, however, pending the outcome of the 1992 presidential elections. Although neither President George H.W. Bush nor newly elected President Bill Clinton argued that NAFTA was essential to U.S. national security interests, they did suggest that the agreement would offer tangible benefits in the form of economic stabilization in the region. Government officials claimed that the deal would help to ease immigration pressures and promote economic growth. However, opponents argued that the treaty posed significant risks for the United States. They warned that the U.S. economy would suffer inestimable losses, including tens of thousands of manufacturing jobs and foreign direct investment to Mexico. Economic security would be rocked by a new level of uncertainty. As the actual ratification campaign heated up in the fall of 1993, so did the intensity of criticisms of the treaty.

The U.S. government was a leading force in negotiation of the U.S.–Canada Free Trade Agreement and the NAFTA. It was also an active participant in multilateral institutions designed to reduce tariff barriers to trade, including the General Agreement on Tariffs and Trade (GATT) and the World Trade Organization (WTO). The United States had established an international reputation for engagement in negotiations on lowering tariff barriers to trade, beginning with the Bretton Woods Agreements after World War II and extending into bilateral and multilateral arrangements in the 1990s. Thus, the U.S. government had helped to create a sort of self-fulfilling prophecy regarding trade liberalization. It was both author and subject of a set of shared norms and expectations about appropriate behavior in this context. Established international legal precedents offered an added level of normative pressure. In this sense, the dual overlapping pressures of normative arrangements and international law created a climate ripe for positive ratification outcomes.

Executive Strategy

The first step toward the NAFTA treaty was actually taken by the Bush (Sr.) administration in 1991. In accord with modifications of the Trade Act of 1974, Congress granted the president fast-track negotiating authority for a free trade agreement in North America. The fast-track process allows the president to negotiate a trade deal that his or her administration considers in the best interest of the nation, but it also requires regular consultation with Congress during the negotiation process.[3]

The NAFTA treaty was finalized by the Bush administration in the hot political summer of 1992. The ratification process in the United States, however, would be managed by a new president. Democratic Party candidate Bill Clinton had been noncommittal on the deal throughout much of 1992, and he recognized that garnering domestic support hinged on satisfying key elements of the Democratic Party base and the electorate. Many Democratic legislators opposed the deal negotiated by the Bush administration, citing domestic concerns about protection of labor and environmental issues. For example, House Majority Leader Richard Gephardt (D-MO) spoke out strongly against the treaty. Gephardt and Henry Waxman (D-CA) cosponsored House Concurrent Resolution 246-100, which cautioned the president "not to submit to Congress any trade agreement that does not preserve existing environmental, health, and labor laws." At the same time, a coalition of supporters in Congress allied themselves with interest groups who favored the overall objectives of NAFTA and saw supplemental agreements as a way to achieve a negotiated settlement.

Once in office, Clinton recognized that the only way NAFTA could be ratified would be through a strategy designed to win over domestic opponents to the deal. Clinton said that he might potentially support the treaty if the three countries held supplemental negotiations on sensitive issues including environmental policies, labor protections, and import surges. Over the objections of the Canadian and Mexican governments, the Clinton administration forced side negotiations for supplemental agreements on the environment and labor. In this sense, the administration practiced synergistic issue linkage, and the administration sought the counsel of Congressional leaders and interest groups during these negotiations. The side agreements were eventually completed and signed on September 14, 1993.

Regime Type: Executive–Legislative Relations

Congress possessed the ultimate power of ratification according to the fast-track process. This was the first major trade agreement between developed countries and a developing economy, and the implications of liberalization of tariff barriers to trade were very significant. Opposition to NAFTA seemed to be growing in 1993, and the Clinton administration faced a serious uphill battle to secure the necessary votes. The president knew that congressional representatives had confronted grassroots opposition during their visits with constituents in the summer recess. Many members pledged to oppose to treaty right up to the final House vote that fall.

In September 1993, President Clinton raised the bar in the NAFTA ratification campaign by holding a high-profile ceremony at the White House. Standing on a podium in the East Room alongside former Presidents Bush, Carter, and Ford, Clinton announced that the treaty offered tremendous benefits for the United States and that he intended to see it passed by Congress in the near future. Behind the scenes, administration officials also began to implement a strategy of carefully targeted side payments to gain support. For example, when representatives from some states expressed concerned that NAFTA would give unfair advantage to Canadian wheat farmers (who enjoyed significant subsidies), the administration offered greater protections for U.S. agriculture.[4] The president also authorized government grants for buildings, infrastructure, and research projects in specific congressional districts. When representatives from Florida expressed concerns over the implications of NAFTA for vegetable and sugar growers from their state, the president pledged that trade representatives would seek assurances from Mexico to protect import surges.[5]

Interest Groups

NAFTA negotiations awakened numerous interest groups to the reality that the deal would have significant implications for labor and the environment. U.S. government officials were pressured by a variety of groups before, during, and after the NAFTA negotiations, but not all groups were hostile to the plan. The Bush and Clinton administrations found support for the trade deal from key lobbies including the U.S. Chamber of Commerce, the National Association of Manufacturers, and even some environmental groups. For example, one survey conducted in September 1992 that found that 72 per cent of U.S. business executives polled supported NAFTA.[6] The Clinton administration also sought to maintain this support by consulting with corporate leaders on NAFTA negotiations through the office of the U.S. Trade Representative (USTR).

A number of interest groups lined up against the treaty, however. Broadly speaking, U.S. interests were concerned about the potential loss of manufacturing jobs given low-wage competition in Mexico. There were concerns about U.S. competitiveness in the textile and apparel markets, the automotive industry, and agriculture (especially competition in fruit and vegetable production).[7] Organized labor groups were highly concerned about the implications of liberalized trade for American manufacturing jobs. They feared that many corporations would move manufacturing facilities to Mexico, where average wages for production workers were only 14 per cent of those in the United States in 1991.[8] Labor groups in the automotive industry, for example, were concerned about increased shifts in the manufacturing of car parts from the United States to the *maquilladora* plants in the border region of Mexico. Studies sponsored by these groups projected the United States could lose up to 500,000 jobs over a ten-year period, with Mexico benefiting from an influx of new foreign investment.[9] American Federation of Labor and Congress of Industrial Organizations (AFL-CIO) President Lane Kirkland believed that Clinton had sold out the Democratic Party through NAFTA. He said: "The best thing that could happen to the Clinton administration is for this agreement to be voted down." Critical of the president's strategy to "buy votes," Kirkland added: "The door to the Treasury has been opened to dole out the pork."[10]

Finally, it should be noted other interest groups expressed mixed positions on the trade pact. Human rights organizations were generally opposed to the treaty on the grounds that the office of the USTR consciously chose not to address human rights standards or the level of democratization in Mexico. Meanwhile, agricultural interests were split, with the American Farm Bureau Federation offering strong support for the agreement, but groups like the California Tomato Growers Association and avocado farmers adamantly opposed. Environmental lobbies were active in NAFTA deliberations as well, but they seem to have been awakened to issues of concern in the trade negotiations somewhat slowly.

Public Opinion

The NAFTA case hints at the extent to which public attitudes in the United States may be shaped by elite discourse. An April 1993 NBC News–*Wall Street Journal* poll found that 27 per cent of those surveyed favored NAFTA and 25 per cent opposed the treaty, with a full 44 per cent of Americans undecided. During that summer an odd coalition of opponents to the treaty was assembled. Former presidential candidates Ross Perot and Patrick Buchanan joined citizen–activist Ralph Nader in speaking out against free trade, and they rallied the support of environmental groups, some labor unions, and human rights organizations. By July 1993 polls showed the public evenly split on NAFTA.

Concerned that support for the deal might be eroding, the Clinton administration took a gamble: In November, Vice President Al Gore challenged Ross Perot to a debate on free trade in a live broadcast on CNN. The debate generated strong public interest, and many believed that Gore had won the contest handily. An NBC-*Wall Street Journal* poll taken after the broadcast on November 15 found that 36 per cent of the public supported NAFTA while 31 per cent remained opposed.[11] The administration appeared satisfied that they had helped to build a permissive consensus for action.

Outcome and Analysis

In the high-pressure days leading up to the vote in November 1993, Clinton's pro-NAFTA forces expected to squeak through with little more than the 218 votes needed to win in the House of Representatives. Clinton spent most of the actual day of the vote on the phone trying to sway supporters and even hosted a last-minute meeting with undecided legislators at the White House. In the end, the House voted in favor of NAFTA implementing legislation by a vote of 234/200. Three days later, the treaty easily passed the Senate by a vote of 61/38.[12]

Clinton had expanded his win-set size for NAFTA ratification through a significant expenditure of political capital. Meanwhile, domestic opponents to the treaty pledged to keep up the fight against liberalized trade policy. At a gathering of groups critical of the NAFTA pact on the day after the historic vote, Ron Carey, President of the Teamsters, warned that the president "turned his back on those folks who got him elected. . . . I can assure you this fight will go on." Joan Claybrook of Public Citizen said, "This was the most anti-democratic process that we've ever seen in the Congress. Secrecy pervades this trade agreement and citizens can't participate."[13] Critics warned that they would hold the president accountable for the outcome of NAFTA and other major trade deals.

Linkages between international pressures and the ratification outcome in this case study are mixed. While the government believed that ratification, although costly, would benefit the U.S. economy in the long run, critics warned that the treaty would create a slippery slope of economic losses. In terms of absolute gains, neorealists would argue that state power would be undermined through this loss of economic security. Liberalized trade meant a decrease in protective barriers to trade as well as political, economic, social, and cultural costs. In contrast, international legal agreements on liberalized trade seemed to offer a clear pathway for U.S. policymakers who favored the potential for agreements. Successive rounds of the GATT regime had helped create a norm of liberalized trade for advanced industrialized economies. The United States had also recently completed the FTA with Canada. Indeed, Clinton's ultimate decision to back the treaty and his dedicated effort to gain ratification can be linked back to the sense of obligation on the part of U.S. government leaders to see the deal through. While many Democrats openly opposed the deal, it was the case that Clinton inherited a plan— a social construct—that defined a liberalized American identity on trade. Thus, the government clearly perceived a pressure to comply with shared norms and expectations about appropriate behavior in this context. There was added incentive to do this based on international legal precedents established through the Canada–U.S. FTA. In this sense, then, the dual overlapping pressure of normative arrangements and international law created a significant amount of pressure to cooperate.

One of the four scope conditions embedded in Level II appears to have influenced U.S. ratification of the treaty. This case strongly illustrates the importance of executive strategies for ratification success. President Clinton practiced all three strategies designed to gain domestic support for the treaty. He used side payments extensively in final bargaining with Congress for support. Indeed, the extent of the administration's "horse-trading" for votes surprised many observers. The president also effectively used synergistic issue linkages in forcing supplemental agreements with Canada and Mexico on labor and the environment. While the administration did not explicitly employ issue redefinition by casting NAFTA as essential to national security, events such as the White House ceremony featuring former presidents certainly helped the president to make the case that ratification was in the long-term interests of the United States.

Other domestic conditions were less significant in shaping the outcome. The Clinton administration recognized serious opposition to the deal in Congress and among key interest groups. Some members of the House of Representatives remained undecided on the treaty right up to the final vote. While the propositions examined for the study would predict defection in cases of division within the government, mobilized interest group and public opposition, there was nevertheless a successful ratification outcome. The key to this surprising outcome appears to be executive action. In summary, the case suggests that the most comprehensive explanation of NAFTA ratification in the United States would incorporate both domestic factors (especially executive strategies for ratification) and international normative pressure.

III. CANADA AND NAFTA

The Canadian government was hesitant about NAFTA from the very beginning. When notified about the initiation of U.S. trade talks with Mexico in

March 1990, Prime Minister Mulroney's first impulse was for his government simply to stay out of them.[14] The push for a continent-wide agreement came virtually on the heels of the successful completion of the U.S.–Canada FTA in 1988. That treaty had allowed a measure of protection for Canadian national and provincial concerns, including limitations in the energy market, labor and environmental issues, intellectual property, and transboundary investment.[15] One former government official said that Canada saw NAFTA as "the FTA on steroids," and worried that the few remaining protections for the Canadian economy surely would be subject to more intense scrutiny in the NAFTA negotiations.[16] At the same time, Mulroney was under fire at home for serious economic and political problems. Critics were increasingly blaming him personally for a three-year-long recession, deep public debt, and the loss of more than 100,000 jobs. Nevertheless, the Canadian government became convinced that the NAFTA negotiations represented an opportunity they could not afford to miss. They hosted the first round of negotiations in Toronto in June 1991.

International Pressure

The Canadian debate over ratification of the NAFTA was clearly influenced by prior experience with the FTA. Generally speaking, elite attitudes in Canada toward that treaty were positive, and government leaders and experts believed that the trade pact would significantly enhance their economy. Prime Minister Mulroney eventually endorsed negotiations for a continent-wide deal based on the conviction that his country stood to gain from the deal. Supporters would argue that Canada would expand its trade volume with Mexico, while at the same time the pact would help insulate the Canadian economy against emerging trade blocs around the world. However, the treaty had a high price for Canada. The deal called for significant economic restructuring throughout North America; Canadian government and economic units would be deeply affected by the transitions in regional economic stabilization arrangements. Protected sectors of the economy would be more vulnerable. New supranational institutions were created to regulate interstate trade, and the deal guaranteed a much higher level of capital, labor, and financial mobility.

For decades Canada had been involved in multilateral negotiations on liberalized trade, including rounds of the GATT, and these deals helped to create a "policy space" in support of greater liberalization. The FTA had also prompted serious political maneuvering (and soul-searching) in Canada, setting the stage for an expansion of the agreement through the NAFTA. More broadly, this trade agreement was consistent with Canadian political identity as an advocate for liberalization, institutionalization of cooperation through agreements, and even the promotion of economic development through engagement with Mexico.

Executive Strategy

Three successive prime ministers sought to shepherd the NAFTA through to ratification and implementation in Canada. Mulroney was faced with the first challenge—the expansion of negotiations to include Mexico, and he had already walked a very fine line to balance domestic and international pressures for the FTA. After a series of consultations with other Conservative leaders and internal government studies, Mulroney announced that Canada would participate in NAFTA talks. The prime minister recognized the trend toward regional trade arrangements in Europe and elsewhere, and he firmly believed that Canada should hitch its wagon to the powerful U.S. economy. The first round of negotiations began in Toronto in June 1991, and Canadian representatives argued for the expansion of trade relations to benefit the regional economy.

The deal was completed in August 1992; by February 1993 Mulroney's popularity had bottomed out (at 12 per cent). Mulroney announced that he would resign from office, but urged Conservative leaders to see the treaty and implementing legislation pass through parliament. Former defense minister Kim Campbell took over the prime ministership with the intent to move forward on ratification. Ratification faced another hurdle, however, when newly elected U.S. President Bill Clinton called for a new round of negotiations for supplemental agreements on labor and environmental issues. Campbell and other Canadian officials initially opposed the reopening of NAFTA discussions. However, the Clinton administration made a strong case for the fact that it would be difficult, if not impossible, for the United States to ratify the treaty without side agreements. Seven rounds of negotiations occurred from March to August 1993, and controversial issues included the development of a Commission on Environmental Cooperation (CEC) that would have independent authority to investigate domestic environmental law compliance in the entire region.

Prime Minister Campbell was able to move the NAFTA bill successfully through the House of Commons on May 27, 1993 (by a vote of 140/124) and received Senate approval on June 23, 1993. The treaty awaited only an official proclamation of ratification by the prime minister. This was delayed, however, pending the outcome of the national election in October. Jean Chrétien and the Liberal Party won a majority in the national elections and swept into government with an agenda of reform. Candidate Chrétien, much like candidate Clinton in the United States, had campaigned on the promise to oppose NAFTA in its current form. During the campaign, Liberals complained openly that the trade agreement might impose significant costs on the Canadian economy without concomitant opportunities for expansion.[17] Once in office, Chrétien suggested that several major provisions of the treaty would have to be renegotiated before he would ratify it. In an interesting, two-level connection, Chrétien was also concerned about President Clinton's ability to ratify the deal in the United States. Chrétien voiced what others had been feeling—that Clinton might try to alter NAFTA and reopen past trade disputes with Canada over things like agriculture, soft-wood lumber, and steel manufacturing in order to secure the necessary votes for ratification.[18]

Regime Type: Executive–Legislative Relations

The role of the parliament in regional free trade agreements was very much a function of legislative majorities of the period. In 1988, Prime Minister Mulroney knew that he had sufficient support in parliament for the U.S.-Canada FTA, and the strong Conservative majority facilitated negotiations and ratification/implementation of the treaty. Chrétien and the Liberals, on the other hand, had a weaker governing majority, and there were questions about whether the new prime minister could guarantee government support if he chose to open the treaty for consideration following his election to office.

Nevertheless, there was surprising agreement about the potential value of free trade among many parliamentarians and government experts. Legislators warmed to the idea of liberalized trade, especially in the wake of economic problems of the early 1980s. Exports to the United States were on the rise. In 1984, Canada exported 76 per cent of all goods to the United States.[19] Studies issued by the Departments of Industry, Trade, and Commerce argued in favor of liberalized trade and noted the trend toward the development of trade blocs in different regions around the world. Parliamentary groups including the Senate Standing Committee on Foreign Affairs issued a series of reports favorable to reduction of trade barriers with the United States. Committees held extensive public hearings in which experts and business leaders championed trade liberalization as beneficial to the Canadian economy.

Another issue that crept into executive–legislative relations in Canada in this period, however, was the role of the provinces in ensuring implementation of the agreement. Throughout the 1970s and 1980s, provincial governments had gained a stronger say in federal government negotiating positions. This evolution of the provincial–federal relationship was based both on economic realities and constitutional arrangements in Canada. While the federal government was granted centralized authority in Ottawa, Article 92 of Canada's 1867 Constitution Act (derived from the British North America Act) states that provincial legislatures "may exclusively make laws in relations to the exploration, development, conservation, and management of non-renewable natural resources."[20] Subsequent reviews of the Canadian Constitution have confirmed provincial jurisdiction over natural resources and the need for consultation in areas such as trade and agricultural policy. The constitutional power of Canadian provinces in the policymaking process is further bolstered by their relative economic power (such as Ontario and Quebec). Thus, while provinces have no formal veto over international agreements finalized by the federal government, they can refuse to implement key elements of such plans, thereby constraining the power of the federal authority to complete binding international commitments without their consent.[21]

Interest Groups

The prospect of a regional free trade agreement generated disputes among interest groups in Canada. The treaty would have significant domestic distributional effects, and lobbies tended to form up along lines consistent with expected payoffs. By the mid-1980s many Canadian business groups, including the Canadian Manufacturers Association, the Chamber of Commerce, the Business Council on National Issues, and the Canadian Export Association, all favored lowered trade liberalization with the United States. These groups were aware that more than two-thirds of all foreign direct investment in Canada came from the United States. They saw many potential benefits for the Canadian economy, including access to the Mexican market, and wider export opportunities for Canadian firms in several key sectors (such as automobiles and financial services).

Meanwhile, opponents of the NAFTA treaty in Canada included an unusual coalition of labor, corporations, and environmental organizations that blamed the FTA for larger economic problems. Corporations in sectors that had been heavily protected by the Canadian government in the past—including the financial services market, textiles, intellectual property, apparel manufacturers, and cultural groups—were deeply concerned about the treaty.[22] Labor groups feared that the Canada–U.S. FTA had been the source of significant job losses. Some studies showed that Canada had already lost as many as 45,000 manufacturing jobs directly as a function FTA arrangements.

Of course, the impact of these job losses was compounded by the general slowdown in the Canadian economy and high unemployment in this period.[23]

Environmental organizations were concerned about the treaty. During the first round of NAFTA negotiations in 1991–2, environmental groups pushed governments to carefully regulate environmental issues. When these issues were papered-over in the treaty produced in August 1992, environmental groups in Canada (and the United States) pushed their governments to renegotiate the plan. But some lobbies were unprepared for the direction these talks took during supplemental negotiations between March and August 1993. Delegates to the talks debated the creation of the CEC, a multinational task force to be delegated the power to regulate environmental disputes. The CEC that was eventually created did have the power to initiate inquiries into violations of domestic environmental laws.[24]

Once again, provincial interests were at work in shaping government policies towards NAFTA. Economically powerful provinces such as Ontario and Quebec expressed concern that the treaty would cause the loss of manufacturing jobs.[25] Provincial leaders heavy on agriculture such as Saskatchewan worried about the implications of lowering tariff barriers to trade and subsidies in agricultural exchange. Indeed, provincial leaders had pushed for a strong level of involvement in the free trade negotiations in North America from the beginning. They warned that Canada's sovereignty—and thereby provincial powers as well—were threatened by treaties like NAFTA.[26]

Public Opinion

There was a steady base of *diffuse* support for liberalized trade in Canada. Some 52 per cent of the public supported the concept of free trade in 1992, increasing steadily to 71 per cent in 1996.[27] However, latent concerns coalesced into serious opposition when any specific prospect of a trade agreement loomed.[28] For example, one could interpret the outcome of the 1988 Canadian federal election—in which Mulroney only received a plurality of support—as a popular vote against free trade. A September 1992 Gallup Canada poll showed that 60 per cent of the people believed that the NAFTA would be bad for the country (an increase of 7 per cent from 1991). A poll in mid-1993 found that a full 62 per cent of respondents opposed NAFTA "somewhat" or "very strongly."[29] Experts have suggested that this is a pattern in similar bilateral agreements in North America—as the final deals loomed larger, Canadians became more "afraid of U.S. economic power and potential political, cultural, and social dominance."[30]

Outcome and Analysis

Canada's completion of the ratification process was the culmination of years of political maneuvering. The negotiations began under Conservative leader Mulroney and continued through a supplemental agreements round under Conservative Prime Minister Campbell. The Conservative-dominated House of Commons voted on implementing legislation in May 1993, and Senate soon followed suit. The final irony in the NAFTA case came when Liberal Party Prime Minister Chrétien promptly dropped his reservations following the "yes" vote in Congress and embraced NAFTA. The prime minister immediately began to argue that remaining issues, such as ensuring Canadian sovereignty over natural resources like water and energy, could be addressed in future negotiations. He also assured his government that the agreement would protect Canada against trade surges in certain sectors.[31] In December 1993, the prime minister proclaimed the treaty ratified.[32]

Normative pressures appear to have played a role in the Canadian ratification of the NAFTA, but material considerations would predict defection from the agreement. Prime Minister Mulroney and his successors clearly perceived normative pressure to participate in the regional free trade negotiations. Through the FTA as well as multilateral trade agreements, Canada had established a reputation as a country supportive of trade liberalization (within limits, of course). Like Clinton, Chrétien's reversal of position to support the agreement may also be reflective of the power of normative pressures and a sense of international obligation. Conversely, neorealism would predict that Canada would not agree to the trade deal given the heavy costs imposed. While the deal might help buffer the Canadian economy from the rising power of regional blocs, economic security was by no means ensured by the treaty. In this sense, Mulroney's initial inclination to stay out of a deal involving Mexico might be characterized as a "rational" Canadian reaction to the plan.

The NAFTA ratification struggle in Canada highlights the importance of two domestic conditions in particular: executive strategies and legislative relations. Mulroney's administration negotiated the treaty fully aware of the political requirements for ratification through passage of implementing legislation. Indeed, some would say that Mulroney became so associated with the promotion of regional free trade agreements that he paid a personal cost when economic conditions soured in the early 1990s. His successor, Jean Chrétien, was forced to consider the use of several instruments of statecraft to achieve the necessary level of domestic support. He suggested the use of synergistic issue linkages through forcing negotiations on side issues and possibility of side payments for those with vested interest in the treaty. The main thrust of

Chrétien's policy toward the treaty, though, was the redefinition of the trade issue as critically important to Canada's future economic security. Once the Clinton administration won its struggle for ratification, Chrétien orchestrated an about-face on the agreement and endorsed its ratification by parliament. In the end, the prime minister was fully aware that his government need not bend too significantly to domestic concerns because it enjoyed executive primacy. Chrétien worked with top advisors to ensure that the treaty and the necessary implementing legislation were formalized by 1993. Here, the ratification game model appears to have captured the importance of the executive strategies and legislative relations, as well as demonstrating a relatively insignificant role of interest groups and public attitudes in shaping Canadian policy.

NOTES

1. Interview with Author, Ottawa, Canada (October 4, 2002).
2. Gary Clyde Hufbauer and Jeffrey J. Schott, *NAFTA: An Assessment* (Washington DC: Institute for International Economics, February 1993), p. 1; for an authoritative perspective on the treaty, see also Jon R. Johnson, *The North American Free Trade Agreement: A Comprehensive Guide* (Aurora, Ontario: Canada Law Book Co., 1994).
3. John J. Audley, *Green Politics and Global Trade: NAFTA and the Future of Environmental Politics* (Washington DC: Georgetown University Press, 1997).
4. Karen Tumulty and Mark Bousian, "Balanced Diet of Deals Whets Appetite for Pact," *Los Angeles Times* (November 17, 1993), p. 1.
5. See Miguel Valverde, "Domestic Politics and the Formulation of Foreign Economic Policy: Negotiating NAFTA," Paper presented at the 39th Annual Meeting of the International Studies Association (March 1998).
6. William P. Avery, "Domestic Interests in NAFTA Bargaining," *Political Science Quarterly*, vol. 113, no. 2 (1998), p. 284.
7. House Committee on Small Business, "The North American Free Trade Agreement," Y4.SM1:102-190 (September 18, 1992); House Committee on Energy and Commerce, Subcommittee on Commerce, Consumer Protection and Competitiveness, "North American Free Trade Agreement," Y4.En2/3:103-110 (February 18, 1993).
8. Sidney Weintraub, "The North American Free Trade Agreement as Negotiated: A U.S. Perspective," in Steven Globerman and Michael Walker, eds., *Assessing NAFTA: A Trinational Analysis* (Vancouver,: The Fraser Institute, 1993), p. 12.
9. Jeff Faux and Thea Lee, *The Effect of George Bush's NAFTA on American Workers: Ladder Up or Ladder Down* (Washington DC: Economic Policy Institute, 1992); see also Timothy J. Kehoe, "Assessing the Economic Impact of North

American Free Trade," in M. Delal Baer and Sidney Weintraub, eds., *The NAFTA Debate: Grappling with Unconventional Trade Issues* (Boulder, CO: Lynne Rienner, 1994), pp. 3–34.

10. William J. Eaton, "Clinton Jilting His Party to Woo NAFTA Votes, Labor Chief Says," *Los Angeles Times* (November 16, 1993), p. A20.

11. Frederick W. Mayer, *Interpreting NAFTA: The Science and Art of Political Analysis* (New York: Columbia University Press), p. 243.

12. *Calgary Herald* (November 18, 1993), p. A1.

13. "News Conference Concerning NAFTA with Various Anti NAFTA Groups," Federal News Service, Federal Information Systems Corporation (November 18, 1993); http://web.lexis-nexis.com/universe/document?_m= b5ee868be2080117426aadca463126da&_docnum=29&wchp=dGLSIS-IslzV&_md5 (accessed July 17, 2002).

14. Maxwell A. Cameron and Brian W. Tomlin, *The Making of NAFTA: How the Deal Was Done* (Ithaca, NY: Cornell University Press, 2000), pp. 64–5.

15. Michael A. Hart, *A North American Free Trade Agreement: The Strategic Implications for Canada* (Ottawa: Centre for Trade Policy and Law, Carleton University, 1990), p. 41; see also Michael Hart, Bill Dymond, and Colin Robertson, *Decision at Midnight: Inside the Canada-U.S. Free Trade Negotiations* (Vancouver, University of British Columbia Press, 1994); G. Bruce Doern and Brian W. Tomlin, *Faith and Fear: The Free Trade Story* (Toronto: Stoddart, 1991).

16. Interview with Author, Ottawa, Canada (October 9, 2002).

17. Leonard Waverman, "The NAFTA Agreement: A Canadian Perspective," in Steven Globerman and Michael Walker, eds., *Assessing NAFTA: A Trinational Analysis* (Vancouver, British Columbia, Canada: The Fraser Institute, 1993), pp. 32–59; see also Johnson, "NAFTA and the Trade in Automotive Goods," pp. 87–129.

18. Jonathan Ferguson, "The Triumph of NAFTA: To the United States, It's a Done Deal. To a Lot of Canadians, It's Time to Call in the Liberals' Promises," *Toronto Star* (November 20, 1993), p. B1.

19. Richard G. Lipsey and Murray G. Smith, *Taking the Initiative: Canada's Trade Options in a Turbulent World* (Toronto: C.D. Howe Institute, 1985), p. 47; see also "Department of External Affairs, A Review of Canadian Trade Policy and Canadian Trade Policy for the 1980s: A Discussion Paper" (Ottawa: Supply and Services, 1983).

20. Department of Justice Canada, 2001, p. 38.

21. Interview with Author, Ottawa, Canada (October 16, 2002).

22. Hufbauer and Schott, *NAFTA: An Assessment*, p. 3.

23. Waverman, "The NAFTA Agreement," p. 33; see also Richard G. Lipsey, "Canada at the U.S.-Mexico Free Trade Dance: Wallflower or Partner?" *Commentary*, no. 20 (C.D. Howe Institute: August 1990).

24. Guy Boileau, "The Interplay Between Domestic Institutions and International Negotiations: A Case of the North American Agreement on Environmental Cooperation," Master's Thesis, Norman Paterson School of International

Affairs, Carleton University, Ottawa, Ontario (September 4, 2001), p. 3; see also Annette Baker Fox, "Environment and Trade: the NAFTA Case," *Political Science Quarterly*, vol. 110, no. 1 (1995), pp. 49–68.

25. Ministry of Industry, Trade and Technology, Government of Ontario, "Background Paper: Assessment of Direct Employment Effects of Freer Trade for Ontario's Manufacturing Industries; Annual First Ministers' Conference, Halifax, Nova Scotia" (November 28–29, 1985).

26. Alan M. Rugman, "North American Economic Integration and Canadian Sovereignty," In M. Delal Baer and Sidney Weintraub, eds., *The NAFTA Debate: Grappling with Unconventional Trade Issues* (Boulder, CO: Lynne Rienner, 1994), p. 114.

27. Matthew Mendelsohn and Robert Wolfe, "Probing the Aftermath of Seattle: Canadian Public Opinion on International Trade, 1980–2000," *International Journal*, vol. 66, no. 2 (Spring 2001), p. 236.

28. John H. Sigler and Dennis Goresky, "Public Opinion on United States-Canadian Relations," *International Organization*, vol. 28 (Autumn 1974), pp. 637–68.

29. Mendelsohn and Wolfe, "Probing the Aftermath of Seattle," pp. 244–5.

30. Rugman, "North American Economic Integration and Canadian Sovereignty," p. 113.

31. *Agence France Presse*, "NAFTA Disputes May Be Settled through Side Deals: Chrétien," November 21, 1993; see also Alan M. Rugman, "North American Economic Integration and Canadian Sovereignty," in *The NAFTA Debate: Grappling with Unconventional Trade Issues*, pp. 97–116.

32. Andrew F. Cooper, "Waiting at the Perimeter: Making US Policy in Canada," In Maureen Appel Molot and Fen Osler Hampson, eds., *Canada Among Nations 2000: Vanishing Borders* (Don Mills, Ontario: Oxford University Press, 2000).

4

The Politics of European Integration

I. HISTORY OF THE MAASTRICHT TREATY ON EUROPEAN UNION

The 1991 Maastricht Treaty on European Union (TEU) represented a dramatic new phase in European politics. The treaty called for intensified political integration, greater centralization of power in Brussels, and monetary union. Leading states including France and Germany hailed the creation of a new entity, the European Union, and made clear their commitment to see the treaty through to full implementation rapidly.

Momentum for the TEU had begun in 1988 when European Commission President Jacques Delors chaired a special working group on the preconditions and timing of monetary union. The work included development of plans for a European Central Bank (ECB) and a common currency. The Commission report, released in April 1989, recommended a series of steps toward integration and was met with a lukewarm response across Europe. The report drew much greater attention several months later, however, when it became clear that Germany might seek rapid reunification after the opening of the Berlin Wall. At a European Community (EC) summit in Strasbourg in December 1989, Chancellor Helmut Kohl and Foreign Minister Hans-Dietrich Genscher sought European support for German reunification but faced difficult questions from regional leaders about their intentions. French President François Mitterrand, a longtime friend of Germany, now openly challenged Kohl regarding multilateral commitments. The French government was particularly adamant that the EC not support a more rapid German reunification program without a firm commitment to monetary policy integration. After extensive deliberation, German and French diplomats announced a compromise: the European Community would support reunification with guarantees on foreign economic policy initiatives in exchange for Kohl's pledge to support a special Intergovernmental Conference (IGC) on European Monetary Union (EMU).

IGC negotiations began in December 1990 and produced a set of recommendations that would evolve into the TEU. The treaty would include three sets of provisions, or pillars, for integration: the first set of provisions focused on the EMU; the second pillar described a program to create a Common Foreign and Security Policy (CFSP); and the third pillar called for cooperation in Justice and Home Affairs. First pillar plans for EMU would be the most direct extension of past progress in the Community. Through the European Monetary System, government leaders had agreed to consider a three-stage process for eventual union and institutional reform. The first stage of the EMU had already begun in June 1990 as part of the Internal Market Program aimed at abolishing the remaining capital controls in the EU member states. The second stage of the EMU was set to begin in 1994, with the establishment of the European Monetary Institute (EMI), with the mandate to review and consider monetary and currency policy reforms as a foundation for a central bank program.[1] The third and most important stage of EMU would implement plans for a new European System of Central Banks (ESCB) consisting of the European Central Bank (ECB) and associated banks in member states. By design, these institutions would then assume full responsibility for monetary policy and foreign exchange operations of the participating member states. Exchange rates among EU member state currencies would be "irrevocably fixed" in January 1999, and all national currencies would be replaced by the *euro* on January 1, 2002.

European leaders also established a set of convergence criteria for participation in the EMU. These criteria would delineate membership in the third stage of EMU implementation in 1999.[2] According to the terms of Article 109j(1) and Protocol 6, member states would need to achieve price stability, steady interest rates, and carefully controlled budget deficits.[3] Furthermore, IGC negotiators agreed that first pillar initiatives would be governed by the integrated community institutions (the European Commission, Parliament, and the Court of Justice), providing a new level of supranational authority over member state foreign economic policies.

European leaders met for an historic summit at Maastricht on December 10, 1991. After a thirty-hour marathon round of negotiations, they announced the completion of the TEU. Leaders agreed to schedule a formal signing ceremony for February 1992, and established the requirement all member states ratify the agreement before it would come into effect.[4] Most believed at the time that the TEU could be ratified and implemented within a few months, but the story would be much more complicated than expected. In the end, completion of the TEU required an additional year of wrangling in governments across Europe, generating legal and political battles with profound implications for the region.

II. FRANCE AND THE TREATY ON EUROPEAN UNION

The TEU ratification struggle in France led to the near collapse of popular support for integration. President François Mitterrand was deeply involved in negotiations for the TEU, yet faced significant skepticism toward the deal at home. France was not alone in this type of struggle. In early June 1992 voters in Denmark shocked the Community by rejecting the treaty. Mitterrand's response to the outcome was defiant: he announced just one day later that France would hold a referendum of its own. This approach was *not* required by the constitution, was opposed by other members of Mitterrand's government, and represented an extremely risky political strategy. Yet the president maintained that the vote would demonstrate to France, and to Europe as a whole, the tremendous groundswell of popular support for integration. In the end, the referendum in September 1992 passed by a narrow 51.04 per cent majority, doing little to strengthen an already-fragile integration program. Six months later, Mitterrand's Socialist Party lost control of the parliament in a landslide victory for the Conservatives.

International Pressure

Signature of the Maastricht Treaty in February 1992 marked the beginning of the post-commitment phase. The French government faced a great deal of international pressure to ratify the agreement, and in some ways the calculation of benefits and costs to French national security was at the core of the debate over ratification. Many French officials believed that the TEU represented tangible security benefits through increased cooperation in regional security initiatives. The CFSP would establish an institutional foundation for coordination of regional security policy, allowing disparate European democracies to "speak with one voice" in foreign affairs. This was particularly salient for the French government on the heels of German unification and the Persian Gulf War (1990–1), not to mention the brewing regional crisis in the Balkans. Critics of the TEU warned, however, that the treaty essentially gutted French sovereignty. The deal would be very costly in economic and political terms for France. It required significant economic restructuring and opened the fiscal and monetary policy floodgates to regional pressures on national economies.

At the very heart of the TEU was the idea that a European Union with greater political, economic, and social power would bring peace and prosperity to the region. Like its counterparts, the French government was influenced by this normative pressure to support the TEU. France had been a central player in regional integration projects—from the European Coal and Steel Community in the 1950s to the Single European Act of the 1980s. European Commission President Jacques Delors, a former Finance Minister in the French government, also helped shape the new institutions and in encouraging France to support the agreement. The French commitment to integration over the decades had also helped to establish a significant regional legal infrastructure that embedded economic and social policies within a larger context. While the concept of deeper European integration clashed to some degree with the French national political culture of independence, supporters argued that France had an obligation to the community that could not be forsaken.

Executive Strategy

The story of TEU ratification in France is one of determined leadership by President François Mitterrand and good fortune in a highly uncertain political showdown. French efforts in the early 1990s must be seen in the context of wider developments. Historically speaking, the themes of monetary integration, austerity, and fiscal conservatism were somewhat new to France. For years after World War II, the French government had employed liberal economic policies focused on growth and modernization, including loose credit policies coupled with a strong social welfare net. Inflation was allowed, even encouraged in some instances, and the government periodically devalued its currency as a monetary tool.[5] France experienced economic growth in the postwar period, but the regime was effectively leveraging its own future.

In the 1970s, however, French leaders began to embrace some measure of macroeconomic discipline in favor of regional economic cooperation and growth. The French *franc* was the second largest currency in the ECU basket of the European Monetary System, and government leaders moved toward austerity as a tool for longer-term growth. Socialist President Mitterrand's election in 1981 was a turning point. After two years of a failed "Socialist experiment" with the economy (involving protectionist trade barriers and currency devaluation), Mitterrand made an about-face and began to pursue initiatives to lower inflation and coordinate monetary policy with France's neighbors.[6]

Mitterrand's leadership on European integration was critical. The president kept France embedded firmly within the EMS in the 1980s in spite of a series of currency crises. He pushed for adoption of the Single European Act in 1985. And it was Mitterrand who advocated for the establishment of the Delors Committee to move forward on EMU. As noted earlier, the Delors Report included proposals to establish clear stages of economic, monetary, and political integration. More directly the report insisted upon a defined monetary union, convergence criteria, and a blueprint for a European Union Central Bank system. Mitterrand's relationship with Chancellor Helmut Kohl helped him convince Germany and other European powers to commit to an intergovernmental conference on deepening European integration. The leaders' personal ties helped France to balance German interests in the region and gain greater control over monetary policy at a politically sensitive time.[7]

What drove Mitterrand's determination to see monetary union through to completion? Some argue that his efforts were catalyzed by the prospect of German unification, but others believe that internal political factors were most important. France faced serious economic problems in the late 1980s and early 1990s, including unemployment coupled with a very rigid labor system that allowed little latitude for employers. In the realm of monetary policy, for example, Mitterrand and top advisors believed that fixed exchange rates would help improve all member states' economies, and the EMS system with the goal of EMU was reflective of this position.[8]

Mitterrand faced serious resistance inside his own cabinet to deepening integration, however. Opponents included Prime Minister Bérégovoy and the head of the French Treasury, Jean-Claude Trichet. Bérégovoy stressed the need for binding agreements on the arrangement prior to the start of the EMU project. He feared that "first pillar" plans such as a common currency and convergence criteria would disadvantage some economies and give disproportionate influence to Germany. Particularly controversial was the timing of the creation of the ECB and the voting structure that would define intensified political integration. Cabinet officials also challenged the automaticity of the TEU with regard to satisfaction of the convergence criteria and possible penalties for violations. On this theme, Mitterrand did eventually allow side deals with other European powers for the inclusion of escape clauses on some convergence criteria.

In the end, though, Mitterrand essentially forced opponents in his government to accept initiatives associated with the TEU. Mitterrand believed that monetary integration "fell clearly into the 'reserve domain' of the President, both as a subject of Community affairs and as a key agenda issue for Franco-German summits."[9] He sought to avoid any government statements that would suggest support for variable speeds on monetary union. Mitterrand pressed Socialist leaders to accept some German conditions, and, with the support of the Finance Ministry, he successfully argued that the creation of an independent ECB would benefit the French economy.[10] Finally, the president made clear that France should support steady progress through the stages of integration with fixed dates and convergence criteria.

The most important stage of the ratification struggle in France came when President Mitterrand decided to pursue a very risky political strategy. On June 3, 1993—one day after the Danish referendum in which voters rejected the TEU—Mitterrand took the bold step of ordering his own referendum on the treaty. Mitterrand proclaimed that a referendum would be the only way to "associate the French with the great European adventure."[11] Publicly, this move was celebrated by other European government leaders as a strong commitment to integration. Privately, however, the referendum decision was highly controversial. Mitterrand was not legally obligated to put the treaty to a vote. But the president believed that support for his government was diminished and that linking his government to this issue would help bolster his party's base.[12] The president also knew that at the time opinion polls showed French voters heavily favoring the agreement. Finally, the president knew that the issue could possibly splinter the political right. France's main center-right parties were deeply divided on the question. Members of the *Union pour la Démocratie Française* (UDF), led by former president Valéry Giscard d'Estaing, generally favored integration, but the neo-Gaullist *Rassemblement pour la Republique* (RPR), led by Jacques Chirac, opposed the plan.[13]

Regime Type: Executive–Legislative Relations

Executive–legislative relations during the debate over ratification were a function of the French parliamentary arrangement. Mitterrand enjoyed a Socialist majority in the National Assembly, and he could be confident that the TEU had sufficient support in the lower house. There was more significant opposition to the TEU in the Senate, however.[14]

The president faced several choices regarding ratification. According to the Fifth Republic Constitution, as head-of-state Mitterrand could simply proclaim the treaty ratified and confirm French implementation of the deal by a vote in the parliament. But the executive's role as guardian of the Constitution also meant that he must ensure that its implementation would not represent a challenge to prevailing French law.[15] In cases of uncertainty, Article 54 calls on the president to request that the French Constitutional Council to review the agreement. While Mitterrand did not personally believe this to be necessary, top advisors urged him to tread carefully.[16] Elisabeth Guigou, the Minister for

European Affairs and a close advisor, pushed him for greater transparency. She believed that "European integration had for too long been an affair for elites only."[17] Mitterrand duly submitted the treaty for review by the Constitutional Council in March 1992, which ruled that several provisions of the TEU did indeed challenge French sovereignty and required a constitutional amendment.[18]

The French president then had two routes to consider for a constitutional amendment. The president could request that the National Assembly and the Senate vote on an identically worded statement for constitutional revision, which would then be subject to a public referendum. Or, the president could call for the two houses of parliament to meet as one (termed a *Congrés du Parlement*) where a three-fifths majority vote would be required to pass a constitutional amendment.[19] In the wake of the Constitutional Court ruling, Mitterrand said in a televised address to the nation that he viewed the ratification of Maastricht as a parliamentary matter that would be best addressed by a *Congrés*. He added that if there were not sufficient support in parliament for the constitutional amendment, he would consult the French people directly through a referendum.[20]

The amendment to the Constitution was proposed as new Article 88, which would make allowances for the government to enter into all measures of the TEU including support for a single European currency, voting rights, and transboundary issues. It was adopted by a three-fifths majority at the special *Congres*, held on June 23, 1992. The final vote was 592 votes in favor, 73 opposed, with 14 abstentions.[21] However, of the 875 members invited to the session, 196 Gaullists chose to walk out instead of demonstrating their party's divisions in a split vote.

Finally, it should be noted that parliamentary opposition reflected a measure of concern about how the TEU would affect French national identity and sovereignty. Mitterrand himself had become associated with strong and determined leadership for France to wager on Europe as its road to future prosperity and stability. But some wondered aloud whether this determined support for Europe came at the cost of French autonomy. As one editorial warned: "Over the past 30 years France has become ever more committed to shaping the European Community; and during Mr. Mitterrand's decade it has allowed that Community to turn round and reshape its shaper. The Frenchness is going out of a France that has pledged itself to Europeanness."[22] One leading figure in the RPR, Philipe Séguin, said that the TEU "violates, in a flagrant manner, the principle according to which national sovereignty is inalienable and imprescritible."[23] Opposition parties believed that these issues would continue to resonate with voters and give them an advantage in the next round of parliamentary elections, scheduled for March 1993.

Interest Groups

As has been described, securing domestic support for the TEU in France was largely a top-down process driven by the technocratic elite. The government quickly engaged key business groups on the issue. For example, former French President Giscard d'Estaing established the Committee for European Monetary Union, a nongovernmental group made up of banking and business conglomerates, to build support for greater monetary and political union. Meanwhile, other interest groups appear to have only slowly awakened to the potential significance of the treaty for the national economy. To the extent that they did become engaged on the TEU, it was largely in groups' consideration of economic vulnerabilities associated with liberalized trade policies and fixed exchange rates. Since the 1985 Single European Act that reduced barriers to trade, France's exports had risen significantly. French exports constituted a very large percentage of its total gross domestic product (in comparison with other advanced industrial economies), which increased the vulnerability of the French economy to regional economic trends.[24]

A key organization of large French employers, the *Conseil National du Patronat Français* (or National Council of French Employers) adopted a neutral stance on the TEU while some farm groups expressed concern about the end of key subsidies and a drop in the price of agricultural products. In September 1992 farmers dumped tons of tomatoes on a highway in Marseilles in a protest against falling import prices and weak protectionist measures that European technocrats had formulated for France. The fishing industry also opposed the deal on the grounds that it might allow cheap seafood imports to flood the French market and that the government was unwilling to offer protections. From 1991 to 1993, French fishermen held a series of strikes protesting against the treaty, some of which turned violent.[25]

Public Opinion

Public opinion played a special role in this case study because of Mitterrand's decision to call the referendum. In general, the government enjoyed a diffuse base of popular support for integration initiatives in the early 1990s. Citizens believed that integration would provide Europe with unprecedented leverage vis-à-vis other potential trade rivals including the United States and Japan. The public also tended to believe that intensified European integration would promote peace in the region. Lindberg and Scheingold characterized popular support at the time as providing a "permissive consensus" for leaders to pursue serious integration projects. The European enterprise was seemingly taken for granted as an accepted part of the political landscape, making it relatively easy to mobilize support for projects to advance or protect the economic programs of the Community.

It was in this atmosphere of permissive consensus that Mitterrand said confidently in early 1992 he believed two out of three French citizens would vote for European unity if a referendum were held. A poll printed in the daily *Le Parisien* that spring suggested that a strong majority favored the treaty (and the idea of submitting the treaty to referendum).[26] However, once the referendum was announced in June 1992 the tide began to turn. Surveys printed in *Le Monde* showed a steady decline of the "yes" vote throughout the summer. In early June 1992, some 69 per cent of respondents said that they would vote "yes" on the referendum; by mid-June, this figure had slipped to 56 per cent; by August, the figure was at a perilous 53 per cent.[27] Demographic surveys conducted at the time showed that those who continued to support the treaty tended to be younger, more educated, and urbanized voters.

The government officially opened its public campaign for support of the referendum in late summer (two weeks earlier than originally planned) in an effort to stem the tide. It launched a massive public information program that included distribution of more than 45 million copies of the treaty to voters. The final poll released prior to the referendum showed public support at 52 per cent for the treaty. Mitterrand's reaction to this last survey was to again warn French voters that a "no" vote would have significant negative repercussions for Europe. He declared, "Europe would lose decades if the no-vote wins," and called the vote "a test of veracity" for France.[28]

Outcome and Analysis

The French referendum on the TEU was held on September 20, 1992. The treaty passed by 51.04 per cent, which Mitterrand immediately chose to interpret as a strong victory. The president proclaimed that France had experienced "one of the most important days" in its history.[29] The outcome clearly did represent a personal victory for Mitterrand, who had staked his own political future on the successful outcome. It also appeared to be a victory for the Socialist party, whose leaders had effectively exploited the rift among Conservatives over the treaty. By November 1, 1993, all member states had ratified the TEU and the European Union was born.

The celebration of the referendum was fairly short-lived for France, however. In early September 1992 a wave of currency speculation led the governments of Italy and Britain to withdraw from the European Monetary System, while Spain and Portugal had to devalue their own currencies in the European basket. A few days after the referendum, speculators forced a run on the *franc*.

Mitterrand knew that withdrawing from the EMS would all but eliminate any chance for real advances on monetary union in the near future. In a set of quiet but assertive moves, the French government appealed to the *Bundesbank* for relief. The *Bundesbank* responded by offering a set of loans to the French government that allowed the *franc* to remain as the second primary currency in the EMS.[30]

These and other events prompted a critical reexamination of the referendum experience in the French polity. Critics suggested that the slim margin of victory for the treaty actually had damaged the Socialist political base. Mitterrand's strategy of taking the issue to the French people had backfired. While he had succeeded in dividing the opposition—perhaps forestalling the resurgence of the nationalist right in France for a few months—Mitterrand's referendum campaign had cost the government dearly. Finally, in the March 1993 national parliamentary elections, the right won a landslide victory over the Socialists. A coalition of conservative parties gained control of 80 per cent of the seats in the National Assembly, two-thirds of the Senate, and many regional governments. The conservative victory led to a two-year period of cohabitation between Mitterrand and the new premier, Edouard Balladur, and it set the stage for the election of Jacques Chirac as president in 1995.

International pressures appear to have played a role in the outcome, although material and normative pressures may have pushed the government in different directions. French leaders believed that they had negotiated an agreement that was in the best interest of the state and campaigned on its behalf in the buildup to the referendum. They made a strong case for the value of regional economic integration as both a way to strengthen the collective and ensure that no one member (an oblique reference to Germany) could come to dominate the European economic engine. However, a more narrow view of the TEU based on material interests would predict that the treaty not be ratified by the government. The TEU represented a fundamental sacrifice of sovereignty at the altar of integration. The French government stood to lose control of fiscal and monetary policy as well as, potentially, foreign and security policy through the CFSP.

The constructivist argument casts a truly curious light on this case study. In some ways, the TEU struggle in France was an extension of past consideration of a series of major agreements on European integration. Past agreements did indeed offer a pathway for policymakers who favored deeper union and a shift of greater coordinating authority to Brussels. However, one could also assert that the very concern about greater institutionalization of the EU became interpreted by opponents as a threat to French national sovereignty. Following in the Gaullist tradition, French foreign policy had remained highly independent for decades, and national political culture offered only a slim margin for enmeshment in European affairs. Here we have a potentially unique case where the very norm of integration became challenged by a countervailing norm of sovereignty in the national interest.

Three scope conditions embedded in Level II seem particularly relevant for this case: executive strategies for ratification, legislative relations, and public opinion. First and foremost, the TEU ratification struggle in France was shaped by French President Mitterrand and his steadfast commitment to see the treaty through to implementation. Mitterrand practiced two of three primary strategies to build policy support. Operating from a position of majoritarian advantage, Mitterrand practiced synergistic issue linkage by promising continued negotiations with other countries for implementation of the stages of monetary policy union. Indeed, bargaining among member states on convergence criteria and the finer details of economic and social policy integration continued for almost a decade. Mitterrand also practiced issue redefinition by aligning French security itself with the interests of the mainstream. Here, the president and treaty supporters addressed issues of French sovereignty and national interests. Mitterrand strove to make the case that ratification was in the long-term interests of France and Europe, and he convinced some skeptics that it would be the only effective route to counter-balance Germany's growing economic power in the region.

Two other domestic conditions had a significant impact on the treaty outcome—executive–legislative relations and public attitudes. Mitterrand knew that the Socialists had political advantage in the National Assembly and that his government could pass a constitutional amendment through the body without much trouble. But he was well aware of latent opposition to the TEU in the Senate where legislators stood opposed to key clauses that would limit French sovereignty. This reality forced the president to carefully consider his options regarding ratification. Ultimately, Mitterrand's choice to call a *Congrés* into session reflected the reality that there remained parliamentary roadblocks to passage.

Public attitudes played a very significant role in the French ratification struggle. In this case, Mitterrand's (seemingly rather impulsive) announcement that France would hold a referendum on the TEU vaulted public opinion into the mix. Indeed, this move seemed to reflect a growing consensus among leaders in the region that they needed greater engagement of the public in the integration process. Several of the president's closest advisors had pressured him to increase the transparency of the process, and the referendum would be a highly public demonstration of support. Furthermore, Mitterrand seemed to trust the results of numerous polls that spring showing strong, if diffuse, support for integration. In the end, the president's maneuver represented an acknowledgement of the power of public opinion even if he expected voters to follow the government's lead in the matter. That said, the outcome of the referendum was fairly ambiguous in terms of defining popular opinion toward further European integration.

III. GERMANY AND THE TREATY ON EUROPEAN UNION

Germany was one of the architects of the TEU, yet it, too, experienced serious domestic political debates in the ratification phase. The German ratification struggle illustrates the role of both international and domestic pressures in post-commitment politics. Chancellor Helmut Kohl became one of the leading proponents for the treaty in Europe in 1992, making numerous appearances on television and at public rallies. However, Kohl's government also became embroiled in debate over the treaty, delaying formal endorsement for more than a year. In the end, Germany was the last European state to submit its instruments of ratification. This section investigates how a treaty that leaders believed matched Germany's own interests faced such a difficult road to ratification.

International Pressure

Germany was under a great deal of regional pressure to ratify the Maastricht Treaty before it was even finalized. Indeed, some of the ideas that evolved into pillars of the treaty were first formulated as a response to concerns about rapid German unification at the end of the Cold War. Mitterrand and Kohl agreed to a grand bargain whereby Europe would accept German unification in exchange for its commitment to enmesh itself in a deepened regional integrative structure. However, the TEU also raised a number of economic security concerns for Germany as it considered monetary and fiscal policy coordination and the elimination of the *Deutschmark* in favor of a new European common currency. The TEU represented a significant ceding of sovereignty from Berlin to key bureaucracies in Brussels.

Germany faced normative pressure to ratify the Maastricht Treaty in accord with its commitments to Europe. Indeed, West Germany had heavily invested in the European enterprise for decades. The government had been a chief architect of past integration programs, including the Single European Act of 1986. Many Germans had come to believe in the *idea* of Europe and accepted the argument that the fates of Germany and the European Union were intertwined. German positions were reflected in the TEU, such as plans for strict convergence criteria for monetary union, and the goal of integration was reflected in German foreign policy decisions. European integration had also established an intricate network of legal standards and processes that fostered continued cooperation. In sum, Germany helped to establish the system of expectations and standards to which they would be held through the ratification process.

Executive Strategy

The TEU represented the most comprehensive reform program in the history of European integration, and Chancellor Kohl returned from Maastricht keenly aware that ratification would require a broad base of support at home. Kohl believed that most cabinet leaders would support the ratification process. In fact, surveys of elite attitudes at the time found that more than 90 per cent of leaders throughout Europe supported deepening economic and political union.[31] At the same time, Kohl was aware of reservations about limiting German influence in the region, about doubts on monetary union inside his own Conservative party, *Länder* opposition, and *Bundesbank* pressures for autonomy.

In a highly pragmatic way Kohl saw these issues in light of the contingent offer of European support for rapid German reunification. Throughout the IGC negotiations and the Maastricht summit, Kohl issued a series of public statements demonstrating strong German support for the plan.[32] Broadly speaking, Kohl believed that deepening European integration was an extension of the German foreign policy of multilateralism. He was comfortable with deepening integration as a payoff for German unification, and he believed that it would benefit all of Europe in the future. In an oft-quoted statement, Kohl said that he viewed unification and European integration as inextricably related. He proclaimed that Maastricht was "proof that the united Germany assumes its responsibility in a united Europe actively, and remains committed to what we have always said, namely that German unity and European unity are two sides of the same coin."[33] Furthermore, Kohl argued that German objectives for the TEU had been attained through the establishment of strict convergence criteria and a rigid timetable for participation in a monetary union plan.

Regime Type: Executive–Legislative Relations

The proportional-representation electoral system in Germany generated a ruling coalition of parties. From 1982 to 1998, the coalition government included the major party, the Christian Democratic Union (CDU), its sister party in Bavaria, the Christian Socialist Union (CSU), and the junior party, the Free Democratic Party (FDP). Each of the party organizations offered support for the Maastricht Treaty, but individual leaders expressed some reservations about the scope and nature of the union.[34] For example, Finance Minister Theo Waigel questioned whether such a treaty would undermine German economic strength at a time of unparalleled performance in Europe. As an extension of economic worries, some Conservatives opposed the loss of sovereignty on economic and monetary policy—a dramatic change in German foreign economic policy in a difficult period of transition. Further-more, they worried that union would ultimately force Germany to change its immigration laws and could potentially undermine its social welfare network.

The opposition Social Democratic Party (SPD) generally favored European integration, but members disagreed about specific elements of the TEU. On the left wing of the party, Saarland Minister-President Oskar Lafontaine and others were skeptical of any treaty commitment that might threaten German social welfare base. The SPD spokesperson for European Union affairs, Heidi Wieczorek-Zeul demanded that Europe place social and economic concerns at the top of integration agenda.[35] Meanwhile, moderates in the party, the so-called New Leftists, including Minister-President of Niedersachsen Ger-hard Schröder and *Fraktion* leader Rudolf Scharping supported the TEU but objected to specific provisions that had been established through the IGC negotiations including unemployment and labor issues.[36] Toying with the issue of the loss of the *Deutschmark*, prominent members of the SPD raised questions about the single currency plan. As Scharping stated publicly, "I would consider it ill-advised to give up the *D-Mark* for some vague idea."[37] And in an interview with the popular news weekly *FOCUS*, Schröder said that he worried that currency union would undermine the *Mark* as one of Ger-many's primary symbols of national identification.[38] In general, there was an absence of party consensus on opposition strategies to the TEU, and members raised a stream of concerns including employment issues, inflation, and the potential negative effects of a single currency.

The ratification struggle became more complicated when SPD opponents in the *Bundesrat* succeeded in converting consideration of the TEU from the status of a treaty (requiring a simple majority in the *Bundestag*) to a consti-tutional amendment (requiring a two-thirds majority vote in both houses of parliament).[39] Given that the Social Democrats controlled a majority of seats in the *Bundesrat* and that *Länder* concerns dominated discourse in the cham-ber, the government automatically became dependent upon the opposition for ratification of the TEU in 1992.

Ensuing negotiations between the government and opposition leaders produced a series of amendments to the TEU in order to garner the necessary
support. Kohl was pressured to modify the treaty to grant the *Länder* more
control over EU legislation and to give the legislature ultimate authority over
monetary and currency union.[40] In a *Bundesrat* session on September 25,
1992, legislators made it clear that TEU approval was contingent on passage
of these plans as constitutional amendments and in the form of implementing
legislation. According to the deal, a new Article 23 was created for the German
Basic Law and devoted to discussion of the ends and means of European integration. The "old" Article 23 had referred to German reunification, and had
been rendered moot with unification in August 1990. The new amendment
focused on the development of a European Union "committed to democratic,
rule-of-law, social and federal principles as well as the principle of subsidiar-
ity." It also emphasized that any transfer of sovereignty from Germany to the
European Union henceforth required the consent of the *Bundesrat*, and any
constitutional changes would require two-thirds majorities in both houses of
parliament.[41] In effect, Kohl's domestic bargain with the opposition produced
an "opt-out" amendment to the TEU that would satisfy critics of the treaty in
the short run and guarantee the long-term ratification and implementation of
the pillars.

Interest Groups

Chancellor Kohl was quite conscious of building domestic support for ratification of the TEU among key interest groups. Government leaders recognized
that groups would have concerns related to the scope and pace of monetary
union as well as social and justice initiatives. These concerns were further
magnified by Germany's uncertain economic situation during the unification
process.

The *Bundesbank* and labor unions in key economic sectors opposed German support for the Maastricht Treaty. *Bundesbank* officials expressed concerns about the pace of EMU and the implications for German economic
stability. Bank officials pressured the Conservatives to negotiate very strin-
gent convergence criteria for the creation of monetary union—half expecting
that the strictness of these measures would prevent European leaders from
reaching a final agreement for the creation of the ECB.[42] Hans Tietmeyer, vice
president of the Bundesbank warned, "all participants must be clear that the
loss of monetary sovereignty will make national efforts to solve domestic economic problems impossible . . . it would be unwise if the hands of the central
banks, and the *Bundesbank*, were tied too fast."[43] When it became clear that

European leaders favored a plan for rapid monetary union, officials turned their attention to other delay tactics.

German labor unions in the steel sector also opposed rapid economic integration. In fact, IG Metall and other groups were worried about an increase in inflation, and the government was locked in negotiations with labor unions in the steel sector regarding pay increases. This further threatened the government with the possibility of labor strikes. Essentially, the bank and other interest groups believed that Germany might exert greater control over monetary integration by slowing the pace of planned union.[44]

Public Support

The German public was disengaged from the TEU ratification process, and public attitudes had little direct effect on foreign policy behavior. In fact, public opinion on the treaty was mixed throughout 1992. Surveys from the period have measured a whole range of opinions from general disinterest, to steadfast belief in the value of European integration, to serious concerns about the economic implications of the treaty.[45] These issues translated into the German public psyche in fascinating ways. After a period of malaise identified with the "Eurosclerosis" of the period, German interest in, and support for, integration began to rise with the Single European Act. By the late 1980s, 72 per cent of Germans believed that membership in the European Community was "a good thing" for their country, and nearly 60 per cent believed that Germany had directly "benefited from membership."[46]

A majority of Germans offered their support for the European Union in surveys in the 1990s, but there was a gap between those generally favoring integration and those who actually expected positive benefits for Germany from the process.[47] At the same time, the German public was clearly skeptical about economic union because of underlying worries about *Unberechenbarkeit* (unpredictability). This issue had always boiled below the surface in postwar Germany; the conventional wisdom being that economic instability was an enabling factor for the rise of the National Socialist party in the 1930s. Predictions about the economic implications of European union were further complicated from 1989 on by uncertainty about German unification.[48]

In addition to cultural orientations, public attitudes toward European integration were also shaped by a lack of information on treaty. Debates about the implications of the TEU occurred mainly behind closed doors inside the government and in university halls, while average Germans remained unaware of many details. According to public opinion polls conducted during the summer and fall of 1992, more than 80 per cent of Germans said that they knew "nothing" or "very little" about the TEU.[49] Nevertheless, public concerns grew after witnessing the failure of the Danish referendum in June 1992 and the slim victory of the French vote in September. Major German newspapers and television reports also began focusing on the potential costs of integration that fall, although primary attention was devoted to economic union. One poll conducted in December 1992 suggested that if the treaty had been put to voters in a referendum, the "yes" vote would win, but only by a slim margin.[50]

Outcome and Analysis

In January 1992, Kohl set about the campaign to secure domestic support for ratification of the TEU by attempting to assure skeptics that it was the best possible outcome for Germany. The chancellor emphasized that the common currency plan, potentially the most salient and divisive issue in the Maastricht package, would only be implemented within a bounded realm of political and fiscal requirements. Kohl linked his own leadership to the treaty with statements like "The construction of European house is a vital issue. My political fate is associated with it."[51]

When the ratification struggle became more complicated by the SPD maneuver in the *Bundesrat* to turn the TEU into a constitutional amendment, Kohl and Genscher stepped up their pressure to support the treaty. The Danish rejection of the TEU in June 1992 was another blow to momentum on the treaty, and economic instability and currency crises worried many supporters. When the TEU was presented for its first reading in the *Bundestag*, respected leaders of the FDP and the Green party spoke out against the treaty as undemocratic while Social Democrats expressed concerns about the social implications of the treaty.[52] Kohl seized on the successful outcome of the French referendum in September to put in a strong legislative push for passage of the treaty, but he was not able to silence disagreements within the cabinet. During the final reading of the bill, Finance Minister Waigel again warned that political symbolism might be driving the decision rather than political caution, while Foreign Minister Klaus Kinkel criticized increased *Länder* involvement in Europe policy.[53]

The fragility of the treaty compromise also seemed to empower the opposition to challenge it on constitutional grounds. When members of the Greens/Alliance '90 and the PDS called for a public referendum, the government flatly rejected the possibility. Opponents then submitted a formal legal challenge to German participation in the TEU before the Federal Constitutional Court. On October 11, 1993, the Court ruled that Germany could legally participate in the organization. The court defined the European Union as a *Staatenverbund*, an association of states falling somewhere between a federation and a confederation. The Court also acknowledged the various limits on EU sovereignty in state government opt-out and local control clauses, saying that member states remained the ultimate *Herren der Verträge* (masters of treaty agreements).[54] In accord with prior rulings, the Court stipulated that significant provisions of European integration must be subject to a vote by the *Bundestag*.

The *Bundestag* finally ratified the Maastricht Treaty as a constitutional amendment on December 2, 1992. The upper house of parliament, the *Bundesrat*, gave the treaty a unanimous vote of approval on December 18, 1992, after a third and final reading in the *Bundesrat*—making it the last of the major EU member states to vote in support of the treaty.[55] In the end, the treaty enjoyed a significant percentage of supporting votes from the CDU/CSU, the FDP, and most members of the SPD. Only the Greens and PDS delegates voted against the treaty. Kohl celebrated the vote by declaring that Germany and the European Union had demonstrated their abilities to act even in "a very difficult time for European politics."[56]

The proposition that states will ratify treaties that represent maximization of national interests does not appear to predict German ratification of the TEU. National security interests played a role in the government's approach to the agreement. Germany helped to design the criteria for economic and monetary policy coordination, and leaders believed that the system offered potential long-term benefits to their national economy. Yet a narrow view of material interests would not predict that a state would support an agreement of this magnitude. The TEU called for a sacrifice of sovereignty to the larger Union, including the loss of control of fiscal and monetary policy and the loss of the *Deutschmark*. In truth, neither policymakers nor economists could predict the future health of the *euro*, and its exchange value plummeted in the first months after it was officially enacted. Deepening integration meant the potential loss of political, economic, social, and cultural influence in the region.

The international relations theory that best explains German actions in this case is constructivism. Indeed, the TEU represented an extension of years of progress toward the institutionalization of international norms. The German government had been highly engaged in major initiatives on integration for decades and had significant influence on the development of pillars for integration and the convergence criteria. In many ways, German leaders were integral to both normative development and implementation. Thus, Kohl's dedicated effort to gain ratification can be interpreted as carrying through on a commitment—a social construct—to deepen European integration. The government clearly perceived a pressure to comply with shared norms and expectations about appropriate behavior in this context.

At the domestic level, the TEU case study certainly illustrates the importance of executive strategies for ratification success in Germany. Like Mitterrand in France, Chancellor Kohl became personally involved in the treaty struggle and his single-minded determination to see this through helps account for the successful outcome. The chancellor practiced all three strategies for ratification. He recognized that domestic opposition was high, especially manifest through *Länder* representation in the *Bundesrat*. Side payments included the development of an opt-out clause to attempt to satisfy the opposition and specific initiatives related to convergence criteria. Second, the chancellor and the foreign minister clearly redefined the issue by linking German national interests with the successful outcome of the treaty. Third, the German government practiced synergistic issue linkage by negotiating in IGCs for an integration program that would meet national interests to the extent possible. For example, German diplomats stipulated on the first day of the Maastricht summit that the ECB should be based in Frankfurt and not Amsterdam (as others, including Jacques Delors, had favored).

Legislative relations, interest groups, and diffuse public support were also important in the German decision-making process. Opponents in the legislature and in the state governments were able to force the federal government's hand by classifying the treaty as a constitutional amendment requiring full legislative approval. The amendment meant that the *Länder* would have an unprecedented say in this foreign policy commitment. Yet in these actions, the process also became more transparent and potentially more democratic. The chancellor had to carefully maneuver around the reservations expressed by *Bundesbank* officials and corporations, while at the same time scrambling to build a coalition of interest groups in support of the TEU. Legislators looked to diffuse public support for the treaty and the larger vision of European integration as legitimation for ratification of the treaty as well. In the end, it appears that all four domestic conditions played a nominally positive role in shaping the ratification outcome.

NOTES

1. Madeleine O. Hosli, "The Formation of the European Economic and Monetary Union: Intergovernmental Negotiations and Two-Level Games," Paper presented at the 39th Annual Convention of the International Studies Association,

Minnesota (March 17–21, 1998); see also Ellen Kennedy, *The Bundesbank: Germany's Central Bank in the International Monetary System* (London: The Royal Institute of International Affairs, 1991).

2. Bank of England, "The Maastricht Agreement on Economic and Monetary Union," *Quarterly Bulletin*, vol. 32, no. 1 (February 1992); see also James Sperling, "German Foreign Policy After Unification: The End of Cheque Book Diplomacy?" *West European Politics*, vol. 17, no. 1 (1994), pp. 73–97.

3. "Vertrag über die Europäische Union," reprinted in *Bulletin*, no. 16 (February 12, 1992), p. 113–19; see also Karl Kaltenthaler, *Germany and the Politics of Europe's Money* (Durham, NC: Duke University Press, 1998).

4. See Colette Mazzucelli, *France and Germany at Maastricht: Politics and Negotiations to Create the European Union* (New York: Garland Publishers, 1997).

5. Wayne Sandholtz, "Choosing Union: Monetary Politics and Maastricht," *International Organization*, vol. 47, no. 1 (Winter 1993), p. 6.

6. These changes were not made without significant political costs, however. The Socialist party lost support from labor unions but gradually built ties with the growing French professional class, the so-called technocrats, and the middle class; Sandholtz, "Choosing Union," p. 7.

7. Interview with Author, Bonn, Germany (June 21, 1992); see also Julius W. Friend, *Unequal Partners: French-German Relations, 1989–2000*, The Washington Papers 180 (Washington DC: Center for Strategic and International Studies, 2001).

8. David J. Howarth, *The French Road to European Monetary Union* (New York: Palgrave, 2001), p. 114; Andrew Britton and David Mayes, *Achieving Monetary Union in Europe* (National Institute of Economic and Social Research, London: Sage, 1992).

9. Howarth, *The French Road to European Monetary Union*, p. 141.

10. Interview with Author, Bonn, Germany (June 18, 1992).

11. FBIS-WEU-92-110: June 8, 1992, "Mitterrand Supports Referendum Despite Risks," in Paris Antenne-2 Television Network (in French) 18:00 GMT (June 5, 1992).

12. John T.S. Keeler and Martin A. Schain, "Presidents, Premiers, and Models of Democracy in France," in John T.S. Keeler and Martin A. Schain, *Chirac's Challenge: Liberalization, Europeanization, and Malaise in France* (New York: St. Martin's Press, 1996), pp. 23–52.

13. "France: A Vote Too Far," *The Economist*, September 26, 1992, p. 48.

14. See Henry Ehrmann and Martin A. Schain, *Politics in France*, 5th ed. (New York: HarperCollins, 1992); see also Vincent Wright, *The Government and Politics of France* (New York: Holmes and Meier, 1989).

15. William G. Andrews, *Presidential Government in Gaullist France* (Albany, NY: SUNY Press, 1982).

16. FBIS-WEU-932-109: June 5, 1992, "Prime Minister on Maastricht Referendum," 07:37 GMT (June 5, 1992).

17. Howarth, *The French Road to European Monetary Union*, p. 50.

18. The Council was especially concerned about provisions of the TEU relating to Community citizens' right to vote and stand in municipal elections, monetary policy integration, and immigration; see Françoise de la Serre and Christian Lequesne, "France and the European Union," in Alan W. Cafruny and Glenda G. Rosenthal, eds., *The State of the European Community: The Maastricht Debates and Beyond* (New York: Longman, 1993), pp. 150–1.
19. Philippe Keraudren and Nicolas Dubois, "France and the Ratification of the Maastricht Treaty," in Finn Laursen and Sophie Vanhoonacker, eds., *The Ratification of the Maastricht Treaty: Issues, Debates, and Future Implications* (Dordrecht: Martinus Nijhoff, 1994), p. 150.
20. Mazzucelli, *France and Germany at Maastricht*, pp. 209–10.
21. de la Serre and Lequesne, "France and the European Union," p. 151.
22. *The Economist*, "A Survey of France," November 23, 1991, pp. 46–52.
23. Eric Aeschimann and Pascal Riché, *La guerre de sept ans: Histoire secrete du franc fort, 1989–1996* (Paris: Calmann-Lévy, 1996), p. 127.
24. David R. Cameron, "The 1992 Initiative: Causes and Consequences," in Alberta M. Sbragia, ed., *Euro-Politics: Institutions and Policymaking in the "New" European Community* (Washington DC: The Brookings Institution, 1992), p. 38.
25. FBIS-WEU-93-036, "EC Might Impose Minimum Prices on Fresh Fish Imports," in Paris AFP 12:55 GMT (February 23, 1993); FBIS-WEU-93-051, "Protests Against Cheap Seafood Imports Turn Violent," in Paris AFP (in English) 15:36 GMT (March 17, 1993).
26. FBIS-WEU-92-108, "Poll: 69% For," in Paris, AFP, 08:07 GMT (June 4, 1992).
27. "Recent Polls on Maastricht Referendum Published [English transl.]," *Le Monde* (August 22, 1992), p. 7.
28. Mitterrand Warns against Rejecting Maastricht," FBIS-WEU-92-178 (September 14, 1992), p. 29.
29. Riding, "Relief in Europe," p. A1.
30. Interview with Author, Bonn, Germany (August 4, 1996).
31. European Commission, *Eurobarometer: Top Decision Makers Survey*: Summary Report (Brussels, 1996); see also Ronald D. Asmus, "In Germany the Leadership's Vision Goes Beyond the Border," *International Herald Tribune* (April 12, 1996), p. 10.
32. Michel G. Huelshoff, Andrei S. Markovits, and Simon Reich, eds., *From Bundesrepublik to Deutschland: German Politics after Unification* (Ann Arbor, MI: University of Michigan Press, 1993); see also Interview with Author, Sankt Augustin, Germany (August 9, 1996).
33. Speech before the *Bundestag*, reprinted in *Stenographischer Bericht*, Plenarprotokoll 12 (December 13, 1991), p. 5705.
34. *The Economist* (December 7, 1991), p. 52.
35. Peter Norman "German SPD threatens to block IGC," *Financial Times* (March 2, 1996), p. 2; Wieczorek-Zeul was the same politician who would later compare the George W. Bush administration to Hitler's Third Reich.

36. Interview with Author, Bonn, Germany (June 20, 1992).
37. Scharping, as quoted in Elke Leonard, *Aus der Opposition an die Macht: Wie Rudolf Scharping Kanzler werden will* (Cologne: Bund Verlag, 1995), p. 114.
38. "Auto Man Revs Up," *The Economist* (February 17, 1996), pp. 45–6; interview with Gerhard Schröder in *Focus*, vol. 45 (1995), pp. 24–5.
39. Rita Beuter, "Germany and the Ratification of the Maastricht Treaty," in Laursen and Vanhoonacker, eds., *The Ratification of the Maastricht Treaty*, pp. 87–112.
40. Interview with Author, Bonn, Germany (June 21, 1992).
41. Quentin Peel, "Bundestag to Vote in Favour of Maastricht: Treaty Approval Has Sting in Tail," *Financial Times* (December 2, 1992), p. 3.
42. *The Economist* (September 22, 1990), p. 60; see also David Marsh, "Kohl Wants Meeting on EMU Put Off," *Financial Times* (December 7, 1989), p. 2; see also Michael J. Baun, "The Maastricht Treaty as High Politics: Germany, France, and European Integration," *Political Science Quarterly*, vol. 110, no. 4 (Winter 1995/1996), pp. 605–24.
43. Tietmeyer quoted in Wolfgang Munchau, "Bundesbank Attacks High-Speed EMU," *The Times of London* (June 12, 1991), p. 8; see also "Bundesbank Demands Firmness in European Monetary Union Talks," *Agence France Presse* (September 18, 1991).
44. David Marsh, "Germany Seeks to Slow the Pace of EC Monetary Union," *Financial Times* (February 22, 1991), p. 4.
45. "Es gibt viele schöne Modelle," *Der Spiegel* (August 24, 1992), pp. 98–101.
46. See European Commission, *Eurobarometer: Trends, 1974–1994* (Luxembourg: European Communities, 1994); see also the European Commission, "Conclusions of the Presidency, Madrid, December 15–16, 1995," *Bulletin of the European Union*, no. 12 (Luxembourg: European Communities, 1995).
47. David R. Cameron, "National Interests, the Dilemmas of European Integration, and Malaise," in Keeler and Schain, eds., *Chirac's Challenge: Liberalization, Europeanization, and Malaise*, pp. 345–8.
48. See Edwina S. Campbell, "United Germany in a Uniting Europe," in Gary L. Geipel, eds., *Germany in a New Era* (Indianapolis, IN: Hudson Institute, 1994), pp. 81–110.
49. Beuter, "Germany and the Ratification of the Maastricht Treaty," p. 102.
50. *Agence France Presse*, "Germany Ratifies Maastricht Treaty," December 18, 1992; web.lexis-nexis.com/universe/document?_m=477680f7d54c0027877b03a9087e b7e8&_docnum=6&wchp=dGLStS-lSlzV&_md5= (accessed July 7, 2002).
51. Ralph Atkins, "Kohl Links his Political Fate to a United Europe," *Financial Times* (November 24, 1992), p. 2.
52. "Debatte des Deutschen Bundestages am 8. Oktober 1992 ueber die Ratifizierung des Maastrichter Vertrages," *Das Parlament*, no. 44 (October 23, 1992).
53. Quentin Peel, "Kohl Rejects Idea of 'Europe ala carte,' " *Financial Times* (December 3, 1992), p. 2.

54. Thomas Risse-Kappen, "Exploring the Nature of the Beast: International Relations Theory and Comparative Policy Analysis Meet the European Union," *Journal of Common Market Studies*, vol. 34 (March 1996), pp. 53–80.

55. Agence France Presse, "Germany Ratifies Maastricht Treaty" (December 18, 1992); web.lexis-nexis.com/universe/document?_m=477680f7d54c0027877 b03a9087eb7e8&_docnum=6&wchp=dGLStS-lSlzV&_md5= (accessed July 7, 2002).

56. Quoted in "EC Summit Reaches Agreement on Central Issues: Denmark Gets a Second Chance," *Deutschland Nachrichten* (December 18, 1992), p. 1.

5

Global Environmental Politics

I. HISTORY OF INTERNATIONAL COOPERATION ON THE ENVIRONMENT

Since the 1972 United Nations Conference on the Human Environment in Stockholm, multilateral negotiations have produced more than ninety major treaties on environmental issues. Optimists suggest that this represents progress toward cooperation on issues of the global commons and point out that there are a surprising number of institutions and procedures in place for coordination of environmental policies.[1] Critics charge, however, that the number of treaties hides the reality that a significant percentage of the agreements signed by government leaders have not been subsequently ratified or implemented.[2] Furthermore, progress in the evolution of the global environmental regime has coincided with increased politicization of intermestic issues. As Chasek argues: "Environmental issues, which combine scientific uncertainty, citizen and industry activism, politics, and economics, may be among the most complicated and difficult to resolve.... Discussions about the best ways of enforcing treaties often fall victim to political rivalries and national sovereignty concerns."[3] Case studies examined here appear to illustrate this complexity.

Global warming is one of the most contentious environmental issues to emerge in recent decades. The theory of global warming is derived from scientific arguments developed in the nineteenth century that increases in carbon dioxide (CO_2) and related greenhouse gas (GHG) emissions lead to higher atmospheric temperatures. Almost a century passed before political leaders began to seriously address the implications of the scientific theory of global warming, however. In 1985, the World Meteorological Organization and the United Nations Environment Programme (UNEP) took the first major step on issue definition by establishing the Intergovernmental Panel on Climate Change (IPCC) to evaluate possible effects of global warming. IPCC reports charting a rise in global surface temperatures triggered UN General Assembly resolutions in the late 1980s and early 1990s calling for negotiations on an agreement to limit GHG emissions.

After two years of pre-negotiations, the UN Conference on Environment and Development was held in Rio de Janeiro, Brazil, in June 1992. Among the issues under consideration was a proposed UN Framework Convention on Climate Change (UNFCCC) to establish limits on GHG emissions. Supporters of the framework convention, including some advanced industrialized countries working alongside environmental groups, argued that cuts in GHG emissions by industrialized states were imperative for future ecological stability. Opponents of the convention believed that the international community should not take radical action based on limited scientific evidence. In particular, they rejected the idea that advanced industrialized countries bear the direct and indirect costs of sustainable development around the globe. After intense negotiations, a compromise framework convention was completed that called for voluntary stabilization of emissions at 1990 levels. The framework convention was signed by 153 countries at the summit and ratified by scores of countries (including all five democracies examined here). The treaty entered into force on March 21, 1994.

In December 1997, government representatives gathered in Kyoto, Japan, to turn elements of the framework convention into a protocol with binding commitments to lower emissions. Not all states favored such a move, however, and summit negotiations were intense. The Kyoto Protocol agreement that was finally hammered-out called for Annex I industrialized countries to reduce overall GHG emissions by 6–8 per cent by 2012, using 1990 levels as a baseline. The plan allowed differentiated target levels for industrialized countries, including an 8 per cent increase for Australia, an 8.2 per cent reduction for key member states of the European Union, a 7 per cent reduction for the United States, and a 6 per cent reduction for Japan. Developing countries would not be required to cut emissions, but they were encouraged to establish voluntary plans for such change.[4] The Kyoto Protocol would officially enter into force when ratified by fifty-five countries (representing at least 55 per cent of global emissions levels). This "double trigger" for enforcement represented a high threshold that essentially demanded participation by the United States and other highly advanced industrialized countries.

While many world leaders celebrated the completion of the Kyoto Protocol, they were all too aware that the plan might never enter into force without ratification of the deal. They also knew from the tough negotiations at the summit that some countries were much more supportive of the plan than others. As one editorial noted on the day after the treaty was signed: "The hard part is over . . . but now comes the hard part."[5]

II. AUSTRALIA AND KYOTO: MISSING
A "THREE-INCH PUTT"

Australia's struggle over the Kyoto agreement in the Howard government may represent a classic case of domestic constraints on international commitments. In the mid-1990s, Australia produced 1 per cent of global GHG emissions, but it ranked as the highest per capita emitter of GHGs in the world. Australia supported early international efforts to address global warming, including the UNFCCC and the 1995 Berlin Mandate. As time passed, however, the government faced tremendous pressure from entrenched interests to resist a protocol. Australian negotiators fought hard at Kyoto to achieve an allowed 8 per cent *increase* in GHG emissions to 2012 along with other stipulations in the treaty language. In spite of these achievements, and more concessions to Australia in subsequent Conference of the Parties (COP) meetings, the government announced its decision not to ratify the treaty in 2001.

International Pressure

Signature of the Kyoto Protocol in April 1998 by the government of Australia marked the beginning of the post-commitment phase. Australia faced international pressure to ratify the agreement, and most observers believed that the government would eventually do so. Supporters claimed that Australia had achieved a good deal in the treaty negotiations and that the economy stood to benefit from a transition to a more climate-friendly orientation. It was also clear that the government risked a degree of isolation by rejecting the international agreement, something that the country often struggled to avoid. Yet behind the scenes, the ratification process became highly politicized, and critics charged that Australia would bear too heavy a burden from the deal. Studies suggested that there would be significant economic costs, borne disproportionately by the energy sector.

Australia was also at the center of a normative storm regarding ratification. It had supported the establishment of the International Panel on Climate Change in 1988. Following on the success of the Montreal Protocol, Prime Minister Bob Hawke ordered the creation of a National Greenhouse Response Strategy, and the government set an Interim Planning Target to reduce GHG emissions to 1988 levels by the year 2000 and another 20 per cent by 2005.[6] Australia ratified the UNFCCC in December 1992. Three years later, Australian negotiators accepted the Berlin Mandate calling for legally binding cuts in emissions. Yet contrary to their perceived role in world politics, once the Protocol was signed Australian diplomats set about an aggressive process to change the international community's plan by pushing for greater flexibility mechanisms. Australia abandoned the multilateral approach to environmental stewardship on climate change and instead opted for a condominium of interests with like-minded countries including the United States.

Executive Strategy

Prime Minister Hawke and his Labor Party government first began to address major environmental concerns, including prospects for climate change, in the 1980s. Australian leaders were aware of their country's vulnerability to climate change based on studies by atmospheric research scientists from the Commonwealth Scientific and Industrial Research Organization (CSIRO). Reports showed that global warming could lead to serious environmental problems for Australia, including intensified ocean storms, extreme weather patterns such as severe droughts or floods, and coastal damage from rising sea levels. Perhaps most salient were the predictions that climate change could produce conditions that would decimate the Great Barrier Reef.[7]

The Hawke government's early activism on the issue generated opposition over time, however. As government officials began to target industries like steel and aluminum for their production of roughly two-thirds of all GHG emissions, energy sector leaders quickly mobilized.[8] Key industrial representatives teamed up with government ministries, cabinet ministers, and members of parliament to counter the emphasis on industrial responsibility for climate change. By the time of the transfer of power from Hawke to Keating in 1992, the government's National Greenhouse Response Strategy had been watered-down. Perhaps most significant was Australia's move to cast its lot with other advanced industrialized countries facing costs from GHG emissions reductions. Australia joined with Canada, Japan, Iceland, New Zealand, Russia, Ukraine, and the United States in a bloc (the so-called Umbrella Group) that demanded concessions, flexibility mechanisms, and cooperation from developing countries in order to achieve a comprehensive solution to climate change.

Victory by the Liberal/National Party coalition in March 1996 signaled another dramatic turn in Australia's environmental policy. The new prime minister, John Howard, was pro-business and shared the concerns of corporations about the implications of any environmental agreement. Characteristic of his leadership style, Howard seemed to have chosen *not* to play a visible role on climate change, and he recognized Cabinet differences on the question from the outset. Howard assigned carriage of the issue to Environment

Minister Robert Hill and tasked him to push back on international pressure for GHG emissions cuts.[9] At the very next COP meeting in Geneva in 1996, Australian diplomats resisted efforts by other countries to establish more assertive guidelines for emissions cuts and even refused to support language borrowed from the Berlin Mandate one year earlier.[10]

The Howard government also adopted a new strategy to achieve *differentiated* emissions reduction targets for industrialized countries in the Kyoto Protocol. Diplomats from the Department of Foreign Affairs and Trade (DFAT) directly lobbied their counterparts in foreign capitals to emphasize their unique situation in relation to climate change. Australia, they argued, was an energy-intensive economy that faced serious competition from many rising Asian economies and had many special needs (such as transportation over long distances between cities).[11] Very few foreign officials bought into the claim, however.[12] In one particularly critical exchange, Timothy Wirth, U.S. Undersecretary of State for Global Affairs said that Australia had not made a good case for differentiated targets. When asked about the U.S. interpretation of Australian economic forecast models, Wirth replied that observers should "look at what those people are smoking."[13] At the time it seemed that efforts by the Howard government to expand Australia's win-set were falling on deaf ears, and some believed that this only further contributed to Australia's international isolation on the issue.

By holding firm on this new position right up to Kyoto, however, the Howard government was eventually able to shift diplomatic momentum back in its favor. Working with their partners in the Umbrella Group, negotiators drove a hard bargain to insert differentiated targets on GHG emission cuts into the Protocol. Australia was one of only three developed countries (along with Iceland and Norway) to secure an allowance to increase its GHG emissions by 8 per cent by 2010. Hill also achieved another last-minute coup for Australia by inserting a clause in the Protocol that would recognize the effects of land-clearing programs in the formula calculating emissions reductions.[14] This so-called Australia clause provided special allowances for the government to receive retroactive credit for ending land-clearing programs in forested and rural areas.[15] Land clearing was an especially serious problem in western New South Wales and Queensland. The net result of this clause was, in reality, a flexible cap that allowed Australia to raise its emissions by as much as 22–33 per cent.[16]

Prime Minister Howard praised the agreement and Australia's negotiating stance, stating: "We fought for Australian jobs every inch of the way and the outcome vindicates the Government's stance." Others were less sanguine. The Labor Party's Shadow Environment Minister, Duncan Kerr, who was an observer on the delegation, said Australia now faced a "three-inch putt" to reach the reduction targets.[17] EU Environment Commissioner and chief EU negotiator Ritt Bjerregaard even said publicly that Australia had been misleading in negotiations but "got away with it."[18] Meanwhile, a spokesman for Greenpeace called it a "low-ground victory...for the Howard Government" that would make Australia a "greenhouse ghetto."[19]

The Australian government signed the Kyoto Protocol on April 30, 1998, in New York. While noting that ratification of the agreement was likely to be "a few years away," Environment Minister Hill maintained confidence in Australia's support for the agreement given the "inevitable momentum about it."[20] From 1998 to 2000, it appeared that the Australian government would indeed ratify the agreement. Discussions were underway inside the government (and within the Umbrella Group) about proposals to create an emissions credit-trading regime. This type of arrangement would allow countries like Australia even more flexibility in meeting the objectives of the Kyoto agreement. The Howard government established the Australian Greenhouse Office (AGO) to study how best to coordinate GHG emissions cuts with major industries and the agricultural sector. To outsiders, these developments signaled the government's resolve to explore its options for ratification and compliance with the Protocol.[21]

Several developments in 2000–1 led to the Howard coalition government decision *not* to ratify the Kyoto Protocol. First, support for the Kyoto Protocol inside the Howard Cabinet collapsed in the lead-up to the Hague Summit of December 2000 (COP-6). There were serious divisions between Cabinet ministers, and between leaders of the Liberal and National parties in the coalition, over a set of new environmental laws that could impact on Australia's compliance with Kyoto. Specifically, cabinet support for the agreement fell away over the question of a "greenhouse trigger" law that would require that all future industrial development projects which might impact GHG emissions receive approval from the federal government. Hill supported the plan, but the ministers for Resources and Energy and Industry sharply opposed the concept of a binding trigger. Industry Minister Senator Nick Minchin referred to a new report that showed that compliance with Kyoto could lower Australia's gross national product and raise prices in the energy sector.[22] Deputy Prime Minister John Anderson of the National Party called it an "environmental veto" of economic development.[23]

Second, the outcome of the 2000 presidential elections in the United States had the effect of delaying any final decision on Kyoto in Canberra. The results of the election race between Al Gore and George W. Bush were so close that they were contested for nearly forty days. Meanwhile, in Canberra the government finalized its negotiating position for the Hague Summit that included demands for a global emissions credit-trading scheme. In words that foreshadowed the turn of events at The Hague, Hill warned that negotiations would be undermined by the deadlock in the U.S. presidential election. He said, "I find it very hard to see how it can reach conclusions now without the United States being a key party".[24]

The Hague COP in late November 2000 represented a very difficult chapter in global efforts to reduce GHG emissions. While the Australian and U.S. governments pushed for flexibility in compliance mechanisms, including allowances for carbon sinks and an emissions credit-trading regime, European Union representatives demanded more concerted action. The conference ended in deadlock, and diplomats returned home uncertain whether an agreement on implementation would ever be possible. The conference also revealed fissures within the Cabinet. Eventually Hill's position inside the government in favor of ratification became untenable. Prime Minister Howard announced his decision to reassign Hill to the Ministry of Defense, effectively ending Australia's public program of championing Kyoto ratification.[25] In March 2001, newly elected President George W. Bush announced that the United States would not ratify the Kyoto Protocol. On June 5, 2002, Prime Minister Howard said in an address to parliament that Australia would not ratify it either. He claimed, "for us to ratify the protocol would cost us jobs and damage our industry."[26]

Regime Type: Executive–Legislative Relations

The Australian political system empowers the executive (prime minister) through majoritarian advantage in the lower house of parliament.[27] From signature of the Protocol in April 1998 to 2000, Cabinet support for the treaty tended to stifle parliamentary debate. But public disclosure of private squabbles over the treaty in May 2000 served to raise the temperature of debates on the floor of parliament. The Labor Party and Greens quickly weighed in on the Cabinet debate by endorsing the greenhouse trigger proposal advocated by Hill. Senator Nick Bolkus, Labor Party environment spokesman, warned that Australia faced a great deal of international hostility if it was to defect from Kyoto. Bolkus warned that the loss of support in the cabinet would mean that "other countries would be waiting in the Hague for Australia with baseball bats. [The cabinet split] shows they're not serious."[28]

Even Labor and the Greens were divided as to whether they should strongly endorse Kyoto. The Protocol did have its costs, after all, and treaty compliance would have serious implications for Labor constituencies. Shadow Minister for Industry Bob McMullan and Minister for Science Martyn Evans argued that there was simply too much uncertainty leading up to the Hague

Summit for it to make a strong public commitment. In late July 2000 the Labor party publicly dropped its commitment to the Kyoto Protocol. It changed its environmental platform simply to a general statement that Labor believed "Australia must act as a responsible member of the world community and commit to greenhouse gas emissions targets."[29] Labor's shift in position certainly echoed the sentiments of a number of business leaders who believed that the Australian government should adopt a more conservative stance on implementation agreements at The Hague. Meanwhile, even the environmentalist Greens were divided over the Protocol given the possibility that Australia might promote nuclear energy as a way to lower GHG emissions. Thus, there was substantial disagreement about the future course. Following several Cabinet meetings, the government announced plans for its own stylized program of GHG abatement measures that included incentives for industry compliance.[30]

Interest Groups

Many interest groups were engaged in the drawn-out debate over ratification of the Protocol in Australia, and the struggle became very bitter indeed. The Australian Industry Greenhouse Network (AIGN) was an umbrella organization of business and trade groups that came out strongly against a tough binding protocol. Other opponents included the Business Council of Australia (BCA), a consortium of corporations with vested interest in Australian energy policies, along with major trade groups representing coal, steel, and aluminum production. BCA leaders held urgent meetings to discuss ways for corporations to craft a unified stand in the midst of Cabinet debates about Australia's negotiating stance for the Hague COP.[31] The BCA released a "blueprint" in September 2000 that essentially laid out conditions for corporate cooperation, demanding that Australia push for an extremely flexible emissions credit-trading scheme at the Hague Summit. The BCA also made it clear that they wanted the Cabinet to formally endorse the pledge not to ratify the Kyoto Protocol before the U.S. government.[32]

Major corporations including BP Amoco, Rio Tinto, and Alcoa joined with consortia to oppose the treaty.[33] Opponents relied on negative economic forecasts to bolster their arguments. In October 2000, the Allen Consulting Group released a new study warning that more than 20,000 jobs would be lost in the Victoria region alone if Australia ratified the Kyoto Protocol.[34] The study predicted significant job losses in coal-fired energy production plants, construction, and mining. The worst job losses would occur in less urban areas, with regional Australia predicted to lose more than 160,000 jobs.

Finally, the study again predicted that the overall gross domestic product of Australia would fall by about 2 per cent annually as a result of ratification and full compliance. While the study created media headlines, it soon became apparent that big corporations and trade consortia (including the Australian Aluminum Council, the Australian Minerals Council, and the Australian Coal Association) had helped sponsor its development.

The government appeared to be tuned in to interest group opposition. Indeed, several representatives of these groups were part of the official Australian delegation to the Kyoto Summit. Cabinet leaders made repeated attempts to placate their opposition. In a very significant move, Energy Minister Senator Parer told coal and oil industry lobbyists in 1998 not to worry because the "Howard government had made a secret cabinet decision not to ratify the Kyoto Protocol unless the United States government did so first."[35] This admission of a linkage guarantee in Australian foreign policy is substantiated by the record but has never been publicly acknowledged by the Howard government.

Supporters of the Kyoto Protocol faced a tougher road. Environmental lobbies had largely been shut out of the consultative process during international negotiations. They urged the government to support GHG emissions cuts and even reluctantly applauded the completion of the Kyoto agreement. But as it became more apparent in 2000 that Australia would take an obstructionist stance at the Hague COP, environmental groups became even more concerned. Greenpeace spokesman Kert Davies charged that Australia and other advanced industrialized interests would sabotage the Summit. He called the emissions credit-trading proposal a "big get out of jail free card."[36] Scientific researchers also joined the debate. For example, researchers from CSIRO continued to produce studies suggested that climate change could lead to more severe storms, increased risk of fire damage, and flooding and erosion. The Queensland Centre for Maritime Studies warned that warmer ocean currents would kill 95 per cent of the coral in the Great Barrier Reef by 2050.[37]

Public Opinion

In many ways, the Australian government stance on this issue can be characterized as dramatically out of step with prevailing public attitudes. Australian public opinion strongly favored international action on the environment. Australians had praised their government's proactive stance on past global issues such as transboundary air pollution and ozone protection. One survey released in 2001 found that 80 per cent of Australians believed that the

Kyoto Protocol should be ratified, even without the support of the United States.[38] The government's rejection of the treaty prompted public outrage that resonated throughout the remainder of the Howard government's term of service.

Outcome and Analysis

Prime Minister John Howard announced in 2001 that Australia would not ratify the Kyoto Protocol, and his government attempted to shift focus quickly thereafter. At this writing, however, climate change has reemerged as a serious debate. The theme came back to public attention in the wake of concerns about the costs of global warming for the Australian economy. Australia's drought has also deeply affected public consciousness on the issue and served to reignite concerns. In the national election campaign in late 2007, the Labor Party candidate for prime minister, Kevin Rudd, pledged to ratify the treaty if elected.

Neorealists predict that a country will not ratify an agreement that poses significant costs versus benefits. After vacillating on the question for several years, it appears that the Howard government bowed to material interest concerns regarding the treaty. The pro-business prime minister acknowledged significant opposition at home to the deal, and this translated into rifts within the cabinet by 2000. In many ways, it appears that Howard was confronted with a classic realist dilemma: whether to support an international treaty that posed significant costs and offered only vague benefits at the risk of losing the support of party ministers and major corporations. In addition, the prime minister was sensitive to international pressures from traditional allies including the United States. Senator Parer's admission that Australia would not ratify the treaty without the United States represents a revealing power politics linkage in foreign policy decision-making.

The prime minister took his decision in spite of significant international normative pressure to uphold the treaty. Indeed, Australia had been integrally involved in early efforts to establish agreements on GHG emissions cuts, and the Hawke government had a very positive reputation as a champion of the environment. Even during the Howard era, Australia faced significant pressure to support the Protocol. Ironically, most of this pressure seems to have fallen on Environment Minister Hill rather than Howard, and the drama over Kyoto played out parallel to the minister's own fate. Australia's rejection of the treaty did contribute to further diplomatic isolation.

Two key domestic conditions played a role in the outcome of Australia's decision on Kyoto: executive strategies for ratification and interest groups. In this case, the Howard government appears not to have engaged in an active or sophisticated approach to try to build support for the treaty at home. Howard remained on the sidelines throughout most of the debate on the issue leading up to the Hague COP. At the same time, interest group activism does appear to have had the anticipated impact on ratification outcome. Major corporations and lobbyists fought the Kyoto Protocol and made it clear that this was a make-or-break issue for them. Finally, there is little evidence that public opinion had an impact on the outcome. Howard's rejection of the treaty flew in the face of the attitudes of most Australians. Informed citizens were aware that despite claims to the contrary, the Liberal/National coalition was doing very little to address GHG emissions cuts.[39] By ignoring the wishes of the international community and its own citizens, critics charged that Australia ran the risk of permanently "relegating itself to global insignificance."[40]

III. CANADA AND THE KYOTO PROTOCOL

The Kyoto Protocol touched off an intense debate over international environmental policy and sovereignty in Canada. In some ways, the ratification of the treaty in December 2002 represented little more than a pyrrhic victory for departing Liberal Party Prime Minister Jean Chrétien. Debates about implementation of the agreement continued for years afterward, especially at the provincial level. The election of a new, minority Conservative government under Prime Minister Stephen Harper in January 2006 made it unlikely that Canada would ever fully comply with the treaty.

International Pressure

International pressures weighed on the Canadian government's decision regarding ratification of the treaty. However, the scope and intensity of these pressures were unclear at the time given the broader scientific debate about climate change. Some Canadian leaders clearly interpreted climate change as a serious and emerging threat to national security. Reductions in GHG emissions, it was argued, would improve the chances of long-term economic stability, territorial integrity, and security. Climatologists warned that Canada, with one of the longest coastlines in the world, would suffer massive economic damage as a result of rising sea levels. Yet, other high-profile players in politics, economics, and science in Canada argued that ratification of the treaty would actually hurt the country. As a major producer of oil and natural gas, Canada's western regional economies stood to lose hundreds of thousands of jobs, and major corporations would be hit hard. Ratification of the deal would have serious domestic distributional effects on the Canadian economy and place high demands on the government to restructure existing policies.

Canada did face normative pressure to ratify the treaty, in part based on its own strong record of support for other environmental agreements including the Long-Range Transboundary Air Pollution (LRTAP) Convention and the Montreal Protocol on CFC emissions. The Canadian government actually hosted an intergovernmental conference on climate change in Toronto in 1988, and delegates produced a final statement calling for a 20 per cent reduction in carbon dioxide emissions within five years. Later, the Canadian government was directly engaged in negotiations to establish the UNFCCC and the Kyoto Protocol, and Canadian leaders articulated a strong "green" political agenda at home. As Reif argues, Canadian foreign policy was greatly shaped by the 1992 Earth Summit: "[E]nvironmental protection became ever more linked with social and economic concerns and there were further increasing numbers of non-state actors and stakeholders voicing their concerns and trying to influence the Canadian foreign policy formation and implementation process."[41]

Executive Strategy

Canadian Prime Minister Jean Chrétien's handling of the Protocol may provide a fascinating illustration of *what not to do* for executives seeking ratification of controversial treaties. Chrétien, head of the Liberal Party governing majority, exhibited little personal interest in climate change negotiations during much of the 1990s. Then, in September 2002, the prime minister surprised many in his own party by announcing his plan to speed the Kyoto Protocol through Parliament for ratification. He also announced plans for retirement after eighteen more months of service. Critics charged that Chrétien was searching for an enduring legacy and believed that the environment was an area where he could make his mark.[42]

This is not to say that Chrétien and his cabinet did nothing toward ratification of the protocol. Rather, the actions that they did take prior to the prime minister's announcement were short-sighted and counterproductive. For example, Chrétien and his cabinet regularly conferred with provincial leaders on policy matters throughout the 1990s, but these meetings seemed to foster the perception that the federal government would be bound by provincial concerns. In the fall of 1997, representatives of the federal government and provinces met to work out a compromise on the government's stance going in to the Kyoto Summit. Chrétien pledged that the federal government would avoid "singling out or weakening one region or one industry."[43] And Environment Minister Christine Stewart reached an agreement with provincial leaders that Canada would only commit at Kyoto to reduce emissions to 1990 levels by 2010, or less than 3 per cent overall.[44] Federal authorities made it clear that following the Kyoto meeting, government agencies would examine the potential impact of the treaty "under a guiding principle that no region should bear an unreasonable burden from implementing the agreement."[45]

At the Kyoto Summit, however, Canadian diplomats went well beyond their mandate and pledged to reduce emissions by a full 6 per cent by 2012. Government ministers knew that the deal would face trouble at home, but instead of returning from Kyoto to launch a carefully coordinated strategy for ratification the administration tried to sidestep the issue. The prime minister did not engage in side payments or issue redefinition in the aftermath of the summit. The government gradually pursued synergistic issue linkages by allying itself closely with other, advanced industrialized states, including Australia, New Zealand, Japan, and the United States, in efforts to water down the treaty by creating highly flexible compliance mechanisms. Canadian delegates worked to craft compliance mechanisms that would include credit for carbon sinks as well as obfuscating source issues. Later, during the Hague COP in 2000, Canada's search for more flexibility drew sharp criticism from environmental groups. The director of the Sierra Club in Canada called Canada's behavior "shameful and embarrassing," warning that his country had become "known internationally as a laggard on environmental issues."[46]

After years of inattention at home, Chrétien announced plans in September 2002 to complete key parts of his political agenda including ratifying the Kyoto Protocol. This pledge was taken without close consultation with his advisors, however, and in many ways contrasted with the reality of the prime minister's political situation at the time. Chrétien and the Liberals faced tremendous pressure from environmental lobbies, key industries in the energy sector, and western provincial governments to reject the treaty. The prime minister also had to contend with serious disagreements inside his own cabinet. Ministers with portfolios with heavy business interests and those representing regions with special concerns opposed the treaty; ministers who worked on environmental and health issues favored it. As one analyst suggested, cabinet ministers were "flummoxed over the political and economic risks of leaning too far in either direction."[47] The simple fact that differences in the cabinet were aired publicly revealed the depth of the problem.

Regime Type: Executive–Legislative Relations

One of the reasons that Chrétien believed his government could speed Kyoto through parliament for ratification was his intimate knowledge of the Canadian political system. As noted in Chapter 2, the Canadian parliamentary system operates on a principle of majoritarianism that rewards the political party receiving the most votes with a ruling majority in the House of Commons. This arrangement ensures that the center of gravity remains with Crown authority. Chrétien and the Liberals had controlled government since 1993. Successful domestic and foreign policy initiatives had secured the Liberal majority through three elections, and in 2002 the party held a majority of forty-three seats in the House of Commons.[48]

All was not unified in the Liberal Party, however. The prime minister's announcement of an eighteen-month "long goodbye" actually suggested a move to hold the party together in the face of disagreements. Chrétien had been under pressure to pass the reins of government on to his Finance Minister, Paul Martin, for some time. As questions about the prime minister's control of the party increased—and as a campaign fund-raising scandal increased in intensity in the fall of 2002—party leaders decided to relax restrictions on members of parliament who crossed party lines for key votes. In November 2002, dozens of Liberal members of parliament sided with the opposition in a vote in the House of Commons to allow chairpersons of committees to be elected by secret ballot. This initiative would effectively limit the power of the prime minister to control parliamentary committee actions. Some believed this was yet another sign that Chrétien had lost control of his party caucus and might resign even earlier than originally planned.[49]

Interest Groups

Canadian interest groups became highly mobilized in the struggle over Kyoto. This reflected not only the intensity of the issue itself but also a broader trend of "Americanization" of interest group lobbying in Canada in terms of organization and effectiveness.[50] Environmental groups who lobbied the Canadian government on the Kyoto Protocol were some of the same nongovernmental organizations (NGOs) that had actively participated in international negotiations on the LRTAP Convention and the Montreal Protocol. The Climate Action Network (a transnational coalition of hundreds of environmental groups) pressured the government to commit to serious GHG emissions cuts. The Sierra Club of Canada also lobbied the government heavily for international cooperation on the environment. As time passed without ratification, these groups regularly reminded the Liberals that other countries had already taken the plunge, including France in 2000; and Germany, the Netherlands, the United Kingdom, and Japan in early 2002.

Opponents included major business groups and oil companies based in Canada's western region. In September 2002, a coalition of dozens of business groups began a public information campaign designed to promote a "made-in-Canada" solution to deal with global warming independent of Kyoto. Key business organizations including the Canadian Chamber of Commerce (with more than 170,000 members) and the Council of Chief Executives argued against a rush to ratification. These groups warned that the Kyoto treaty might cost Canada some $30 billion in lost economic activity and as many as 450,000 jobs in the manufacturing sector.[51]

The energy sector was deeply opposed to the Kyoto Protocol and put particular pressure on Cabinet leaders and officials from the Ministries of the Environment and National Resources. In addition to challenging the scientific validity of the theory of global warming, representatives of Canada's oil patch region in the western provinces warned that it would be "catastrophic" for regional economies. A leading energy company executive from Calgary's western oil patch region was quoted as saying: "[I am] upset and offended at the way environmentalists pin blame on the coal industry for climatic change.... I don't think Canadians, much as we like to be boy scouts, will want to make irrational commitments in Kyoto without understanding the implications for the way we live."[52] Dee Parkinson-Marcoux, president of Calgary's Gulf Heavy Oil, added, "when you become a target, you can suddenly get terribly interested in an issue."[53]

Finally, Canadian provincial economies were closely connected with corporate interests, particularly in the oil patch region. The rift between federal and provincial government positions on Kyoto was particularly salient because of the constitutional arrangement in Canada that vests provincial governments with authority over natural resources. In preparation for the 1997 Kyoto conference, for example, the federal government negotiated a compromise with provincial leaders that Canada would only agree to reduce emissions by 3 per cent. But the treaty that was finalized in Kyoto actually committed Canada to a 6 per cent reduction—well beyond the limit agreed to by the provinces.

The prime minister's decree in September 2002 that the protocol would be ratified by the end of year created an avalanche of criticism from provincial leaders. Led by Alberta's Premier Ralph Klein, provincial leaders warned that the deal might ruin regional economies and was politically unacceptable. In a thinly veiled threat, Klein warned that Alberta might consider secession from Canada and warned of a possible constitutional crisis over the deal.[54]

Nova Scotia Premier John Hamm said that his province's economy might be "decimated" if Ottawa ratified the Kyoto Protocol without consideration of provincial and sectoral needs.[55] And Ontario's premier, Ernie Eves, warned that his provincial government would simply refuse to implement terms of the Kyoto Protocol without federal government compensation for antici-pated job losses and economic damage. While federal government officials attempted to negotiate a compromise plan with key ministers of the provinces throughout the fall of 2002, consensus was elusive. Key legal and political questions remained unanswered as the Canadian regime marched toward ratification.[56]

Public Opinion

Public attitudes toward the Kyoto Protocol reflected the struggle between vested interest groups and the government. The government enjoyed diffuse public support for action on environmental issues. According to a Gallup survey in the early 1990s, for example, 58 per cent of Canadians viewed global warming as a "very serious" issue, and another 27 per cent believed it was "somewhat serious."[57] Surveys of public sentiments nationwide showed that more than 56 per cent supported ratification in September 2002, and a poll conducted in early November 2002 by Environics/CROP suggested that 78 per cent of Canadians favored ratification.

However, opposition to the protocol was high in certain provinces that faced dire projections about domestic distributional effects. Regional attitudes seemed to be greatly shaped by elite discourse that same year. For example, a May 2002 poll found that 72 per cent of Albertans favored Kyoto, but a poll taken six months later found that the same majority had decided to oppose the treaty because they feared it would put Canada at a distinct disadvantage.[58] Ultimately, much of the public voice on these matters seemed to be condi-tioned by interest group activity as well as elite discourse.

Outcome and Analysis

After extensive debate on the Protocol, Chrétien and the Liberal Party majority pushed through a parliamentary vote in favor of the treaty and implementing legislation on December 10, 2002. On December 17, Canada's environment minister submitted the instruments of ratification of Kyoto to the United Nations.[59] Since ratification, however, Canada, along with other countries including Japan, the United States, Australia, and New Zealand have focused their efforts on creating side arrangements for carbon sinks and the emissions credit-trading regime from international programs to reduce GHGs. One of the most controversial moves by the Canadian government was an effort to seek credit for emissions reductions for the sale of nuclear reactors to developing countries.

By 2005 Canada's GHG emissions had actually risen more than 24 per cent above baseline 1990s levels. The powerful energy sector along with western provinces have resisted fundamental reforms and successfully fought for the development of oil sands projects (a particularly high source of CO_2 production).[60] Finally, the election of a new government under conservative Stephen Harper effectively signaled the end of the treaty debate in Canada. Harper made it clear that their government had moved on to new, alternative approaches to address climate change. Canada has joined with like-minded advanced industrialized states, including the United States and Australia, in pushing for a global solution to the problem that would include participation by developing countries.

The proposition that states are more likely to ratify treaties that represent a maximization of national interests does not clearly explain Canadian actions in this case study. While the prime minister pledged his support for the treaty, there is little evidence to suggest that government officials believed this to be a value-maximizing action. Major voices in Canada contended that ratification of the treaty would actually hurt the regime. Indeed, corporations in the energy sector in Canada's western provinces stood to lose hundreds of thousands of jobs. These constraints were very clear to provincial leaders during the ratification struggle, yet the federal government appeared not to waver in its plan to ratify the treaty by December 2002.

At the same time, the constructivist approach emphasizing the power of norms in shaping Canadian foreign policy offers some measure of explanation in this case. But it does not account for the five-year delay and the stop–start nature of the ratification process. Canada's leadership in international environmental policy fostered a norm of "liberal environmentalism" that began to take shape during the 1980s, coalesced in the Rio summit, and continued to influence Canadian policies in the 1990s.[61] Key members of the Chrétien government were influenced by this tradition, especially Environment Minister Stewart and Natural Resources Minister Goodale, in the buildup to Kyoto as evidenced by their willingness to pledge to reductions far beyond their mandate. Yet following the signature of the treaty, the Canadian government focused not on rapid ratification but rather on the exploration of flexibility mechanisms that would make compliance more attractive. Thus, the constructivist perspective explains the ultimate outcome of this case study but does little to account for the timing and scope of ratification.

This study suggests that two of four scope conditions at Level II may have influenced the outcome of the Kyoto ratification struggle in Canada. Unlike many other cases, executive strategies did not seem to effect ratification success. Prime Minister Chrétien appears not to have employed any sophisticated strategy to build domestic support for this program. There is no evidence of explicit efforts at side payments to build domestic support, and NGOs were the only actors really involved in articulating this as a national security concern (i.e., issue redefinition). Chrétien's government was involved in synergistic issue linkage through attempts to water down compliance mechanisms at COPs following Kyoto, but there is little evidence to suggest that the prime minister himself was involved in directing these efforts. Meanwhile, executive–legislative relations were critical in shaping the ratification struggle. Liberal leaders knew that they could overcome the opposition in a final vote on the treaty, and they even allowed a fairly lengthy floor debate and set of speeches by the opposition. However, the administration's hands were virtually tied when it came to dealing with provincial leaders resisting implementation. These problems extend to the present day, and at this writing it appears unlikely that Canada will ever fully comply with the treaty.

Interest groups were actively involved in the ratification debate. Environmental lobbies including the Climate Action Network and the Sierra Club favored cooperation with the Kyoto Protocol in the tradition of other major environmental agreements. However, these groups were matched by major business consortia and industry representatives from the energy sector who sought to prevent ratification. The Canadian Council of Chief Executives and the Chamber of Commerce mobilized heavily to prevent ratification in the fall of 2002, warning (with some evidence) that Canada would face serious economic costs of compliance. Finally, public opinion had little if any measurable impact on the ratification outcome. Most Canadians expressed diffuse support for international agreements to lower GHG emissions, but some constituencies were deeply opposed to specific tenets of the protocol. Public opposition was especially intense in certain provinces—increasing the likelihood that agreements would not be implemented by provincial leaders.

IV. FRANCE AND THE KYOTO PROTOCOL

France was a leading player in EU diplomacy that helped to develop the Kyoto Protocol, and it was instrumental in pushing for ratification by all EU member states. French President Jacques Chirac enjoyed bipartisan support for the plan in the legislature. Indeed, the French government had effectively co-opted major interest groups to support the managed reduction plan. Especially important in the government's calculation of costs and benefits of the deal was the centrality of the French nuclear industry. Accordingly, French officials championed a rigorous climate change protocol and discouraged much flexibility in the compliance system. Beyond the regional and international debates over the treaty, the Chirac government itself was able to move quickly to ratify the agreement.

International Pressure

French government officials recognized climate change as a serious challenge. Along with its EU partners, France endorsed concerted action on GHG emissions cuts in the late 1980s, years before some other governments. France seems to have approached the climate change question aware of its implications for national security and economic prosperity. France was also heavily invested in the development of institutionalized responses to climate change. The French government had established a strong track record on environmental cooperation, including support for the LRTAP Convention and the Montreal Protocol. Government leaders worked closely with their European counterparts in articulation of the institutions and norms governing GHG emissions, and they were enmeshed in both legal and institutional networks promoting cooperation.[62]

Executive Strategy

French support for international agreements on climate change began under the Mitterrand presidency. In general, the government accepted its share of responsibility on the issue as the fourth largest producer of GHGs in Europe, behind Germany, the United Kingdom, and Italy.[63] European diplomats began addressing the issue in the late 1980s, including consideration of policies designed to promote energy conservation and even a regional carbon tax. In June 1990, the European Council called for early adoption of strategies to limit emissions of GHGs and established the European Environment Agency to provide monitoring functions and to help facilitate member state implementation of environmental law.[64] At the Joint Council of Energy and Environment Ministers that October, officials issued a communiqué that called for stabilization of emissions by Community members "by the year 2000 at 1990 levels."[65]

In this action the European Community recognized the challenges of climate change and agreed on concerted action well before many other governments had begun to address the issue. By confronting the issue head-on, France and its partners also sponsored some of the first negotiations on questions of flexibility mechanisms to promote treaty compliance and a regional or national carbon tax. Mitterrand favored a carbon tax that would be imposed on all energy production facilities, while other European capitals were pushing for a broader energy tax. In the end, the European Council was deadlocked on the issue and finally resolved not to impose any regional tax plan, opting instead for voluntary tax programs in member states.[66]

The French government signed the Kyoto Protocol on April 29, 1998, making it one of first advanced industrialized countries to do so. France also joined with EU member states to endorse regional as well as national solutions to the GHG emissions-cut challenge. Article 4 of the Protocol actually allowed parties to negotiate a side agreement in which they pledged to fulfill their Kyoto mandate as a group. Emissions reduction levels for the EU as a whole were set at −8 per cent, yet member states were left the latitude to determine how best to distribute the burden. In June 1998 the Council finalized a plan that required countries like Germany and Denmark to cut emissions by 21 per cent, while others including Spain, Portugal, Ireland, and Sweden would actually be allowed an increase in emissions. The goal for France was a 0 per cent change in GHG emissions to 2012. The government and key industries were pleased with what they believed was a manageable objective, yet environmental groups charged that France could (and should) go much further.[67]

Fifth Republic institutions provided Chirac and his Prime Minister Lionel Jospin with the political capital necessary to achieve domestic support for the treaty when they sought it. Indeed, the debate in France never seemed to center on *whether* the government should support the treaty but rather *how* to achieve Kyoto targets. The primary issue of contention in the 1990s was flexibility mechanisms. During the course of the first several COPs, the French government position was that the mandate for GHG emissions cuts should be as rigid as possible, thereby forcing many countries to make difficult choices about energy policy and the environment.[68] French diplomats pushed their counterparts in the EU to resist the creation of an emissions credit-trading scheme, for example, as preferred by some Umbrella Group member states. Bettina Laville, environment advisor to Prime Minister Lionel Jospin, was an outspoken opponent of flexibility mechanisms like carbon sinks.[69] The French position was bolstered by the fact that the government perceived its own goal as manageable (especially given its heavy reliance on nuclear energy).

By 1998, however, it had become clear that flexibility mechanisms of some sort would be necessary to offer any hope that major Annex I states would support the protocol. Once EU diplomats accepted that achievement of the objectives of the Kyoto Protocol would be contingent on compromise on flexibility mechanisms, the debate turned to exactly what form they might take.[70] The Umbrella Group continued to push for an allowance for carbon sinks, but French officials including Environment Minister Dominique Voynet rejected the proposal.[71] A related issue under discussion at COPs focused on the creation of a Clean Development Mechanism (CDM). The CDM was a proposal to provide relief of the GHG emissions cuts burdens for advanced industrialized states that would help developing countries develop cleaner energy technologies. The question essentially forced France's hand on the matter of flexibility mechanisms, and the Chirac government let it be known that they favored nuclear energy programs as part of a comprehensive program of reforms.

The EU moved steadily toward ratification by member states and the institution as a whole. French leaders joined with their counterparts in a pledge at the COP-5 meeting in Bonn in 1999 to ratify the Kyoto Protocol within three years. In May 2000, the European Commission established the European Climate Change Programme (ECCP), an initiative to promote implementation of, and compliance with, the Kyoto Protocol.[72] Chirac used the 2000 meeting in The Hague as an opportunity to push France's position, saying:

I arrive in The Hague with a sense of urgency.... Since 1992, we have fallen too far behind in the fight against global warming. We cannot afford any further delay. That is why, I can confirm to you here, Europe is resolved to act and has mobilised to fight the greenhouse effect. Europe calls upon the other industrialised countries to join with it in this fight.... Of course, there are the inevitable difficulties of adaptation and constraints attendant upon the necessary process of development. Of course, we have to contend with pressures from those with a vested interest in taking the easy route or immobility, the immediate interests of those who earn a rent on energy wastage. But we must not allow this to stand in our way. Today, at The Hague, the international community, represented by the world's environmental ministers, has a moral and political duty to move forward in the right direction.[73]

Chirac's statements were intended both to rally support for action toward the larger cause and to encourage the EU and Umbrella Group member states to find common ground. At the same time, however, Dominique Voynet, the French environment minister and head of the EU delegation, stood firmly opposed to some types of flexibility mechanisms advocated by the United States. The Hague conference ultimately deadlocked over the question. Finally, it is worth noting that by 2003 the EU had endorsed a wide variety of mechanisms as enticements for major emitters to join the regime and even accepted a program of emissions credit-trading among EU member states.[74]

Regime Type: Executive–Legislative Relations

The National Assembly played a marginal role in French environmental policy. Indeed, the French government had a long tradition of ministerial autonomy that essentially guaranteed a dominant role in policymaking for the Ministry for the Environment and Regional Development. Dominique Voynet, a member of the Green party in France, was appointed minister for the environment and regional development in Jospin's cabinet in 1997. This was a highly significant move for the conservative government and one that testified to the centrality of environmental issues for France and the EU in the 1990s. In 1999, the National Assembly also reviewed a set of coordinated policy initiatives developed by the European Commission and approved the government's own national plan to uphold Kyoto mandates and comply with environmental law.

Interest Groups

At least two factors served to limit the influence of interest groups in the ratification process for the Kyoto Protocol in France. First, French politics were dominated by the executive, making consideration of ratification of the Kyoto Protocol a relatively closed process. Discussions inside the government were driven by the technocratic elite and allowed few points of entry for key interest groups.[75] The Chirac government did selectively engage leaders of key industries during negotiations, including appointing them as official members of delegations to COPs. Second, electoral laws dictate a strong role for major party organizations, and so many interest groups traditionally sought affiliations with parties in order to have their voices heard.[76]

Those groups who did become active on the climate change issue did so from the perspective of outsiders to the political process. France had experienced a rise of new social movements in the 1980s and 1990s dedicated to issues such as ecology and pacifism. Yet while there remained a political culture of mobilization and protest to effect political change in France, the actual climate change response seemed to attain little traction.[77] One contentious, related issue was France's reliance on nuclear power for nearly 80 per cent of all its energy. The government saw this as a position of strength in the climate change debate. Yet environmental groups saw the nuclear issue as vexing, both in its immediate terms in France and in a wider context as a possible "solution" to GHG emissions worldwide. Environmental groups found it especially troubling that the government had stated that it would like to see nuclear projects as part of the CDMs—a program designed to grant developed countries easier emissions targets in return for providing developing countries with good technologies.[78] Groups including the World Wildlife Fund Climate Change Campaign and Greenpeace opposed nuclear energy as a solution to climate change.[79]

Public Opinion

French public opinion regarding the dangers of global warming was consistent with that across much of Europe. French citizens expressed concern about climate change and supported general solutions. According to 1995 Eurobarometer survey data, for example, 44 per cent of French citizens said that they were "very worried" about global warming, while another 34 per cent were "somewhat worried." These figures were higher than responses in several other countries, yet below the European average by several points.[80] Seventy-eight per cent of respondents in France also characterized environmental protection as an "urgent problem."[81]

Outcome and Analysis

On May 31, 2002, France joined with other members of the European Union in ratifying the protocol. President Chirac trumpeted this achievement in a variety of international meetings that year, including the Johannesburg Summit on Sustainable Development and the Group of Eight summit in Canada.[82] He joined with his European counterparts in lobbying leaders of the United States, Russia, and Japan to ratify the treaty.

The proposition that states are more likely to support treaties that represent a maximization of national interests does not appear to explain French ratification of the Kyoto Protocol. A neorealist perspective focused on absolute gains would contend that France would be disadvantaged by the agreement. France faced significant costs associated with GHG emissions cuts coupled with uncertainty regarding worldwide compliance with the regime. Conversely, the constructivist approach emphasizing the power of norms offers some measure of explanation in this case. The French government had engaged in multilateral negotiations on climate change for a decade and continued to emphasize a norm of strict compliance (with limited flexibility mechanisms) well past the effective life of the discussion. Through initiatives including the UNFCCC and the European Climate Change Programme, France repeatedly demonstrated its commitment to the emerging norm.

This study suggests that three of four scope conditions at Level II may have influenced the outcome of the ratification struggle. Executive strategies seemed to have little bearing on this case in that Chirac and Jospin appear to have assumed the domestic support necessary for ratification success. There is no evidence of side payments or issue redefinition associated with the deal. To the extent that synergistic issue linkage was under discussion at COPs, the French government tended to withhold its support. Confidence on the part of the executive appears justified when one looks at the landscape of other relevant domestic conditions, however. Chirac enjoyed significant influence in the National Assembly, and his government had effectively co-opted key interest groups in support of the deal. The government also enjoyed a permissive public consensus for action. In sum, normative pressures coupled with a supportive domestic political arena appear to explain the steady course of French policy in ratifying the Kyoto Protocol.

V. GERMANY AND THE KYOTO PROTOCOL

The Federal Republic of Germany produced the largest volume of GHG emissions in the European Union in the 1990s, yet it emerged as a lead state on climate change. German Chancellor Helmut Kohl was instrumental in crafting the Kyoto Protocol and encouraging his government to ratify the treaty along with other members of the European Union. The new Social Democratic Party (SPD)–Green Party coalition government elected in 1998 propelled this agenda forward, and Germany ratified the protocol in 2002.[83] To date, Germany and its European allies have continued to lead other advanced industrialized countries—sometimes pulling, and sometimes pushing—toward real limits in GHG emissions.

International Pressure

From the time of the UNFCCC to the signature of the Kyoto treaty in 1998, German leaders perceived benefits to completion of an agreement on the reductions of GHG emissions. Far earlier than some other governments,

Germany and its European neighbors appear to have bought into the scientific assessments that stressed the potential peril of ignoring GHG emissions. However, the treaty would be very costly for the German economy, and it represented a significant sacrifice of sovereignty over environmental regulations at home and in the region. At the same time, Germany had worked with other EC partners to address issues in the previous decade including transboundary air pollution and CFC emissions. On climate change, the Kohl government was actually ahead of most other advanced industrialized states in defining the problem and proposing solutions. As a lead state, Germany helped formulate the standards that would guide international action on the matter. In many ways, Germany was both a contributor to the establishment of the norm of cooperation on climate change and a participant in the regime. Furthermore, the LRTAP and CFC agreements had established international legal foundations for cooperation on the environment that set a precedent for Kyoto. In this sense, then, the German government faced dual overlapping pressures of normative arrangements and international law.

Executive Strategy

Germany's support for international environmental action began in the 1970s. West German leaders, including Chancellor Helmut Schmidt (SPD), created a federal environmental program to address critical issues at the time including air and water pollution. While election victories for the Christian Democratic Union (CDU, or Conservatives) led to a period of retrenchment on environmental issues, the Conservative position evolved significantly after the Chernobyl nuclear reactor accident in the Soviet Union in 1986.[84] The German government created the *Bundesministerium für Umwelt, Naturschuts und Reaktorsicherheit* (the Federal Ministry for the Environment, Nature Conservations, and Nuclear Safety, or BMU), a new cabinet-level ministry that increased the profile of environmental issues.

In June 1990, the Kohl government announced a bold unilateral program to reduce GHG emissions by a dramatic 25 per cent by 2005, working from a 1987-level baseline. This plan included a move to higher emissions standards for automobiles, a carbon tax proposal, and other programs to boost energy efficiency.[85] The cabinet also created a new Climate-Gas Reduction Strategies Inter-ministerial Working Group, to be chaired by Environment Minister Klaus Töpfer. He became the public voice of the government pushing hard for reductions in GHG emissions throughout the 1990s.[86]

How could a conservative chancellor and cabinet come to embrace dramatic unilateral cuts in GHG emissions? Scientific research showed that

Germany was responsible for more than 20 per cent of GHG emissions in Europe, and it was clear that for any regional or international agreement on GHGs to succeed the government would have to endorse major cuts. Germany's ability to significantly cut its CO_2 emissions was also aided by reunification in that the government could shut down or convert many inefficient eastern industrial facilities.[87] In other words, government experts believed that reductions could be achieved at marginal cost. Finally, Kohl's embrace of climate change was not only a recognition of the seriousness of the issue—it was also a maneuver to counter increasing pressure from the political left for environmental and energy policy reform. This was particularly important in the buildup to the 1990 federal elections (the "unification election"), as the Conservatives sought to shore up their support across the political spectrum.[88]

Having established a clear commitment to address the global warming issue at home, Kohl took his message abroad. The Chancellor placed climate change high on his agenda for the G-7 summit in Houston in July 1990 (in spite of resistance by the Bush Sr. administration). German officials maintained a position of support for dramatic emissions reduction plans through the 1992 Earth Summit and 1997 Kyoto meeting, and through forums including European Commission, the UNEP, and head of state summits. Later, Germany continued to lead the European Union to consider ratification and implementation of the Kyoto Protocol. Töpfer moved from his post in the BMU to become director of UNEP, further raising Germany's international profile on the environment.

Regime Type: Executive–Legislative Relations

Chancellor Kohl controlled a governing coalition of parties including the CDU, the Christian Socialist Union (its sister party in Bavaria), and the FDP. The chancellor knew that the legislative majority he enjoyed would be sufficient to ratify the Kyoto Protocol. However, parliamentary stances on climate change were inextricably linked with several other issues. First, scientific research published in the 1980s called attention to growing evidence that Germany's forests were in peril from environmental causes like air pollution and acid rain (the *Waldsterben* crisis). This news created widespread public concern as forest lands were tied not only to economic health but also a sense of German national identity. Second, the Chernobyl accident produced intense debates across Europe over the safety and future of nuclear energy programs. In Germany, the CDU maintained a pro-nuclear stance in the 1990s, and some conservatives even argued that the construction of more nuclear facilities would help ease GHG emissions problems associated with coal-burning power

plants. At the other end of the political spectrum, the Greens were vocal opponents of nuclear power, and their concerns were only magnified in the wake
of the Chernobyl accident.[89] The Greens became particularly adept at forcing
the hands of larger parties by tapping into public concerns and working with
consortia of interest groups to pressure the government.[90]

In fact, the *Bundestag* became the first public forum for exploration of
climate change and proposed responses during the latter half of the 1980s,
well before the cabinet seized the issue as their own. In June 1987, the *Bundestag*'s Enquete Commission for Preventative Measures to Protect Earth's
Atmosphere was created. The commission included eleven members of the
Bundestag from all major parties along with eleven climate research scientists.
This group held hearings to collect evidence on global warming and offer
a series of proposed solutions. They released an influential report in 1988
that called for a full 30 per cent reduction by the year 2005, with particular
attention to reductions in the newer states. The commission also explored the
highly controversial matter of whether the government should institute a carbon tax to raise revenue for environmental cleanup and efficiency programs.
These bipartisan initiatives helped pave the way for cabinet leaders to move
forward on climate change with backing from the parliament.

Interest Groups

Significant changes in energy and emissions policies would affect a number of domestic interests in Germany. The first organized effort to engage
the government on climate change actually came from a group of research
scientists in 1979. The Energy Working Circle (*Arbeitskreis Energie*) of the
German Physics Society, made up of physicists from universities, industry, and
the public sector launched a public information campaign aimed at raising
concern about climate change. As noted earlier, the Chernobyl accident and
the *Waldsterben* helped advocacy groups concerned about global warming to
reach a much larger audience of concerned citizens in the 1980s.

The effects of interest groups on government policy were limited, however,
by several, fascinating dynamics of the political system in this period. First,
global warming itself never became a rallying theme for groups either in favor
of, or opposed to, major cuts in gas emissions. In fact, NGOs and environmental interests were distracted by other issues during this same period.[91] The
climate change issue was overshadowed by a parallel, noisy debate about an
environmental tax during this same period. Some groups such as the German
Confederation of Small and Medium-Sized Enterprises (BVMW) and service
worker unions favored renewable energy strategies and even the possibility

of an energy tax. At the same time, the Federation of German Industry (*Bundesverband der Deutschen Industrie* or BDI) and the German Chamber of Industry and Commerce first opposed any energy tax proposal. Once it became clear, however, that the federal government was moving toward the adoption of some kind of levy or tax, they altered their tactics to focus on a regional or international levy program that would not specifically disadvantage German businesses.

Public Opinion

Support for international environmental cooperation in Germany actually started at the grassroots level. In the 1960s, local citizen action groups (*Bürgerinitiativen*) organized to address local environmental problems. By the 1980s, these groups had developed into a nationwide network of citizens concerned about such issues as nuclear weapons, nuclear energy, acid rain, and water pollution. The election of the Greens to the *Bundestag* in 1983 signaled that these issues had moved into the mainstream. Environmental activism increased significantly after Chernobyl and grew with the controversy of NATO's modernization of intermediate-range nuclear forces in the region in the late 1980s.

By the 1990s, many Germans had begun to focus on climate change itself. According to a 1992 survey, some 73 per cent of Germans called climate change "very serious," while another 21 per cent categorized it as "somewhat serious." Combined, these figures ranked Germans as one of the most concerned publics among advanced industrialized states.[92] In the period following Kyoto, German public opinion strongly supported a reduction of GHG emissions, although respondents were split over specific initiatives such as a carbon tax. Attention to the environment only increased with the 1998 election of the SPD–Green coalition government. The Greens gained some influence over environmental policy (including the assignment of the Environment Ministry portfolio), and the government directed resources to research on renewable and alternative energy sources (including wind power, solar energy, and biomass).[93]

Outcome and Analysis

In the wake of the Kyoto Summit, there was a large degree of political consensus in Germany on the need for dramatic GHG emissions cuts. The new SPD-Green coalition took up the issue almost immediately upon their election in

September 1998. Chancellor Gerhard Schröder and his Green Party Foreign Minister, Joschka Fischer, were influential in orchestrating policy changes. In the years that followed, Germany reduced its commitment to coal energy from approximately 36 per cent of all primary energy in 1990 to around 21 per cent in 2005, and it closed inefficient and highly polluting (lignite coal) energy plants in eastern Germany. In early 2002, both the *Bundestag* and *Bundesrat* voted to ratify the Kyoto Protocol. Germany joined with many of its EU partners to submit their instruments of ratification that spring, in advance of the UN World Summit on Environment and Development in Johannesburg.[94]

Germany continued to play a leadership role in international negotiations to establish a compliance regime for the protocol. In 1998, diplomats from EU member states worked closely together to develop a common position on the question of the emissions credit-trading regime prior to the COP-4 meeting in Argentina.[95] During the period of German presidency of the European Council in May 1999, the EU Council of Ministers developed a joint implementation plan for the protocol.[96] The German government hosted the COP-5 meetings in Bonn in October–November 1999, and devoted a great deal of energy to negotiations on flexibility mechanisms built into the regime.[97] With strong encouragement from the EU, the Russian government ratified the protocol in November 2004. This fulfilled the double-trigger for ratification (fifty-five countries ratified, representing more than 55 per cent of global GHG emissions), and the Kyoto Protocol formally went into effect on February 16, 2005.

International pressures seemed to guide Germany in two different directions on Kyoto. While German leaders recognized that climate change was a critical issue, the government also faced significant costs in exchange for uncertain outcomes. Germany was Europe's leading emitter of GHGs, and energy policy would have to be restructured. Meanwhile, normative pressure predicted German cooperation with the treaty. Germany had a strong record on the environment, and the Conservative/Liberal government was outspoken in its support for national and regional action on climate change.

Domestic conditions were very influential in the German ratification of the protocol. First, this case illustrates the importance of executive strategies for ratification success. The Kohl cabinet announcement in June 1990 that Germany would unilaterally make dramatic cuts in GHG emissions showed the importance of determined leadership. The Chancellor subsequently practiced all three strategies designed to gain domestic support for the treaty. The government adopted a bipartisan approach to the project from the outset. Töpfer's interministerial working group represented various constituencies with vested interests in changes in energy policy. In the process of investigating the problem and possible solutions, the Kohl government clearly integrated side payments into the development of the GHG emission planned cuts. By playing a dominant role in regional negotiations on implementation, the chancellor expressed willingness to use synergistic issue linkages to encourage other advanced industrialized democracies to commit to the agreement. Later, Chancellor Schröder and Foreign Minister Fischer embraced the concept of issue redefinition by casting GHG emission cuts as essential to national and regional security. In many ways, this was the story of determined leadership to achieve key environmental policy objectives.

Ratification of the Kyoto Protocol was also facilitated by the role of the legislature, the distraction of interest groups, and diffuse public support. Indeed, the *Bundestag*'s Enquete Commission was a key player in investigation of climate change even before the Conservative–Liberal coalition took action. This panel made it clear that the government could undertake GHG emissions cuts with bipartisan support. The election victory of the SPD–Green coalition in 1998 helped ratchet up pressure on all players in the German system to support the protocol. Interest groups, meanwhile, had become somewhat distracted by related, complex issues. Some industry groups mobilized to fight the proposed carbon tax, while others were caught up in lobbying the government over continued funding of coal-powered energy plants. Finally, it should be noted that there was strong, if diffuse, support among the German public for action on climate change. Germans themselves had embraced action on the environment beginning in the 1960s, and they were satisfied to support initiatives in the late 1990s and beyond. Public support for action was also facilitated by significant media coverage of environmental problems.

VI. THE UNITED STATES AND THE KYOTO PROTOCOL

The U.S. record on climate change is rife with contradiction. The government supported the UNFCCC but resisted a binding agreement limiting GHG emissions throughout most of the 1990s. Critics charged that emissions cuts would have serious economic costs and that a treaty forcing advanced industrialized countries to shoulder the costs of sustainable development around the globe was inherently unfair. Nevertheless, the Clinton administration did sign the Kyoto Protocol in 1998, setting a target of roughly 7 per cent emissions cuts by the United States by 2012. World leaders celebrated U.S. accession to the treaty, but they were aware that domestic constraints were a serious hurdle to ratification and compliance.

International Pressure

No country has faced greater international pressure to ratify the Kyoto Protocol than the United States. The U.S. Senate ratified the UNFCCC, and Clinton administration officials participated in COP meetings throughout the 1990s. Vice President Al Gore signed the Kyoto Protocol on behalf of the U.S. government in November 1998, but the administration knew that the treaty— and the very *idea* of a treaty of this nature—offered a mix of opportunities and challenges. Opponents of the Protocol argued that it would significantly harm U.S. economic security as well as create a double standard for the rest of the world. Advanced industrialized economies would bear the costs for reducing GHG emissions while developing countries might very well continue along the same path of industrialization. The treaty, they contended, would hurt the U.S. economy and major businesses. At the same time, scientific skepticism about global warming further muddied the water of calculations of costs and benefits.

The United States faced serious normative pressure to ratify the Kyoto Protocol. The U.S. government had a good track record on some environmental issues, including its leadership on the Montreal Protocol to cut CFC emissions a decade earlier. U.S. diplomats were actively involved in negotiations at the COPs to craft what would become the Kyoto Protocol. Past agreements on regulatory regimes in other environmental areas had become sedimented as layers in the broader normative network of global action on the environment. Thus, the subsequent reversal of U.S. policy in spite of persistent normative pressure for international cooperation on climate change left many experts looking for explanations in the ratification struggle itself.

Executive Strategy

The Clinton administration's approach to climate change could hardly be characterized as an effective strategy. After gaining ratification of the UNFCCC, the President appeared to support moves toward a binding international protocol on GHG emissions cuts. Indeed, with very little advance consultation, the president authorized U.S. diplomats at the 1995 Berlin COP to commit to establish a binding protocol for advanced industrialized states that offered an exemption for less developed countries. Rocked by Congressional scolding, the President retreated from the commitment for several years. Even though the administration hailed the completion of the Kyoto Protocol, the President Clinton chose not to sign it for almost one year. Once the administration did sign the protocol in the fall of 1998, it offered only halfhearted attempts to build grassroots support for the treaty in the years that followed. Publicly, President Clinton promoted strong international cooperation on the environment and hailed the Kyoto Protocol as a "golden opportunity to conquer one of the most important challenges of the 21st century." The executive branch issued a series of statements in favor of the treaty but appeared to do little else to move it to ratification.

Privately, however, the administration recognized that the protocol would be politically unacceptable in its present form. It posed significant costs to the government, and its true impact was yet unknown. In direct contrast to the Australian government approach, the chairwoman of the president's Council of Economic Advisors, Janet Yellen, said publicly that economic forecasting on Kyoto was futile. There was no way, she contended, that economic models could "give us a definitive answer as to the economic impacts of a given climate change policy."[98] U.S. diplomats quietly pushed to water down the treaty by crafting highly flexible mechanisms for implementation at subsequent international conferences. At home, Clinton's approach to Kyoto ratification was essentially to conduct an end run around opponents in Congress by building grassroots support for the treaty through proposed tax cuts, market incentives, and close cooperation with industry. Sugarcoating the deal might satisfy key corporate leaders and interest groups over time, it was hoped, thereby reducing pressure on Congress to oppose the treaty. Furthermore, Clinton hoped that Democratic control of the House and Senate or even a Gore presidential victory in 2000 would create a better political climate for ratification.[99]

Regime Type: Executive–Legislative Relations

The Clinton administration knew that relations between the White House and Congress would be crucial for its strategy to build domestic political support for the treaty. But they also knew that they would have to overcome incredible opposition in the Senate. This opposition rested on several key arguments. First, congressional critics maintained that scientific evidence on global warming was actually quite limited and not a firm foundation on which to establish a plan for drastic changes in industrialization policies. Second, congressional leaders opposed plans that would hurt key sectors of the U.S. economy including manufacturers, the energy sector, and agriculture.[100] Third, some demanded that any treaty on climate change be universal in application. Any initiative to target industrialized nations over developing countries would be inconceivable, warned critics. Fourth, some Congressional leaders took exception to proposals floated at the Rio Summit for industrialized countries to provide significant financial resources to fund sustainable development initiatives in the global South. Calls for technology transfer and grants for progress in developing countries would be challenged by U.S. legislators.

Congressional anxiety over Clinton administration environmental policies grew in the wake of the Republican sweep of the 1994 elections. The 1996 Geneva agreement to establish a legally binding protocol set off alarm bells in Congress regarding environmental negotiations. Senator Jesse Helms (R-NC), Chairman of the Senate Foreign Relations Committee, lambasted the administration's action as a dangerous "capitulation" to international concerns. He said:

[T]his means that any new treaty commitments regarding greenhouse gas emissions will set forth legally binding emissions levels that must be met by industrialized countries only. The U.S. position turns basic principles of sound economic policy on its head since it directs industrialized countries to subsidize developing countries by polluting less while incurring higher costs so that developing countries can pollute more without incurring costs.[101]

Helms and other key Congressional leaders were greatly concerned about the direction of Clinton environmental policies, and by 1997 they had constructed a coalition in the Senate against any serious cut in gas emissions. In June 1997, Senators Chuck Hagel (R-NE) and Robert Byrd (D-WV) cosponsored Resolution 98, a bipartisan, nonbinding resolution that warned the administration not to sign any climate change treaty that limited restrictions on emissions to developed countries without extending limits to developing states. Byrd was particularly concerned that the Clinton administration would support a perceived "free ride" given to the developing states (by Berlin Mandate) in the upcoming Kyoto negotiations. He argued that it was wrong to allow "big carbon dioxide emitters" like Brazil, China, India, Mexico, South Korea, and Indonesia to continue to expand inefficient fossil fuel combustion while the developed countries had to pay the costs of reductions, and he worried aloud about the possibility of the loss of U.S. jobs.[102] The Hagel–Byrd resolution emphasized the possible economic implications of such a deal, and they demanded that the Clinton administration provide a financial impact study on the deal if the Senate were to consider it for ratification. The resolution passed the Senate by an overwhelming margin of 95–0.[103] Once the deal was finalized in Kyoto that December, even Senator John Kerry (D-MA) predicted, "What we have here is not ratifiable in the Senate."[104]

Interest Groups

The Kyoto Protocol catalyzed a number of interest groups in the United States to action. Those who favored the Kyoto Protocol included NGOs and scientists who believed that concerted international action must be taken. The Natural Resources Defense Council, Greenpeace, the Environmental Defense Fund, the Sierra Club, and the World Wildlife Foundation all rallied support for the treaty. Groups opposed to Kyoto included trade associations and companies in the energy sector. Perhaps most notable was the emergence of an unusual coalition of interests opposed to the treaty including both labor and management. Thomas Donohue, president of the U.S. Chamber of Commerce, said, "This agreement is bad for the American economy, American workers, and American families."[105] Major union leaders in the United States, including Richard Trumka of the AFL-CIO, warned that an "agreement that shifts production and jobs out of the industrialized world to the developing world without environmental benefit is a trade treaty—not an environmental treaty."[106] They pledged to fight Senate ratification and implementation of the protocol, and their voices were prominent in subsequent Congressional hearings on the treaty.

Key corporate and energy interests mobilized through front associations including the Global Climate Coalition (representing more than 200,000 companies and trade associations) and the conservative Climate Council. Gail McDonald, president of the GCC, led an active campaign against ratification that included several national speaking tours. Similar to the arguments of Senate opponents, McDonald pointed to the targeted selectivity of the protocols in exempting developing countries from the deal—yet by 2012, they would be responsible for more than 60 per cent of emissions.[107] Countries like China, India, Brazil, Mexico, and South Korea would get an unfair advantage in economic growth. The only true results of the treaty, opponents argued, would be economic losses in the United States.

Public Opinion

The American public offered diffuse support for action on climate change, but surveys showed that citizens believed they lacked detailed knowledge of the issue on which to judge. According to the Gallup 1992 Health of the Planet report, 47 per cent of Americans believed global warming was a "very serious problem" while 31 per cent saw it as "somewhat serious."[108] Data from the Bush administration reflected more specific attention to global warming. A *New York Times*/CBS News poll conducted in June 2001 found that 72 per cent of respondents believed that immediate steps were necessary to fight global warming, rather than delays for more extensive scientific study, 52 per cent of respondents favored U.S. ratification of the Kyoto Protocol, and only 39 per cent of those polled approved of Bush's handling of the environment.[109] More than 66 per cent of respondents believed that Bush and Vice President Cheney were "too beholden to oil companies."[110] However, when asked whether they would support higher prices or taxes for consumer products in exchange for lowering GHG emissions, a majority of Americans opposed any change.

Outcome and Analysis

Faced with overwhelming domestic opposition to the Kyoto Protocol, President Clinton chose not to submit the treaty to the Senate for ratification during the remainder of his term. Instead, he focused on his two-track strategy to build public support for the treaty through targeted tax cuts and flexible compliance mechanisms at the international level.

The Kyoto Protocol debate in the United States was essentially brought to an end by the new George W. Bush administration. In March 2001, just three months after taking office, President Bush announced that the government was formally withdrawing its support of the Kyoto Protocol. While officials in the new administration had debated a range of policy options up to the decision, President Bush felt compelled to establish a clear resolve on energy policy and international obligations. The president said that he believed it was wrong to label carbon dioxide a pollutant subject to domestic and international regulations, and his administration would no longer be subject to any prior agreements on targeted emissions cuts. Instead, Bush announced a U.S. plan for voluntary measures to slow GHG emissions based on "the common-sense idea that sustainable economic growth is the key to environmental progress...economic growth is the solution, not the problem."[111]

The proposition that states are more likely to ratify treaties that represent maximization of national interests seems to help explain this case of defection. A review of the ratification struggle shows the degree of controversy within the U.S. polity over support for the treaty. Supporters of the treaty had the most difficult challenge—arguing that short-term economic costs were in the long-term interests of the United States. Opponents were able to make a much more concrete case that the deal would hurt the U.S. economy while at the same time providing loopholes for developing countries. The constructivist argument that the stronger the international norms, the more likely it is that the state will successfully ratify an international agreement does not seem to be supported by this case study. The Kyoto Protocol resulted from a decade of negotiations on the environment, and the United States had been enmeshed in climate change diplomacy throughout this period. The U.S. government had been a leading and progressive voice on ozone depletion and transboundary air pollution in the prior decade, so many naturally assumed that it would fulfill its "obligations" on climate change. Indeed, when the Clinton administration gave its support for the Berlin Mandate and signed the Protocol, some supporters were under the mistaken assumption that the norm of environmental stewardship had won the day. Yet in the end, President Clinton's rhetorical support for the agreement seemed constrained by the hard reality of domestic politics.

Three domestic political conditions seem particularly relevant for this case: executive strategies for ratification, legislative relations, and interest group behavior. First, the Clinton administration adopted a very curious stance toward the treaty. The President seemed to accept that little could be accomplished short of some dramatic shift in Congress and among vested interests. Clinton attempted to practice two of three strategies to build domestic support. He employed side payments targeted largely at corporations that might ease the pain of eventual compliance. These included targeted tax-cut proposals and other incentives. But Clinton's primary focus was on synergistic issue linkage whereby U.S. representatives could negotiate highly flexible compliance mechanisms, including the Clean Development Mechanism and emissions credit trading.

Executive–legislative relations appear to be critical to understanding this case. The Clinton administration faced serious opposition to the treaty in Congress, and initiatives like the Hagel–Byrd resolution demonstrate the depth of Senate resistance. Indeed, one of the more interesting questions that emerge from this case is how the administration believed that it could ever achieve Senate support in the face of these challenges. Even sympathetic Senators like John Kerry (D-MA) warned the President that the treaty might present an insurmountable challenge. Finally, interest group opposition can be seen as directly linked to the Senate's position in this matter. Interest groups like the GCC and a coalition of labor and corporate groups were deeply opposed to the treaty. These groups, including some traditional supporters of the Democratic Party, were able to lean on the administration both publicly and privately to seek an alternative path on climate change. Together with Congress, these groups effectively drew a line in the sand (in spite of administration initiatives to widen the win-set through synergistic issue linkages).

NOTES

1. Lynton Keith Caldwell, *International Environmental Policy* (Durham, NC: Duke University Press, 1991); see also Arild Underdal and Kenneth Hanf, eds., *International Environmental Agreements and Domestic Politics: The Case of Acid Rain* (Aldershot, UK: Ashgate Publishers, 2000).

2. Patricia M. Wolff, "Uncovering Determinants of International Environmental Cooperation: The Disjuncture Between Treaty Signing and Treaty Ratification," Master's Thesis, Department of Political Science, University of Oregon (June 1996).

3. Pamela S. Chasek, *Earth Negotiations: Analyzing Thirty Years of Environmental Diplomacy* (New York: United Nations University Press, 2001), p. 2; see also Miranda A. Schreurs and Elizabeth Economy, *The Internationalization of Environmental Protection* (Cambridge: Cambridge University Press, 1997).

4. Peter D. Cameron and Donald Zillman, eds., *Kyoto: From Principles to Practice* (The Hague: Kluwer Law International, 2001); see also Warwick J. McKibbin and Peter J. Wilcoxen, *Climate Change Policy After Kyoto: Blueprint for a Realistic Approach* (Washington DC: Brookings Institution Press, 2002).

5. Cameron Barrand and Lawrence J. Goodrich, "The Future of the Kyoto Climate Accord Is Still Up in the Air," *Christian Science Monitor* (December 12, 1997), p. 8.

6. Ros Taplin, "Greenhouse: An Overview of Policy and Practice," *Australian Journal of Environmental Management*, vol. 1, no. 3 (1994), p. 145; Mark Diesendorf, "A Critique of the Australian Government's Greenhouse Policies," in Alexander Gillespie and William C.G. Burns, eds., *Climate Change in the South Pacific: Impacts and Responses in Australia, New Zealand, and Small Island States* (Dordrecht, Netherlands: Kluwer Academic Publishers, 2000), pp. 79–93.

7. Harriet Bulkeley, "The Formation of Australian Climate Change Policy: 1985–1995," in Gillespie and Burns, eds., *Climate Change in the South Pacific*, pp. 33–50; see also Ching-Cheng Chang, Robert Mendelsohn, and Daigee Shaw, *Global Warming and the Asian Pacific* (Cheltenham, UK: Edward Elgar, 2003); interview with Author, Sydney, Australia (February 15, 2007).

8. Clive Hamilton, *Running from the Storm: The Development of Climate Change Policy in Australia* (Sydney: University of New South Wales Press, 2001).

9. Interview with Author, Canberra, Australia (March 20, 2007).

10. William Hare, "Australia and Kyoto: In or Out?," "Forum: The Kyoto Protocol: Politics and Practicalities," *Forum: The University of New South Wales Law Journal*, vol. 24, no. 2 (July 2001), pp. 17–21.

11. Australian diplomats relied on data in these meetings from an economic model prepared by the Australian Bureau of Agricultural and Resource Economics (ABARE), a federal government research agency. Sadly, it was later revealed that major sponsors of the ABARE study included oil companies and Australian coal and aluminum industries; Hare, "Australia and Kyoto," pp. 17–21.

12. Hamilton, *Running from the Storm*, p. 54.

13. *Sydney Morning Herald* (July 24, 1997), p. 10.

14. Stephen Lunn and Robert Garran, "Our 1:42 am Greenhouse Coup," *The Australian* (December 12, 1997), p. 1; for further discussion, see Hare, "Australia and Kyoto," pp. 17–21.

15. Tony Beck, "The Kyoto Conundrum Continued," *The Australian* (December 16, 1997), p. 13.
16. Harriet Bulkeley, "The Formation of Australian Climate Change Policy," pp. 33–50.
17. As quoted in ABC News, "Australian Government Forces Its Position at Climate Summit," ABC News, www.abc.net.au/news/features/kyoto/default.htm (accessed March 28, 2007).
18. As quoted in Hamilton, *Running from the Storm*, p. 89; see also E. Papadakis, "Global Environmental Diplomacy: Australia's Stances on Global Warming," *Australian Journal of International Affairs*, vol. 56, no. 2 (July 2002), pp. 265–77.
19. Lunn and Garran, "Our 1:42 am Greenhouse Coup," p. 1.
20. As quoted in "Australia Signs on Greenhouse Gases," *The Daily Telegraph* (April 30, 1998), p. 2; see also Cameron Stewart, "Rift Over Green Gas Controls," *The Australian* (May 1, 1998), p. 9.
21. "Australian Government Considering Emissions Trading System," AAP Newsfeed, *Finance Wire*, December 21, 1999, web.lexis-nexis.com/universe/document?_M=2e2f9dc709174ee10375b8f4a854ca09&_docnum=187&wchp=dGLbVzz-zSkVb&_md5=b5f4bba378 (accessed December 7, 2006).
22. Senator Nick Minchin, "Responding to Climate Change: Providing a Policy Framework for a Competitive Australia," *Forum: The University of New South Wales Law Journal*, vol. 2, no. 2 (July 2001), pp. 13–16.
23. "Fed: Split Emerges in Cabinet Over Greenhouse Gases Plan," AAP Newsfeed (May 23, 2000).
24. "Cabinet Finalises Greenhouse Stand," *Australian Financial Review* (November 13, 2000), p. 6; Hill repeated this statement of concern in April 2001; Robert Hill, Speech presented at the Equity and Global Climate change Conference, Washington DC (April 17, 2001), www.pewclimate.org/events/hill.cfm.
25. Interview with Author, Canberra, Australia (May 17, 2007).
26. As quoted in Hare, "Australia and Kyoto: In or Out?" p. 20.
27. Senate Legal and Constitutional References Committee, Parliament of Australia, Trick or Treaty? Commonwealth Power to Make and Implement Treaties (1995), pp. 300–4.
28. "Australia Failing on Greenhouse Promise," *Sydney Morning Herald* (May 25, 2000), p. 8.
29. "Labor Drops Commitment to Greenhouse Protocol," *Sydney Morning Herald* (July 29, 2000), p. 13.
30. Interview with Author, Sydney, Australia (February 15, 2007).
31. "Companies in Fresh Look at Greenhouse," *Australian Financial Review* (July 25, 2000), p. 5.
32. "Labor Drops Commitment to Greenhouse Protocol," *Sydney Morning Herald* (July 29, 2000), p. 13; "BCA Heavies Release Blueprint on Greenhouse Trading," *Australian Financial Review* (September 22, 2000), p. 3.

33. Program Transcript of "The Greenhouse Mafia," Four Corners Series, Australian Broadcasting Corporation, date aired: February 13, 2006, www.abc.net.au/4corners/content/2006/s1566257.htm (accessed April 26, 2007).
34. Allen Consulting, 2000, "Greenhouse Emissions Trading," Melbourne, January 2000; see also DFAT and ABARE, 1995, *Global Climate Change: Economic Dimensions of a Cooperative International Policy Response Beyond 2000* (ABARE: Canberra); "Victoria Facing Huge Job Losses," *The Age* (October 12, 2000), p. 6.
35. Hamilton, *Running from the Storm*, p. 134.
36. "Says Saltbush Can Save the World," *The Age* (November 18, 2000), p. 5.
37. Kathy Marks, "Warmer Pacific Ocean Threatens to Wipe Out Coral on Great Barrier Reef within 50 Years," *The Independent* (February 23, 2004), p. 24.
38. Newspoll Market Research, "Greenhouse Gas" (Kyoto Protocol Study prepared for Greenpeace Australia Pacific, 6–8 April 2001), www.geocities.com/jimgreen3/greenouse2.html (accessed March 11, 2007).
39. Interview with Author, Sydney, Australia (February 15, 2007).
40. Interview with Author, Canberra, Australia (March 20, 2007).
41. Linda C. Reif, "Environment Policy: The Rio Summit Five Years Later," in Fen Osler Hampson and Maureen Appel Molot, eds., *Canada Among Nations 1998: Leadership and Dialogue* (Toronto: Oxford University Press, 1998), p. 269.
42. Interview with Author, Ottawa, Canada (October 11, 2002).
43. Chrétien, quoted in "A New Mantra: Canadian Government's Strategy for Reducing Greenhouse Gases," *Maclean's*, vol. 110 (November 17, 1997), pp. 28–9.
44. Interview with Author, Ottawa, Canada (October 8, 2002); see also Bruce Wallace, "Inside the Kyoto Deal: A Landmark Agreement Receives Mixed Reviews," *Maclean's*, vol. 110 (December 22, 1997), pp. 22–5.
45. National Climate Change Process, "Canada's National Implementation Strategy on Climate Change" (Ottawa: Government of Canada, 2000), p. 2; see also Bruce Doern, "Seven Key Issues and Challenges: Canadian Energy Policy in the Sustainable Development Era," Paper prepared for the Carleton Research Unit on Innovation, Science, and the Environment (CRUISE) Conference on Canadian Energy Policy in the Sustainable Development Era (October 17, 2002), p. 19.
46. Lee-Anne Broadhead, "Canada as a Rogue State: Its Shameful Performance on Climate Change," *International Journal*, vol. 56, no. 3 (Summer 2001), p. 475.
47. Bruce Wallace, "Facing Off Over Greenhouse Gases: Pressure to Curb Emissions Splits the Liberals," *Maclean's*, vol. 110 (November 3, 1997), pp. 12–14; see also Wallace, "Inside the Kyoto Deal: A Landmark Agreement Receives Mixed Reviews," *Maclean's*, vol. 110 (December 22, 1997), pp. 22–5.
48. Jeffrey Simpson, *The Friendly Dictatorship* (Toronto: McClelland & Stewart, 2001).
49. Interview with Author, Ottawa, Canada (October 20, 2002); Bill Curry, "56 Liberals Rise Against PM," *National Post* (November 6, 2002), p. A1.

50. Interview with Author, Ottawa, Canada (October 8, 2002).
51. Brian Bergman, "The Cost of Kyoto: How Far Are Canadians Willing to Go to Help Prevent Global Warming?" *Maclean's*, vol. 115 (March 18, 2002), pp. 38–9.
52. Wallace, "Inside the Kyoto Deal," p. 24.
53. Ibid., p. 24.
54. Bergman, "A Gathering Storm Over Kyoto," p. 20.
55. *National Post* (October 10, 2002), p. A1.
56. Interview with Author, Ottawa, Canada (October 11, 2002).
57. Riley E. Dunlap, George H. Gallup, and Alec M. Gallup, "Health of the Planet Survey: A George H. Memorial Survey" (Princeton, NJ: Gallup International Institute); see also EKOS Research Associates Inc. 2003. *Canadian Attitudes Toward Climate Change: Spring 2003 Tracking Study. Final Report.* March; IPSOS-Reid, "The Public's Year-End Agenda," *Issue Watch* vol. 17, no. 6 (November/December 2002).
58. Environics West survey, quoted in Gillis (October 5, 2002), p. A5.
59. Climate Action Network Europe, Brussels Belgium; www.climnet.org/EUenergy/ratification/calendar.htm (accessed July 14, 2003).
60. Clifford Krauss, "Was Canada Just Too Good to be True?" *New York Times* (May 25, 2005), p. A8.
61. Steven Bernstein, "International Institutions and the Framing of Domestic Policies: The Kyoto Protocol and Canada's Response to Climate Change," *Policy Sciences*, vol. 35, no. 2 (2002), pp. 203–36; see also Bernstein, *The Compromise of Liberal Environmentalism* (New York: Columbia University Press, 2001).
62. See Nigel Haigh, "Climate Change Policies and Politics in the European Community," in Tim O'Riordan and Jill Jäger, eds., *Politics of Climate Change: A European Perspective* (London: Routledge, 1996), pp. 155–85.
63. Scott Barrett, "Political Economy of the Kyoto Protocol," *Oxford Review of Economic Policy*, vol. 14, no. 4 (2000), p. 3; see also Climate Change Secretariat website: www.unfcc.de
64. See Mikael Shou Andersen and Duncan Liefferink, eds., *European Environmental Policy: The Pioneers*, Issues in Environmental Politics (Manchester: Manchester University Press, 1997).
65. "Declaration by the European Council on the Environmental Imperative," *Bulletin of the European Community*, vol. 23, no. 6 (1990), pp. 16–18; see also M.S. Andersen and D. Lieffereink, eds., *European Environmental Policy: The Pioneers* (Manchester: Manchester University Press, 1997).
66. See D. Wilkinson, "Maastricht and the Environment: The Implications for the EC's Environmental Policy of the Treaty on European Union," *Journal of Environmental Law*, vol. 4, no. 2 (1992), pp. 221–39.
67. Peter G. G. Davies, "Climate Change and the European Community," pp. 27–38, in Peter D. Cameron and Donald Zillman, eds., *Kyoto: From Principles to Practice, International Environmental Law and Policy Series* (The Hague: Kluwer Law International, 2001).

68. John Vogler, "The European Union as an Actor in International Environmental Politics," *Environmental Politics*, vol. 8, no. 3 (Autumn 1999), pp. 24–48.

69. Affrontement en vue Sur le Climat, *La Tribune* (October 13, 2000), p. 4.

70. Susan McInerney, "G-8 Approves 'Flexible Mechanisms' to Cut Greenhouse Gas Emissions," *International Environment Reporter*, vol. 21, no. 11 (May 27, 1998).

71. Michael McCarthy, "Climate Conference: Europe Rejects U.S. Call to Alter Pollution Targets," *The Independent* (November 22, 2000), p. 1.

72. Climate Action Network Europe, "European Climate Change Programme," www.climnet.org/euenergy/ECCP.html (accessed October 20, 2006).

73. Speech by Mr. Jacques Chirac, French President, to the Sixth Conference of the Parties to the United Nations Framework Convention on Climate Change, The Hague, Netherlands, November 20, 2000, transcript on www.elysee.fr (accessed August 4, 2007).

74. Andrew C. Revkin, "Treaty Talks Fail to Find Consensus in Global Warming," *New York Times* (November 26, 2000), p. 1.

75. Dana R. Fisher, "Global and Domestic Actors Within the Global Climate Change Regime: Toward a Theory of the Global Environmental System," *International Journal of Sociology and Social Policy*, vol. 23, no. 10 (November 2003), pp. 5–30.

76. See Graeme Hayes, *Environmental Protest and the State in France* (New York: Palgrave Macmillan, 2002).

77. See Sarah Waters, "New Social Movements in France: The Rise of Civic Forms of Mobilisation," *West European Politics*, vol. 21, no. 3 (July 1998), pp. 170–86.

78. Andrew Appleton, "The New Social Movement Phenomenon: Placing France in Comparative Perspective," in R. Elgie, ed., *The Changing French Political System* (London: Frank Cass, 2000), pp. 57–75.

79. Lars H. Gulbrandsen and Steinar Andresen, "NGO Influence in the Implementation of the Kyoto Protocol: Compliance, Flexibility Mechanisms, and Sinks," *Global Environmental Politics*, vol. 4, no. 4 (November 2004), pp. 54–75.

80. Eurobarometer 43.1, Survey conducted by INRA (Europe) a European Network of Market and Public Opinion Research Agencies (1995), p. 95.

81. Ibid., p. 91.

82. European Parliament, 2002, Report on the Proposal for a Council Decision Concerning the Conclusion, on Behalf of the European Community, of the Kyoto Protocol to the United Nations Framework Convention on Climate Change and the Joint Fulfillment of Commitments Thereunder, A5-0025/2002.

83. Nigel Haigh, "Climate Change Policies and Politics in the European Community," pp. 155–85 in Jill Jäger and Tim O'Riordan, eds., *Politics of Climate Change* (London: Routledge, 1996), pp. 161–2; see also Loren Ray Cass, "The Politics of Climate Change: The Origins and Development of Climate Policy in the United Kingdom, Germany, and the United States," Doctoral Dissertation,

Brandeis University (2001), p. 132; Christiane Beuermann and Jill Jaeger, "Climate Change Politics in Germany," in *Politics of Climate Change*, pp. 186–227.

84. Helmut Weidner, "Die Umweltpolitiker konservativ-liberalen Regierung," *Aus Politik und Zeitgeschichte* (November 17, 1989), pp. 16–28.

85. Bundesministerium für Umwelt, Naturschutz und Reaktorsicherheit [BMU], "Bericht des Bundesministers für Umwelt, Naturschutz und Reaktorsicherheit zur Reduzierung der CO_2-Emissionen in der bundesrepublik Deutschland zum jahr 2005: Erster Bericht auf der Grundlage des Beschlusses der Bundesregierung zu Zielvorstellungen fuer eine erreichbare Reduktion der CO_2 Emissionen (Bonn: Federal Environment Ministry, June 13, 1990).

86. Klaus Töpfer, quoted in "International Meeting Yields Debate over Global Climate Change Positions," *International Environment Reporter*, vol. 13, no. 5 (Berlin: Bureau of National Affairs, May 9, 1990), p. 201; see also Michael T. Hatch, *Politics and Nuclear Power: Energy Policy in Western Europe* (Lexington, KY: University Press of Kentucky, 1986).

87. Loren Ray Cass, "The Politics of Climate Change," p. 136; *Frankfurter Allgemeine Zeitung*, "Souberere Kraftwerke ohne Gewalt und Dennoch Wirkungsvoll (February 26, 1990), p. 2.

88. Interview with Author, Bonn, Germany (July 2, 1996).

89. German Bundestag, *Protecting the Earth's Atmosphere: An International Challenge* (Bonn: German Bundestag, 1989); Edda Mueller, "Umweltreperatur oder Umweltvorsorge? Bewaeltigung von Querschnittsaufgaben der Verwaltung am Beispiel des Umweltschutzes," *Zeitschift für Beamtenrecht*, vol. 38 (June 1990), pp. 165–74.

90. Their election to the government coalition in September 1998 represented the high watermark of environmental concerns, and once again they attempted to use this forum as an opportunity to order the shutdown of nuclear power plants across the country; interview with Author, Bonn, Germany (October 8, 1998).

91. Interview with Author, Bonn, Germany (July 3, 1996).

92. Brechen, "Comparative Public Opinion," p. 110.

93. Staffan Jacobsson and Volkmar Lauber, "Reaction of German Society and Politics to Social and Economic Crises Resulting from Conventional Energy Use Since the 1970s," *Energy Policy*, www.iff.ac.at/socec/backdoor/sose05-ringsozoek/9_lauberLibDirReaktionderdtPolundGt.pdf (accessed July 12, 2006); see also John Gummer and Robert Moreland, "The European Union and Global Climate Change: A Review of Five National Programmes," Pew Center on Global Climate Change Report, June 2000, www.pewclimate.org/document.dfm?documentID=183 (accessed July 2, 2006).

94. See Johann-Christian Pielow, "Germany: Political Incentives Concerning the Implementation of the Kyoto Protocol," in Peter D. Cameron and Donald Zillman, eds., *Kyoto: From Principles to Practice* (The Hague: Kluwer Law International, 2001), pp. 73–85.

95. EC Energy Monthly, "EU Firms Up Flexible Mechanisms Negotiation Position for Buenos Aires," *Financial Times Energy Newsletters-EC Energy Monthly* (October 1, 1998), pp. 7–8.

96. "Environment: Agreement on Climate and Commission Proposals," *Europe Report* (May 19, 1999), no. 2408.

97. BMU (Federal Ministry for the Environment, Nature Conservation, and Nuclear Safety), "Germany's National Climate Change Program" (Berlin: Government of the Federal Republic of Germany, 2000); "Climate Change: Delegates in Bonn Express Guarded Optimism for Year 2000," *Europe Energy* (November 10, 1999), no. 547; see also "EU Ministers Agree Deal to Share Out Kyoto Plan," *Power Economics* (July 31, 1998), p. 17.

98. William K. Stevens, "Cost Uncertainties Delaying Action on Global Warming Policy," *New York Times* (October 6, 1997), p. A1.

99. Interview with Author, Washington DC (July 16, 2001).

100. This opposition developed through Congressional hearings and investigations of the potential implications of the Kyoto Protocol; see, for example, "Road from Kyoto: Hearing before the Committee on Science, U.S. House of Representatives," 105th Congress (Washington DC: Government Printing Office, 1999); "The Kyoto Protocol: Is the Clinton–Gore Administration Selling Out Americans?" Parts I–VI; Hearing before the Subcommittee on National Economic Growth, Natural Resources, and Regulatory Affairs of the Committee on Government Reform and Oversight, House of Representatives, 105th Congress, April 23, May 19, May 20, June 24, July 15, September 16, 1998 (Washington DC: Government Printing Office, 1999).

101. "Global Climate Change," *Congressional Record*, S11490 (September 27, 1996).

102. Interview with Author, Washington DC (July 17, 2001).

103. "Senate Resolution 98—Expressing the Sense of the Senate Regarding the United Nations Framework Convention on Climate Change," *Congressional Record* (June 12, 1997), p. S5622.

104. Jake Thompson, "Winning Friends, Influencing Senate Freshmen Sen. Chuck Hagel Crafts a Reputation as a Consensus Builder," *Omaha World Herald* (July 26, 1997), p. 1.

105. Ibid., p. 8.

106. Ibid., p. 8.

107. Gail McDonald, as quoted in Geeta Sharma-Jensen, "Business Leader Assails Global Climate Treaty," *Milwaukee Journal Sentinel* (January 19, 1998), p. 6.

108. Steven R. Brechen, "Comparative Public Opinion and Knowledge on Global Climate Change and the Kyoto Protocol: The U.S. Versus the World?" *International Journal of Sociology and Social Policy*, vol. 23, no. 10 (2003), pp. 106–43; see also R. Dunlap, G. H. Gallup, and A.M. Gallup, "Health of the Planet Survey: A George H. Memorial Survey (Princeton, NJ: Gallup International Institute, 1993).

109. Lydia Saad, "Poll Analyses—Americans Sharply Divided on Seriousness of Global Warming—Only One-third Consider the Problem Grave," Gallup

News Service (March 25, 2002), www.gallup.com/poll/releases/pr020419.asp (accessed September 3, 2002).

110. *New York Times*/CBS News Survey, June 2001; results reported in Steve Kettmann, "Will Bush Support the Kyoto Protocol? Pressure Here and Abroad May Leave Him No Choice," July 18, 2001, www.salon.com/news/features/2001/kyoto (accessed March 4, 2004).

111. Andrew Revkin, "Bush Offers Plan for Voluntary Measures to Limit Gas Emissions," *New York Times* (February 15, 2002), p. A6.

6

The Comprehensive
Nuclear-Test-Ban Treaty

Struggles over ratification of the 1996 Comprehensive Nuclear-Test-Ban Treaty (CTBT) illustrate the politicization of international agreements, even in an area of so-called high politics where many believe that national security imperatives drive state behavior. By the 1990s, countries around the world had supported a number of agreements designed to limit the spread of nuclear weapons and technology. The CTBT was interpreted by many as the logical next step in the deepening of the nuclear nonproliferation regime. U.S. President Bill Clinton called it "the longest-sought, hardest-fought prize in arms control history."[1] Others warned, however, that the treaty circumscribed the latitude of major nuclear powers to conduct test explosions at the very time that the international security environment had become more uncertain. To date, the CTBT has not entered into force, in part because of decisions by select governments not to ratify the agreement.

I. HISTORY OF THE COMPREHENSIVE
NUCLEAR-TEST-BAN TREATY

The first discussions of a nuclear test ban emerged in the aftermath of World War II. Western leaders recognized the awesome destructive capability of atomic weapons and knew that a nuclear arms race would bring an entirely new set of international security challenges. Some conscientious rulers had a change of heart regarding atomic weapons after Hiroshima and Nagasaki, and they began to advocate for an absolute ban on weapons testing and development. Prominent scientists who had been involved in the Manhattan Project also spoke out in favor of strict international controls on nuclear technology. In addition, United Nations commissions explored ways to avoid a nuclear arms race while at the same time administering nuclear energy programs for civilian uses.

At the start of the 1950s, Cold War tensions impeded significant progress on a test-ban agreement. The United States, the Soviet Union, and the United Kingdom all engaged in aboveground nuclear-test detonations on remote sites and quickly expanded their arsenals. France made progress toward its own nuclear weapons capability. U.S. President Eisenhower's New Look strategic profile gave nuclear weapons a central role in defense plans for Western Europe. Practically speaking, governments on both sides of the Iron Curtain believed nuclear weapons testing to be an essential part of their deterrence profile. And over the decades nuclear weapons states would conduct more than 2,000 critical nuclear tests (with thousands more subcritical tests).

By the end of the decade, several factors pushed leaders to reconsider negotiating a test ban. First, it appeared that more and more countries might rapidly develop nuclear weapons. Western leaders were particularly concerned about the research and development program in the communist People's Republic of China. Optimists believed that by delimiting the conditions for nuclear testing they could effectively raise the threshold for would-be proliferants. Second, the Soviet Union and the United States had begun testing a new generation of bombs that were incredibly powerful and threatened an intensified arms race. Third, scientific research began to show the harmful effects of radiation on human health and the environment.[2] These and other considerations helped move recalcitrant governments toward consideration of arms limitation, and pre-negotiations began between western and Soviet diplomats. In 1958, Great Britain, the Soviet Union, and the United States agreed on a one-year moratorium of nuclear testing.[3]

Nuclear weapons states completed a series of arms control treaties in the 1960s and 1970s. For example, the United States, the Soviet Union, and Great Britain negotiated a Partial Nuclear-Test-Ban Treaty (PTBT) in 1963. The agreement banned nuclear tests above ground in the atmosphere, in space, and under water. The only remaining venue for testing would be through controlled, underground blasts with scientific monitoring. The United States and the Soviet Union also signed a Threshold Test-Ban Treaty (TTBT) that limited underground tests to under 150 kilotons. In the 1970s, U.S. and Soviet negotiators also completed several bilateral arms limitation agreements, including a peaceful nuclear explosions treaty (PNET).[4]

The end of the Cold War created a new window of opportunity for arms limitation agreements. In 1990, the TTBT and PNET were ratified by the U.S. Senate. President George H.W. Bush signed a nuclear testing moratorium bill into law in 1992 that called for nine-month suspension of tests and urged international progress on a comprehensive test ban. Other nuclear weapons states followed suit. Meanwhile, the UN Conference on Disarmament (CD) focused its attention on negotiation on a comprehensive nuclear test ban.

When the CD became deadlocked over specifics, supporters decided to present the text of the agreement as a resolution to the United Nations General Assembly instead.

The CTBT outlined fundamental obligations for all states to cease nuclear testing and to discourage efforts to test on the part of others. To ensure compliance, the core of the agreement focused on verification and compliance. Part I of the treaty established an International Monitoring System that would include more than 300 seismic and acoustic monitoring systems around the world. Part II established a system of verification through an on-site inspections program. Treaty clauses established standards of privileges and immunities for teams: overflight rights for test monitoring, with details on what the aircraft can carry in terms of monitoring; managed access to inspection sites; and collection, handling, and analysis of samples. Part III of the treaty provided confidence-building measures including notification of large explosions and location and transparency of the monitoring program.[5] The agreement also established a Comprehensive Test-Ban Organization (CTBTO), based in Vienna, to administer the program.

The CTBT received overwhelming support in a vote in the United Nations General Assembly in September 1996; 158 countries voted for the treaty resolution and only three against (India, Libya, and Bhutan). The treaty was then opened for signature at the plenary meeting. Within five years, more than 165 countries had signed the agreement, and 93 of them had ratified it.[6] However, the treaty also stipulated that it would only enter into force when all nuclear-capable states (a total of forty-four countries) signed and ratified the treaty. According to the Article XIV of the agreement, because this did not occur three years after it was opened for signature the UN convened a series of annual conferences to discuss ways to accelerate the ratification processes in participating states to achieve speedy entry-into-force of the treaty. To date, the treaty has not been signed by some nuclear-capable states and not ratified by others. What follows is a brief synopsis of ratification dilemmas in five key signatory countries.

II. AUSTRALIA AND THE CTBT

The story of Australia's engagement with the CTBT has several fascinating dimensions. Publicly, Australia was a strong advocate of the CTBT as a reflection of its commitment to the nonproliferation regime. The treaty was signed by the Howard government in 1996 and then advanced quickly for ratification. These actions glossed over an important historical episode, however: In the

1960s, Australia had developed the technological capability for a complete nuclear fuel cycle and even tried to acquire nuclear weapons of its own. Even after signature and ratification of the CTBT, critics charged that the Howard government was pushing for an expansion of Australian export policies and greater involvement in the global nuclear fuel cycle.

International Pressures

The Australian government faced significant international pressure to ratify the CTBT. Supporters argued that the treaty would provide Australia with increased security through constraints on the proliferation of nuclear weapons. They charged that the treaty offered tangible benefits by raising the bar on nuclear weapons research. As a major nonnuclear weapons state, Australia was a vocal participant in the nonproliferation regime. Diplomats had helped to negotiate major treaties in the past including the PTBT and the Treaty of Raratonga establishing a South Pacific Nuclear Weapons Free Zone. At a deeper level, the CTBT was not only about material constraints on nuclear capabilities, it was also a pledge by participants not to conduct nuclear weapons tests. In this way, it reinforced the nonproliferation norm that had been developing over decades, and Australian leaders clearly perceived an obligation to support the treaty.

Executive Strategy

Prime ministers from both major parties, the Liberal Party and the Australian Labor Party (Labor), supported a global nuclear-test-ban treaty. In the 1980s and 1990s, Labor Prime Ministers Hawke and Keating, along with Foreign Minister Gareth Evans, were outspoken advocates for nuclear nonproliferation. Upon election to office in March 1996, Liberal Party Prime Minister John Howard and Foreign Minister Alexander Downer took up the cause and promoted the finalization of negotiations on the CTBT. While Howard's foreign policy rhetoric on nuclear issues was more muted than that of his predecessors, he tasked Downer to help break the deadlock on the draft treaty in the Conference on Disarmament and move the treaty forward for signature in the UN General Assembly in September 1996.

On the surface, Prime Minister Howard's support for the CTBT was entirely consistent with his government's stance toward nuclear weapons. But Australia's nuclear history was actually much more nuanced. Australia first became involved in nuclear research in 1944 when the government sponsored a large-scale exploration program for uranium for use in the Manhattan Project. Exploration for uranium continued after World War II, and large deposits were discovered, mined, and exported to the United Kingdom and the United States for use in weapons programs.[7] In 1951, under the leadership of Prime Minister Robert Menzies, Australia signed a security pact with the United States and New Zealand (ANZUS) that saw the establishment of permanent U.S. military bases in Australia. Menzies also invited Great Britain to test nuclear weapons in his country (based on very little consultation with his own government). The first British bomb was tested in 1952 on Montebello Islands off Western Australia. Later tests were conducted at Woomera and Emu Field in South Australia.[8] The 1950s also saw a joint program between the Australian and British government to develop and test nuclear-capable long-range missiles.[9]

In 1953, the Australian government created the Australian Atomic Energy Commission (AAEC) to explore atomic energy research and development. Conservatives in the Australian government, especially Sir Philip Baxter, a nuclear physicist and chairman of the AAEC, believed that nuclear weapons should be the centerpiece of a modern military force. They interpreted their Cold War strategic situation as similar to that of Western European countries, which had seen the deployment of substantial nuclear weapons (as well as chemical and biological warheads) for defense against a Communist bloc onslaught.[10] The government established its first nuclear research reactor, supplied by the United Kingdom, five years later. Australian leaders also began to make secret requests to their allies to obtain nuclear weapons of their own. As one expert characterized it: "Far from lolling about 'on the beach', the long succession of Liberal Party governments during the first quarter century of the Cold War invested Australia heavily in the Free World's nuclear deterrence plans against the Communist threat . . . and even tried to foment an Australian nuclear weapons program."[11]

The development of the Nuclear Nonproliferation Treaty (NPT) in 1968 posed a new challenge for the Australian government. On the surface, the NPT was an international agreement that fit with Australia's declared position of anti-nuclearism. However, Liberal Prime Minister John Gorton opposed the treaty because he believed that it might unduly limit Australia's plans for construction of nuclear reactors using domestically produced fuel, a possible expansion of uranium exports, and even eventual acquisition of nuclear weapons.[12] Gorton maintained that the NPT would not stabilize global or regional security because he feared China, India, and others in the region would not sign on, or comply with, the treaty. Along with prominent cabinet ministers, Gorton appears to have resolved that forsaking all interest in nuclear weapons was shortsighted. The prime minister resisted signing the treaty until February 1970 and even then continued to keep his nuclear options open by refusing to ratify the agreement. Australia only ratified the treaty in 1973 under the leadership of a new prime minister, Gough Whitlam.[13] The record shows that in the three-year period between signature and ratification, some military strategists remained committed to the pursuit of a nuclear arsenal.[14]

The Labor government moved away from nuclear energy in favor of multilateral commitments to nonproliferation in the 1980s.[15] In 1985, for example, Australia joined with other countries in the region to support a South Pacific Nuclear Free Zone Treaty.[16] Signatories pledged not to manufacture or acquire nuclear weapons, to prevent territorial stationing of any nuclear device, to prevent nuclear testing in the region, and to ban on radioactive waste dumping at sea. The 1986 disaster at the Chernobyl nuclear reactor in the Soviet Union deepened worldwide concern about the costs of nuclearism. By the 1990s, the Australian Labor government under Prime Minister Paul Keating had become an outspoken advocate of a global nuclear test ban. Indeed, Australian diplomats figured prominently in negotiations in CD meetings, and scientists made significant contributions to plans for the international verification regime.

Prime Minister Keating and Foreign Minister Evans found their voices heard in CD proceedings on the draft CTBT text. The Conference operated on a principle of consensus, whereby all forty-four nuclear-capable countries would have to agree on a draft treaty before it would be submitted to the United Nations for endorsement. Evans and Australian diplomats helped to design a plan to overcome CD opposition by drafting a replica of the treaty language and submitting it to the General Assembly as a resolution for a vote. When the Liberal National coalition took control of government in March 1996, responsibility for this plan shifted to Foreign Minister Downer (who subsequently received most of the credit). This device became the CTBT which was passed by a huge majority in September 1996 and opened for signature.[17]

Foreign Minister Downer signed the CTBT on behalf of his government in September 1996. He then ordered a series of government reviews of the implications of the treaty for publication. According to the government's own National Interest Analysis on the treaty, the "CTBT is important to Australia's national security interests and for global security. In particular, Australia has a strong security interest in ensuring that nuclear weapons are not acquired by countries that could use them against Australia." The government emphasized its historic commitment to the nonproliferation regime as well as its future role as host of more than twenty international monitoring stations for the CTBT (the third largest concentration in the world). The NIA also described the treaty as having "indispensable normative value." Signing the agreement would constitute "a political and moral commitment to renounce nuclear explosions."[18] Based on the recommendations in the NIA, the Howard government tabled the implementing legislation for the treaty to be ratified on May 13, 1998.

Regime Type: Executive–Legislative Relations

Australia's signature of the CTBT opened a brief period of post-commitment politics. The CTBT required little in the way of substantive changes in Australian security policies, and so the government advanced enabling legislation to the parliament for endorsement in May 1998. From the beginning, the concept of a test ban enjoyed bipartisan support in the Australian parliament. Parliamentarians were pleased with the developing profile of Australia as a major voice in the global nonproliferation enterprise. They recognized the value of playing a strong role in international negotiations, coupled with achievements including the indefinite extension of the NPT and promoting binding treaties on chemical and biological weapons. Members of parliament joined with the government in condemning late nuclear tests by France and China, and they endorsed the prime minister's statements of protest of the French decision (in particular).

The subject was so popular, in fact, that Australian support for the CTBT was taken as a given by many in the public sector, and there was only limited review. The Joint Standing Committee on Treaties (JSCOT) reviewed the treaty as part of its regular mandate; in several hearings, JSCOT members received testimony from a range of supporters of Australia's commitment to the nonproliferation regime. The committee summarily recommended the treaty for ratification.

Interest Groups

The CTBT generated only a mild degree of interest among businesses and nongovernmental organizations. While protestors decried France's nuclear tests, they did not really rally in favor of the Australian decision to endorse the CTBT. Notably, the Keating and Howard governments worked hard to foster a cooperative relationship with various interest groups and organizations who did attend to the issue. The government invited representatives of industry to participate in a regular set of meetings of a Panel of Experts that advised DFAT officials of their perspective on the treaty. The government subsequently enjoyed the public endorsement of the deal by groups who favored the treaty and the IMS system such as the Australian Mining Industry Council. The treaty also enjoyed the support of peace activists and groups of academics such as those from the Peace Research Centre at the Australian National University. By consulting with the groups during the negotiations at the CD, the federal government seems to have assuaged any relevant concerns about the deal.

Public Support

In many ways, the government's nonproliferation agenda seemed to resonate with Australia's national political identity. There was so much support for nonproliferation that it almost outstripped the pace of the government policies, in fact. In the wake of the French decision to launch a new round of nuclear testing, for example, thousands of Australians took to the streets. French consulate offices were the target of protests and vandalism, and groups threatened boycotts of French goods.

Opponents of the French testing decision put tremendous pressure on the Keating government for some type of response. While Keating was unwilling to sever diplomatic ties with the French government, he did develop a creative approach to the larger issue at hand: Australia invited a number of international nuclear weapons experts to Canberra to discuss ways to achieve the goal of complete nuclear disarmament.[19] The formation of the "Canberra Commission" represented both an honest effort to host an international forum on disarmament and a carefully calculated political move to assuage public frustration with the French testing decision.[20] The Commission meetings began in January 1996 and attracted a high-profile collection of experts and former government officials from around the world. Unfortunately, the defeat of the Labor Party in the March national elections undermined the potential impact of the commission's recommendation for global nuclear disarmament.

Outcome and Analysis

The Australian government ratified the CTBT on July 9, 1998. Prime Minister Howard and Foreign Minister Downer used the occasion to speak out publicly on the issue of indefinite extension of the NPT, and an accelerated timetable for entry-into-force of the CTBT.

Both material and normative pressures appear to have played a role in Australia's decision to ratify the CTBT. Howard believed that the treaty offered tangible security benefits to Australia and its allies. Indeed, by raising the bar on nuclear testing, only established nuclear weapons states with advanced arsenals and sophisticated computer technology for test simulations stood to benefit. This meant that Australia could continue to count on the United States and the United Kingdom for military security while at the same time other countries would be barred from crossing the threshold by the treaty. Furthermore, the CTBT was completely consistent with Australia's diplomatic stance as a nonnuclear weapons state that favored arms controls. Australia was both architect of the institutional and normative structure that defined the nonproliferation regime and a member of that community. In many ways, the government would have perceived an obligation to support a treaty of such potential significance as the CTBT.

The CTBT ratification process in Australia highlights the importance of three domestic conditions in particular: executive–legislative relations, interest groups, and public opinion. Executive strategies appear not to have played a prominent role in this case partly because the treaty needed no special endorsement for passage through government. In some ways, the CTBT seemed the embodiment of the nonproliferation norm for the government and therefore required little engagement by the prime minister for passage. More importantly, Howard knew that there was bipartisan consensus in favor of ratification of the treaty in parliament, that there were very few interest groups who were concerned about the implications of the treaty, and that his government enjoyed strong public support for the agreement.

III. CANADA AND THE CTBT

The ratification process for the CTBT in Canada was noncontroversial. Canada was a strong advocate for a test ban in the 1990s in spite of the fact that the government had actually co-owned nuclear warheads with the United States and supplied uranium and plutonium to its allies during the Cold War. In 1996, Prime Minister Jean Chrétien appeared committed to advance the nonproliferation norm. In December 1998, Canada deposited its instrument of ratification of the treaty with the United Nations.

International Pressure

Canada was a nonnuclear weapons state and a strong supporter of the non-proliferation regime over decades. The Canadian government believed that their country stood to gain tangible benefits from the test ban. They also knew that their strongest ally, the United States, had a massive nuclear arsenal as well as the most sophisticated computer testing models available for future weapons modernization. In this sense, supporters believed that the CTBT would effectively only constrain developing countries and "rogue states" seeking to develop weapons of mass destruction, further enhancing Canadian security.

Executive Strategy

Prime Minister Chrétien and the Liberal party supported a test-ban agreement. Canadian officials pushed for the completion of the treaty during the two-year negotiation process in the UN Conference on Disarmament. When that effort failed, Canada supported the translation of the document into a General Assembly resolution and voted in favor of the treaty in September 1996. The straightforward nature of the case belies a fascinating history, though, that included a decade in which Canada possessed its own nuclear weapons. One expert has characterized Canada's position as a kind of "nuclear schizophrenia" in which two contradictory dynamics shaped Canadian foreign policy toward nuclear weapons: the acquisition of nuclear weapons and government efforts to strengthen the nonproliferation regime.[21]

Canada's nuclear history began when it supplied scientific expertise as well as uranium ore and plutonium for the Manhattan Project during World War II.[22] With the backing of the United States and Britain, the Canadian government constructed the first nuclear research reactor outside the United States, the Zero Energy Experimental Pile at Chalk River on the Ontario–Quebec border. In 1949, Canada became a partner in the North Atlantic Treaty Organization (NATO). Nine years later, the United States and Canada established the North American Aerospace Defense Command (NORAD), a system of early warning detection and monitoring facilities for missile strikes aimed at North America. Defense cooperation also included the forward basing of U.S. strike aircraft in Canada.[23]

By the 1950s Canada had developed a full-fledged nuclear research program. The Chalk River facility was capable of producing plutonium for export for atomic weapons. The government also expanded its Great Bear Lake mine and emerged as one of the world's major suppliers of uranium. Canadian scientists also developed a prototype nuclear energy plant, the Canadian Deuterium Uranium (CANDU) reactor, for export to developing countries, including India, Pakistan, Argentina, and South Korea. Unfortunately, CANDU reactors ran on heavy water (that could be used to produce weapons-grade plutonium) and could be refueled-under-load, allowing the clandestine removal of plutonium for use in nuclear weapons.[24]

During the 1950s and 1960s, a succession of Canadian governments had even more direct links to nuclear weapons. Beginning in the 1950s, government officials were encouraged by the United States to acquire nuclear weapons as part of a larger commitment to NATO defense.[25] Prime Minister John Diefenbaker and his Progressive Conservative Party-led government believed that Canada should participate to some degree, but the prime minister was reluctant to acquire an independent nuclear force. After some debate, Diefenbaker made a decision in 1958 to purchase two nuclear-capable missile systems and leave open the question of whether or not to acquire nuclear warheads.[26] In the end, the prime minister ordered the deployment of these systems in Europe and Canada but authorized them to carry only conventional warheads.[27] Diefenbaker's successor, Liberal Party Prime Minister Lester Pearson, took a more proactive stance on the nuclear issue. Pearson finalized a deal whereby Canada would acquire four weapons systems to be fitted with nuclear warheads (under joint command control) in August 1963. Experts believe that this totaled between 250 and 450 nuclear warheads.[28] According to a Defence Department White Paper from 1964, "Having accepted responsibility for membership in a nuclear armed alliance, the question of nuclear weapons for Canadian Armed Forces is a subordinate issue."[29] Canadian troops possessed these weapons from 1963 to 1972 (although the last of the weapons were not removed from the country until 1984). This situation was reversed in the 1970s by Liberal Prime Minister Pierre Trudeau, however. Trudeau was a vocal critic of Canadian possession of the weapons, and in 1971 he announced a plan to transfer all of them back to U.S. control.

At the same time, Canada also strongly supported the international nuclear nonproliferation regime. Canadian officials participated in two United Nations commissions that were attempting to broker a strategic arms limitation deal between the Soviet Union and the United States in the decade after World War II.[30] Canadian diplomats and scientists were also directly involved in the establishment of the UN Atomic Energy Commission in January 1946.[31] In the late 1950s, Canadian diplomats supported the development of a limited nuclear-test-ban treaty. And even as NATO moved to heavily rely on nuclear weapons for defense, the Canadians continued to measure their cooperation.

Trudeau's decision to renounce Canadian nuclear capabilities coincided with an increasingly vocal role for his country in global arms control and disarmament initiatives. The Canadian government supported the NPT as "most effective international instrument to achieve Canada's fundamental objectives of nuclear disarmament and non-proliferation."[32] Trudeau himself became one of the world's leading advocates for limits on nuclear testing and disarmament. In 1978, he gave a high-profile speech to the United Nations General Assembly in which he advocated a "strategy of suffocation" for nuclear weapons development by threatening to choke off the supply of fissionable material. Trudeau bragged that Canada was "not only the first country with the capability to produce nuclear weapons that chose not to do so, we are also the first nuclear-armed country to have chosen to divest itself of nuclear weapons."[33]

In the 1990s, Prime Minister Chrétien and Liberal Party officials supported the U.S. moratorium on testing and praised the agreement between the United States and Russia to pressure the international community to complete a treaty by the end of 1996. Canadian officials vocally condemned the last rounds of Chinese and French nuclear testing. Canadian diplomats were also responsible for inserting a key clause in the CTBT that called for annual conferences of the parties (so-called Article XIV Conferences) to review the status of the treaty if it did not enter into force within three years of opening for signature. Finally, Canada was one of the first countries to sign the CTBT in September 1996, and Chrétien along with Foreign Minister Lloyd Axworthy pushed the government steadily toward passage of implementing legislation in the fall of 1998.

Regime Type: Executive–Legislative Relations

Canada's signature of the CTBT in September 1996 was the catalyst for a careful review of Canada's nonproliferation policies. Foreign Minister Axworthy invited the parliamentary Standing Committee on Foreign Affairs and International Trade (SCAIT) to conduct a comprehensive study of Canada's nonproliferation policies. In December 1998, the committee published a report entitled "Canada and the Nuclear Challenge: Reducing the Political Value of Nuclear Weapons for the 21st Century," which reflected parliament's position that arms control was consistent with Canadian security interests. Canada should continue to participate in alliances including NATO, the report argued, while preparing to meet new security challenges in the new century. SCAIT confirmed the long-term position that the NPT was the centerpiece of the nonproliferation regime—offering constraints on the spread of weapons and technology while committing nuclear weapons states to the objective of nuclear disarmament. At the same time, parliamentary advocates called the CTBT an "indispensable part of the non-proliferation regime...a more effective obstacle to the qualitative development of nuclear weapons than all previous disarmament treaties."[34] Facing no serious opposition, the implementing legislation passed through parliament very quickly.

Interest Groups

The Canadian government found support for the CTBT and its nonproliferation policies from a loose association of academic groups and policy institutes. As with other cases, the decision to support the CTBT was taken as a given by many in the military-industrial complex, and it did not fundamentally challenge their interests. The SCAIT inquiry also found widespread support for broad goals of nonproliferation and disarmament.

Public Opinion

By the 1970s, public opinion had crystallized firmly around an antinuclear weapons stance. Canadian diplomat William Epstein believed that Canada's nuclear policies "reflected nationwide abhorrence of these weapons, the desire to prevent their proliferation, and to see them entirely eliminated, and the hope to benefit from the promising peaceful uses of nuclear energy."[35] In this environment, prime ministers continued to walk a fine line between outright support for the United States and its nuclear strategy and the global goal of proliferation control and stability. The 1980s brought these tensions into stark contrast as Conservative Prime Minister Brian Mulroney struggled to maintain strong ties with the Reagan administration and at the same time general public opinion had shifted against nuclear weapons. Similar to Prime Minister Diefenbaker's actions two decades earlier, the Mulroney government actually dragged its heels in terms of cooperation with the Reagan administration on the Strategic Defense Initiative and related projects.[36]

Outcome and Analysis

In the fall of 1998 the parliament moved forward with passage of implementing legislation and demanded that the international community follow suit. Foreign Minister Axworthy made clear his government's commitment to a nuclear test ban as part of a larger agenda of international security. He said, "The CTBT is an important part of Canada's efforts over the past years to construct an effective international nuclear nonproliferation and disarmament regime. . . . By ratifying, Canada will help to enhance the strength of this regime."[37] Canada also took on the stewardship of the CTBTO. The CTBTO would be primarily responsible for managing the network of monitoring stations around the world and running the international verification regime. Canadian diplomats led negotiations to establish a $28-million-budget program for the organization with costs to be shared among key signatories.[38]

International pressures seemed to influence Canadian decisions regarding the CTBT. First and foremost, Canada was a nonnuclear weapons state that believed in the value of the global nonproliferation regime. Canadian diplomats worked hard in support of treaties on nuclear weapons; they were central in international negotiations including the 1995 NPT review conference. Canada also saw tangible benefits to the agreement, including the raising of the threshold of nuclear weapons development by would-be proliferants. At the same time, the Canadian regime knew that its ally the United States and other countries with advanced technology could effectively conduct virtual tests in the future if modernization were needed. Canada's actions toward the CTBT appear to be entirely consistent with constructivism, whereby the government was a long-term supporter of the nonproliferation norm and willing to work with its friends and allies to promote greater international compliance with its tenets.

Several domestic political conditions appear to have been significant. Prime Minister Chrétien was confident that his Liberal Party government would support the treaty given Canada's long-term stance toward nonproliferation. Thus, he appears to have exerted little to no executive pressure nor employed sophisticated strategies to achieve this outcome. In essence, support for the treaty was taken as a given by the executive. Propositions regarding interest group activity and public opinion appear to be upheld by this case. In sum, it appears that the issue generated only academic debates in Canada at the time in spite of the fascinating, dynamic, and controversial history of Canadian nuclear weapons policy.

IV. FRANCE AND THE CTBT

France conducted its first nuclear test explosion in 1960. President Charles De Gaulle believed an independent French nuclear force to be consistent with his notion of a foreign policy of *grandeur* and a tradition of self-sufficiency in security policy. The government established a rigorous nuclear testing program based first in the desert of Algeria, then later in the South Pacific. While claiming to support CD negotiations on a global test ban, President Chirac announced in 1995 that his government would have to conduct another round of nuclear tests before it could sign on to the CTBT. In the end, he carried through on both pledges: the government completed the testing cycle and signed the CTBT in 1996. Along with the United Kingdom, it was one of the first nuclear weapons states to ratify the treaty.

International Pressures

Security calculations clearly influenced France's position on the CTBT. Consistent with the Gaullist tradition, the president maintained that testing was necessary for ensuring the viability of a new warhead, the TN-75, and for refinement of computer simulation systems for future tests.[39] Government supporters also argued that France was helping to ensure European security—that is, by testing their own nuclear weapons, France could claim that they were actually looking out for broader regional security interests.[40] At the same time, France had long supported the international nonproliferation regime and treaties including PTBT and the NPT. In 1995, they faced significant normative pressure not to conduct further nuclear tests and to support the CTBT. World leaders were particularly outraged that the French government had supported the indefinite extension of the NPT only one month before announcing its new testing plans.[41] And the international community roundly condemned French testing plans as provocative and potentially environmentally hazardous.

Executive Strategy

French President Jacques Chirac's decision to order a final round of nuclear tests in 1995 and then sign the CTBT one year later was consistent with foreign policy patterns developed over decades. Under the leadership of Charles De Gaulle, France established a foreign and security policy grounded on self-reliance. As head of the French provisional government, De Gaulle had ordered the creation of a French civilian atomic energy commission in October 1945. While he may not have envisioned an independent nuclear capability at the time, De Gaulle clearly wanted his country to be "in the nuclear game."

A rapid flurry of events in the early 1950s triggered the French government to move toward an independent nuclear program. First, a plan to create a European Defense Community that would join France, Germany, and other states together in a collective security pact collapsed under a weight of mistrust. Echoing other conservative sentiments across Europe, the French National Assembly firmly rejected the deal. The United States soon announced its support for the rearmament of West Germany and its entry into NATO as well as the New Look strategy (that placed nuclear weapons as the centerpiece of European defense). French forces also suffered defeats in Indochina that led to their withdrawal from the region.[42] In 1954, the government of Prime Minister Pierre Mendés France and President De Gaulle ordered the establishment of an independent nuclear program. France first tested a nuclear device in February 1960. Leaders and citizens quickly warmed to the idea of a French nuclear deterrent and came to see it as synonymous with the French national identity.[43]

By the 1980s, France had established a significant *force de frappe* (strike force) and was regularly testing warheads for modernization programs. These actions drew the attention of antinuclear grassroots organizations based in Europe. NATO's plans for modernization of its intermediate-range nuclear forces in the 1980s increased public concerns about proliferation, especially in western Europe. Nongovernmental organizations were especially active in protesting the continuing French testing regime. Tensions between the French government and these organizations came to a boil in 1985 when a Greenpeace protest vessel, *The Rainbow Warrior*, was sunk in the port of Auckland, New Zealand. The vessel had been in port as part of a planned protest to sail into the testing zone at Mururoa Atoll in French Polynesia. When evidence emerged that French secret intelligence agents had carried out the action, France was again the target of intense international criticism.

From the French perspective, the end of the Cold War created both new opportunities and new uncertainties in international security. The changed strategic environment prompted a new round of debates regarding a test ban. Socialist Party leaders believed that the global arms race was at an end. In April 1992 Prime Minister Bérégovoy announced Mitterrand's decision to suspend tests for the remainder of the year. In early 1993, Mitterrand extended the moratorium, and the government ceased nuclear tests for two more years. While this decision was challenged by continued nuclear testing by China, it matched the emerging profiles of all other major declared nuclear powers.[44] In 1994, Mitterrand predicted that France would never again test nuclear weapons, stating: "France will not want to offend the world by relaunching the nuclear arms race and by disdaining the countries of the third world. I have confidence in my successors. They will not be able to act otherwise."[45]

In May 1995, Jacques Chirac and his Gaullist party coalition swept to power in France with a massive conservative majority. One of the key planks in the election platform had been the call for a fresh take on military policy including modernization of the French nuclear arsenal. Just weeks later, on June 13, 1995, Chirac announced his "irrevocable decision" that France would conduct a series of eight nuclear tests at the Mururoa Atoll in the coming year. He claimed that civilian and military experts consulted by the government "were unanimous that a further limited series of tests is indispensable" for national security. Primary justifications for the tests were twofold: the new round of testing would help to ensure the reliability of the French nuclear deterrent and refine the computer simulation technology necessary for future artificial testing.[46] At the same time, Chirac insisted that the tests would "not alter France's commitment to a complete nuclear test ban treaty now under discussion in Geneva."[47] As if to underscore his government's commitment to non-proliferation, Chirac tasked French diplomats to help negotiate an agreement for the indefinite extension of the NPT.[48] The international community completed the extension agreement in August 1995. Chirac repeatedly promised that his government would sign the CTBT once the testing program was completed.[49]

Chirac was true to his word, and France was one of the first governments to sign the CTBT at the United Nations in September 1996. Chirac's government maintained its support for the agreement throughout the post-commitment period. Indeed, there was little doubt the agreement would be ratified by the legislature given the president's high-profile commitment to the deal. On January 21, 1998, the French cabinet adopted a bill authorizing ratification of the CTBT and advanced the legislation to the parliament for endorsement.[50] Chirac also played a leadership role in encouraging other governments to sign the treaty and move it forward for rapid entry into force.[51]

Regime Type: Executive–Legislative Relations

Chirac's dual-track plan to complete a new round of nuclear tests coupled with a pledge to sign the CTBT enabled most parliamentarians to support the initiative. At a philosophical level, parliamentarians seemed comfortable with a diplomacy linking military readiness with a policy of nonproliferation in the post-Cold War era. At a practical level, Chirac and his prime minister, Alain Juppé, managed a conservative majority of nearly 80 per cent of seats in the National Assembly and two-thirds of the Senate. The opposition Socialist Party leadership also supported the CTBT.

It is the case that the prospect of an agreement brought traditional debates about French military strategy in the National Assembly to the surface. Members explored a wide range of issues regarding military strategy and nuclear weapons, including minimal deterrence and the potential for an EU nuclear defense program. While Chirac supported French participation in the CTBT, he also acknowledged the legitimacy of arguments regarding strategic flexibility. Meanwhile, leading Gaullist conservatives expressed concern that a test-ban treaty might circumscribe French strategic flexibility (such as limiting tests on new nuclear warheads). Critics also questioned whether the treaty would curb would-be proliferants.[52] Notably, these debates also played out inside government ministries, including a general division between the conservative Ministry of Defense stance and the more flexible commitment from the French Foreign Ministry to the outlines of a test-ban agreement.

Interest Groups

As was the case in other democracies, interest groups in France were most vocal in condemning the announcement of testing—not the ultimate decision to ratify the CTBT. Key opponents of French nuclearism included nongovernmental organizations like Greenpeace along with a loose coalition of domestic peace movements. These groups were joined by other organizations including trade unions and student groups. For example, a major protest was held on June 20, 1995, in which tens of thousands took to the streets. Some of the more colorful banners carried by protestors suggested: "If your tests are risk-free, carry them out in Paris" and "We are all Polynesians."[53] In stark contrast, France's signature of the CTBT and the subsequent drive for ratification generated far less interest-group participation in the political process. Hearings by National Assembly committees reviewing the treaty generated little political heat, and the government proceeded quickly to ratification.

Public Opinion

As noted above, the French public was largely disengaged from the debate over ratification of the CTBT. If newly elected President Chirac had hoped that his announcement of plans for testing coupled with eventual signature of the treaty would boost his approval ratings, however, he was mistaken. Public approval of the president declined sharply during Chirac's first six months in office. The president took office with an approval rating of 59 per cent in May 1995, but by September that figure had dropped to only 33 per cent of French voters.[54] In spite of the commitment to strengthen its national defense and restore a measure of grandeur to the French deterrent profile, the government was facing serious problems with unemployment and a massive budget deficit. Those who did attend to proliferation concerns were mobilized much more by the announcement of tests in 1995 than the signing of the CTBT one year later. For example, in a survey conducted in September 1995, 60 per cent of French citizens said that they believed testing was wrong.[55]

Outcome and Analysis

Chirac's government persevered in its plans to complete a final round of tests. Chirac justified his decision in the dark days of public protest, arguing, "The peace that has existed for the past half century is based on nuclear deterrence. And a great modern country like France, fortunate enough to possess a high quality nuclear deterrent, enjoys both a security and a political weight in the world which are two essential elements of the nation's future."[56] True to its word, the French government moved quickly toward ratification of the treaty in January 1998.[57] On April 6, France and the United Kingdom deposited their instruments of ratification. The French government also officially closed its nuclear weapons test site on Mururoa Atoll.[58]

International relations theories appear to offer mixed results in this case study. Neorealism helps to explain the French government's resistance to commit to a test-ban treaty before it believed that its modernization test rounds were complete. Chirac justified the decision largely on the basis of national security concerns, warning: "A country that wants to live in security should not lower its guard...in a very uncertain world."[59] Defense Minister Charles Millon called testing "indispensable to enable us to guarantee the reliability and safety of our nuclear arms in the long term. Nuclear deterrence guarantees our independence and the ultimate protection of our vital interests."[60] Yet neorealism does not seem to account for the ultimate sacrifice of sovereignty in ratifying the test-ban treaty. This puzzle can be more easily accounted for from a constructivist perspective focusing on French action as the fulfillment of a long-term commitment to the nonproliferation norm.

Domestic conditions seem to offer several additional layers of explanation of this complex case. For example, executive strategy for ratification was critical to the ultimate realization of the government's goal of support for the treaty. Chirac's plan for a final round of testing represented a challenge to the Socialist Party's moratorium and satisfied conservatives and military advisors who sought final, critical tests to confirm modernization objectives. The government's willingness to order the tests—and to weather the storm of international criticism that followed the announcement—demonstrated Chirac's commitment to the overall enterprise. At the same time, the president knew that he could employ this strategy successfully given the strong conservative majorities in both houses of parliament. Interest groups that rallied against the plan for testing largely did so from outside the government, and these groups enjoyed little influence within policymaking circles. Finally, while the French public opposed the testing decision in at least one survey, they also supported the larger goals of nonproliferation including the completion of the CTBT.

V. GERMANY AND THE CTBT

The Federal Republic of Germany, with its sizable nuclear energy program, was one of the first countries to sign the CTBT in September 1996. The government moved quickly to ratify the treaty in August 1998. German Chancellor Helmut Kohl (CDU) and Foreign Minister Klaus Kinkel (FDP) made clear the government's commitment to nonproliferation and encouraged other countries to support for a rapid entry into force of the treaty.

International Pressures

Germany faced significant international pressure to ratify the CTBT, especially given its commitment to nuclear nonproliferation and its own special status in the decades after World War II. Germany had been divided and demilitarized by the victorious allies after the war. The three western zones were incorporated in a new entity, the Federal Republic of Germany, in 1949. Chancellor Konrad Adenauer pursued close political, economic, and security ties with western allies. West Germany joined the NATO alliance in October 1954 following its public renunciation of any intent to pursue weapons of mass destruction. In the 1960s and 1970s, German leaders were personally engaged in building bridges between the East and West, an essential foundation for arms control agreements in the decades that followed. Thus, many German officials were responsible for stewardship of the nonproliferation norm, and their successors were committed to its fulfillment in ratification of the CTBT.

Executive Strategies

The CTBT was negotiated under the Kohl coalition government that had been in office for sixteen years (1982–98). Chancellor Kohl's foreign minister in the mid-1990s, Klaus Kinkel, represented the junior party in coalition and strove to maintain the profile of reliability and continuity in foreign policy that been developed by his long-time predecessor, Hans-Dietrich Genscher. Kohl and Kinkel provided steadfast support for the negotiation of the CTBT as well as ratification, both within Germany and by member states of the European Union.

Germany had a somewhat unique historical experience with nuclear weapons. Indeed, one could argue that the nuclear arms race began there. During World War II, Nazi party leaders funded a top-secret research project to harness the atom for a weapon of immense destructive capability. Concerns in the west (articulated most notably by Albert Einstein) about the Nazi scientists' progress prompted the United States government to launch the Manhattan Project. With the end of the war came the elimination of the German project. In October 1954, Chancellor Konrad Adenauer issued Germany's formal renunciation of interest in all weapons of mass destruction at the London Nine-Power Conference.[61] Ironically, this did not stop Germany's allies from deploying thousands of nuclear warheads in the country as part of the planned NATO defense of Western Europe. Indeed, Kamp contends that Germany *insisted* on "a massive U.S. nuclear presence in Europe, including the deployment of a substantial number of nuclear weapons on German soil, because this was seen as increasing the credibility of the U.S. nuclear commitment."[62] As a result, Germans lived on the front lines of the Cold War for decades.

West German leaders maintained strong support for the NATO alliance and its relationship with western powers throughout the Cold War. Indeed, they were deeply dependent upon their allies for their security. Yet it was exactly because of this unique geopolitical situation that some Germans became outspoken advocates for nuclear arms limitation and even disarmament. A significant grassroots movement against military rearmament and nuclear weapons grew up in the 1950s in the famous *Kampf dem Atomtod* protests, for example. Millions of German citizens mobilized against the very idea that their NATO allies would deploy nuclear weapons in the theater and against the stockpiling of these weapons around the world.

This paradox in Germany's orientation toward nuclear weapons came to a head in the form of debates over the NPT. Like their counterparts in Australia, some German leaders in the 1960s were reluctant to support the NPT because they envisioned future scenarios in which Germany might need to control or acquire nuclear weapons. Karl-Heinz Kamp summarizes German reservations to the treaty at the time as including the fear of being cut out of a U.S.–Soviet–British condominium on nuclear weapons, concern that the NPT would "codify the inferior status of the nuclear have-nots" (which German leaders misinterpreted as the "second Versailles that would discriminate against Germany"), and the fear of damage to Germany's nascent nuclear power industry.[63] As a result, German diplomats were heavily involved in the negotiation of the NPT, representing the voice of concerned nonnuclear weapons states. They also sought to maintain some latitude for the European Community to establish its own defense program (that might include nuclear weapons).[64]

Following unification, the German government attempted to take a diplomatic lead in fostering the expansion of the nonproliferation regime. Kohl and Kinkel announced a new ten-point diplomatic plan designed to address a range of concerns in 1993. The government called on "rogue states" to freeze their nuclear weapons development programs in exchange for engagement by the European Union. The government encouraged others to support the indefinite extension of the NPT in the upcoming review conference. It called for stronger binding agreements on control of chemical and biological weapons and a potential fissile material production cutoff treaty. At the same time the government advocated a program to create a nuclear weapons register under the auspices of the United Nations and called for the completion of negotiations on a CTBT by 1995.[65]

Germany's nuclear diplomacy continued to be a delicate balancing act, however. At the beginning of CD negotiations on the CTBT, for example, German diplomats pursued an ambitious agenda. They argued that even preparatory activities for a nuclear test should be outlawed by the treaty and that the treaty should call on nuclear weapons states to make progress toward global nuclear disarmament. Under pressure from allies including the United States, however, the German position shifted toward a more conservative statement of ideals.[66] German leaders' frustrations about the French announcement of a new round of nuclear tests in 1995 were tempered by broader concerns about upsetting the balance of cooperation with their European partners. German leaders stopped short of condemning the French government, saying only that they were "not happy" about the decision.

Regime Type: Executive–Legislative Relations

Ratification of the CTBT would require a simple majority vote in both houses of the German legislature. This was not a challenge, however, as Kohl's government enjoyed near-universal support for the treaty in parliament. Critics contend that this support was the product of a blind spot on nuclear weapons. For example, Kamp charges that in Germany "nuclear weapons and their role in the framework of a common European defence structure have been a non-issue since unification in 1990. There has hardly been any speculation— leave alone a substantial debate—on the future of nuclear forces in European security."[67] The CTBT enjoyed the support of all major parties. Some FDP leaders thought the government should pressure its allies to go further by supporting a fissile material cutoff treaty and negotiations toward complete nuclear disarmament.[68]

Interest Groups

The CTBT did not generate a great deal of interest group activity in Germany. Ratification seems to have been taken as a given by most groups. Some antinuclear groups used the post-commitment phase to call attention to new issues including the creation of a nuclear ownership registry. For example, Erwin Häckel of the German Council on Foreign Relations argued that the CTBT was a strong step toward greater regulation and control of nuclear weapons worldwide. Building on recent progress with the Conventional Forces in Europe (CFE) Treaty that would regulate conventional military deployments, supporters believed that even the goal of nuclear weapons disarmament might now be attainable. Others countered that at best German interest groups displayed ambivalence on the question of disarmament in the mid-1990s. As Mueller argues, "Between Nibelungen-like loyalty to the Western alliance's first-use option and a spirited tussle for greater transparency in the nuclear powers complex, there is a palette of opinions and attitudes for which there is no clear common denominator."[69] German interest groups, like some government officials, walked a fine line in balancing their need for the assurance of a western nuclear deterrent with the larger goals of arms control and disarmament.

Public Opinion

There was no substantial nuclear debate in Germany surrounding ratification of the CTBT, and there is limited data regarding public attitudes in this case study. One survey conducted in 1993 found that only 14 per cent of Germans wanted their country to have its own nuclear capability.[70] The lack of opposition to the CTBT appears consistent with general government foreign policy orientations at the time. Indeed, one expert describes the post-unification era as a period of "nuclear apathy" on the part of the public.[71]

Outcome and Analysis

Germany officially ratified the CTBT in August 1998, making them the eighteenth state to ratify the agreement. In accord with the plans, Germany began construction of four IMS monitoring facilities including a seismic station, a radionuclide station, and two infrasound stations. Ironically, the ratification of the CTBT was one of the last acts of the Conservative/Liberal government. In October 1998 the coalition was defeated by the opposition Social Democrats and Greens. The new government continued to support its larger stated goals of a nuclear-free world.

International pressures appear to have influenced German decisions regarding the CTBT. Germany had traditionally relied on its western allies for defense guarantees, including the extension of the U.S. nuclear umbrella. But Germany was a nonnuclear weapons state that saw advantages in completion of an international agreement to ban critical nuclear tests. In this context, German leaders perceived tangible security benefits from a treaty that would effectively bar would-be proliferants from obtaining nuclear weapons while at the same time ensure the U.S. nuclear arsenal's viability for decades into the future. German diplomats were also instrumental in helping to articulate the international nonproliferation norm, and some emerged as outspoken advocates of an even more extreme position at the time—including call for a fissile material cutoff treaty and even complete nuclear disarmament.

At least three domestic political conditions appear to have influenced the outcome of treaty ratification in Germany. While Chancellor Kohl and Foreign Minister Kinkel did not have to expend many government resources to ensure cooperation from the parliament, the legislature did play a role in the final vote on ratification. In this case the Conservative/Liberal government knew that the treaty had bipartisan support. Indeed, some legislators claimed that it did not go far enough in achieving nonproliferation goals. Propositions regarding interest group activity and public opinion were also supported by this case. The treaty generated little or no domestic opposition, appears not to have "awakened" certain constituencies to action, and enjoyed diffuse public support.

VI. THE UNITED STATES AND THE CTBT

The United States was one of world's leading nuclear powers in the Cold War. In the 1980s, the U.S. military had amassed more than 20,000 nuclear warheads with the capability to deliver them to any target in the world. Yet the United States was also one of the driving forces behind the development of the global nonproliferation regime. Diplomats negotiated a series of arms control treaties during the Cold War, and in many cases presidents conducted effective strategies to build Senate support for ratification. Prior to the CTBT, the Senate had ratified a range of agreements, from the PTBT in the 1960s to the Chemical Weapons Convention in the 1990s. The proposal for a comprehensive test ban, however, faced a wall of conservative opposition in the U.S. Senate, and the treaty was rejected on October 13, 1999.

International Pressure

The United States faced serious international pressure in relation to the CTBT. Supporters both inside and outside the United States argued that the treaty represented an opportunity to tighten the global nonproliferation regime. They contended that the agreement would bar some countries from conducting critical nuclear tests, create a new system for monitoring potential violations of the regime, and strengthen the international legal network for prosecution of violations. However, from the standpoint of national security, critics believed that the United States stood to lose an edge on potential rivals. The treaty might not prevent some groups or countries from conducting clandestine low-yield tests at the same time that the U.S. nuclear arsenal was left to decay, they argued. Critics firmly believed that the treaty would leave the United States less secure. Conversely, the United States faced strong normative pressure to cooperate with the agreement. The record of U.S. support for arms control treaties was very strong during the Cold War. Optimists believed that the new political climate might allow countries to develop an entirely new system of management and control of nuclear weapons proliferation.

Executive Strategy

President Clinton's support for ratification of the CTBT was consistent with decades of leadership on arms control and nonproliferation issues. Indeed, President Eisenhower was the first to suggest international negotiations on a nuclear test ban in the 1950s. Eisenhower and his advisors were sensitive to the prevailing trends in proliferation. More countries were on the path to a nuclear weapon, including the communist People's Republic of China. The superpower arms race required an incredible investment of resources, yet the world did not seem much safer.[72] As a gesture of good faith, Eisenhower agreed to a one-year moratorium on testing in 1958, followed in kind by Great Britain and the Soviet Union.[73] In the 1960s and 1970s, U.S. leaders extended on this through treaties including the PTBT (Presidents Kennedy and Johnson), the Strategic Arms Limitation Treaty (President Nixon), and verification protocols for the TTBT and PNET (President Reagan).[74]

The end of the Cold War created a new window of opportunity for progress on test limits. U.S. President George H. W. Bush signed a nuclear testing moratorium bill into law in October 1992 that called for nine-month suspension of tests and international progress on a comprehensive test ban. In 1993, newly elected President Bill Clinton announced an extension of the testing moratorium, and other countries including Russia and France followed suit. Broadly speaking, this reflected a newfound sense of optimism regarding the potential for a test-ban agreement. Diplomats at the United Nations agreed that negotiations on a comprehensive nuclear-test-ban treaty should begin in early 1994.

President Clinton was the first government leader to sign the CTBT in September 1996. The president appeared confident at the time that the agreement would receive support in Washington as well as in many other capitals around the world. However, the record shows that the administration did very little to advance the treaty to ratification over the subsequent three-year period. The president announced that he would submit the treaty for ratification by the Senate in September 1997, but administration officials knew it would be an uphill battle. The State and Defense departments subsequently turned their attention to other foreign policy priorities. According to one expert, "Ironically, having achieved half a victory [signing CTBT], Clinton essentially abandoned the fight, allowing a host of personal and political issues to vie for his attention until it was too late to save the treaty."[75] Officials would offer statements in support of the deal from time to time, but this failed to translate into substantive policy initiatives.

As 1998 wore on, the administration actually lost ground on the treaty due to a number of complicating factors. First and foremost, the Monica Lewinsky scandal became a public relations nightmare for the administration and created a serious political standoff between the White House and Congress. The Senate launched impeachment proceedings while the president continued to deny wrongdoing. Second, the world was rocked in May 1998 by a series of nuclear tests in India and Pakistan. Secretary Albright made a halfhearted attempt to link the fate of the CTBT to the issue of India and Pakistan nuclear testing, arguing: "If we want India and Pakistan to stop testing and keep others from starting [Senate ratification of the CTBT] is the most basic, minimal, obvious step we can take on this critical issue at this perilous time. American leadership should be unambiguous, decisive, and clear."[76] But to most observers it appeared that momentum for treaty ratification in the United States had been lost.

The Clinton administration and key Senate allies again pushed a ratification vote in 1999. This time, however, they got more than they had bargained for: Senate Republican leaders made a strategic decision that they could defeat the treaty by fast-tracking it to a floor vote. The administration's first response to this move was optimistic: they conducted a short but intense campaign in favor of Senate ratification. Top officials including Secretary of Defense William Cohen and Secretary of State Albright rushed to Capitol Hill to lobby the Senate. President Clinton began to court undecided senators and argued in favor of the treaty in a series of public statements. On October 6, 1999, the White House held a high-profile ceremony that featured prominent supporters of the treaty, including past and present administration officials and even Nobel Prize-winning nuclear physicists.[77]

Critics of the treaty, and of the president's handling of the issue, characterized these efforts as too little, too late, however. Just days after the White House ceremony the administration made an about-face and turned its full energies to a drive to *postpone the Senate vote on the treaty*. The administration realized that the treaty had nowhere near the required number of votes for passage (67), and it believed that stakes were too high to lose the treaty on a simple parliamentary maneuver. Yet conservative opponents of the president would not budge; they sought a promise in writing from Clinton that he would not bring the CTBT up for Senate vote during the remainder of his term in office. The president refused. In response, Senator Jesse Helms (R-NC) commented: "the president appears to be playing poker with the Senate, but he does not have a winning hand and I think he knows it." He added, "It must be made clear that this CTBT is dead and the next president will not be bound by its terms. Without such concrete assurances, I will insist that the Senate proceed as planned and vote down this treaty." The White House continued to argue in favor of ratification on the merits of the treaty, but seemed to recognize that it was a losing battle.

Regime Type: Executive–Legislative Relations

The CTBT required a two-thirds majority vote in the Senate for ratification. This would be nearly impossible to achieve in the political climate of 1999. The positions of the two camps in the Senate on the CTBT could not have been more diametrically opposed. Supporters believed that the treaty was an appropriate extension of the nonproliferation regime, that the United States had sufficient technical capabilities for testing through computer simulation, and that it would work by constraining other groups and countries seeking to develop weapons. For example, moderate Senator Jim Jeffords (R-VT) argued that the international verification and monitoring regime was an effective new dimension of the agreement.[78] Senator Barbara Boxer (D-CA) said during the late stages of the debate that the United States had a "stark choice. We can continue to lead the world in stopping the spread of nuclear weapons by supporting this treaty or we can start a nuclear chain reaction by opposing it. I pray that we will support this treaty." Supporters also cited a report issued by the Departments of Defense and Energy in December 1998 that certified U.S. nuclear weapons would remain "safe" and "reliable" for the foreseeable future.

The treaty faced significant opposition in the Senate, however. Its most formidable opponent was Senator Helms, the chairman of the Senate Foreign

Relations Committee, who effectively blocked consideration of the treaty by refusing to hold committee hearings on it. Helms believed deeply that the treaty undermined U.S. national security interests and "was exceedingly harmful to the United States." Helms maintained that his committee would only consider the CTBT for ratification if the administration would also submit two other controversial treaties for a Senate vote: the protocols to the ABM Treaty and the Kyoto Protocol.[79] To the administration it appeared that Helms intended to hold hostage (or even kill) all three initiatives in the Senate. In September 1998, Senator Helms, Trent Lott (R-MS), and John Kyl (R-AZ) sent an open letter to the president arguing that the Indian and Pakistani tests in May had shown unequivocally that the CTBT would not be verifiable.[80] The treaty might still make it technically possible for simple fission weapons to be constructed without actual nuclear tests. The cases of South Africa and Pakistan seemed to illustrate this point.

Opponents made their move to fast-track the CTBT to a floor vote on September 30, 1999. Senate Minority Leader Tom Daschle (D-SD) countered that this move violated standard procedures including a period of advance notification of legislative business and the lack of committee hearings.[81] It was in this back and forth in early October that the extent of opposition to the treaty became clear to the White House. For example, Senator Richard Lugar (R-IN), a traditional supporter of bipartisanship in foreign policy and an advocate of arms control, argued that he did not believe the CTBT was "of the same caliber as the arms control treaties that have come before the Senate in recent decades." He added his concern that, "[p]residential leadership has been almost entirely absent on this issue. Despite having several years to make a case for ratification, the administration has declined to initiate the type of advocacy campaign that should accompany any treaty of this magnitude."[82] While Senate Republicans agreed to change the committee hearing plan, to allow longer floor debate, and to hold a final vote days later, the outcome nevertheless seemed predetermined.

Interest Groups

A number of groups lined up on both sides of the CTBT debate. Supporters were able to muster a significant brain trust in favor of the treaty. Clinton garnered the support of the current and former Joint Chiefs of Staff and a range of prominent former administration officials in favor of the treaty. The treaty also received backing from a group of more than thirty Nobel laureates from the American Physical Society, who sent an open letter of support to the Senate and media outlets.[83] The administration also enjoyed the backing of policy research institutes including the Arms Control Association, Brookings Institution, the Carnegie Endowment for International Peace, the Center for Defense Information, and many others. Lobbyists from a range of NGOs and peace activist organizations including the Union of Concerned Scientists, the Council for a Livable World, and Physicians for Social Responsibility kept up pressure on the Senate for their support.

Opponents of the treaty included past (and future) administration officials including former Defense Secretaries Dick Cheney and Donald Rumsfeld, former National Security Advisor Brent Scowcroft, and Richard Perle. According to a spokesman for Governor George W. Bush of Texas, the would-be presidential candidate supported the moratorium but opposed a permanent ban on nuclear testing. Opponents also played on existing differences within the administration about the treaty. For example, some experts from the Department of Energy argued that the verification regime established by the treaty could never be considered foolproof as it might be possible to conduct small nuclear explosions (in the 1 to 10-kiloton range) without detection from the outside world.

Public Opinion

The Clinton administration enjoyed strong public support for the international nonproliferation regime and the CTBT. For example, a poll from July 1999 showed that 80 per cent of Americans supported ratification of the CTBT.[84] The flames of public support were also fanned by Democratic Party activists and by organizations that favored arms control. Peace groups sponsored a series of demonstrations where Congressional representatives appeared to lobby the public on the treaty (and raise the media profile of the events). It is interesting to note, however, that throughout this campaign, some Republican leaders remained convinced that popular support for the treaty would be fleeting. They believed that they could hold out against the tide of popular opinion on this issue and remain secure in the defeat of the treaty in the face of upcoming national elections.

Outcome and Analysis

The CTBT ran up against a wall of conservative opposition in the U.S. Senate. On October 13, 1999, the U.S. Senate rejected the treaty by a vote of 48–51, dealing a severe blow not only to President Clinton's foreign policy legacy but also to the global nonproliferation regime.[85]

The president's response to the defeat was swift and angry. In a White House press conference, Clinton said:

In recent days members of the Congressional majority have displayed a reckless partisanship. It threatens America's economic well-being and now our national security. Yesterday, hard-line Republicans irresponsibly forced a vote against the Comprehensive Nuclear Test Ban Treaty. This was partisan politics of the worst kind because it was so blatant and because of the risks it poses to the safety of the American people and the world. What the Senate seeks is to abandon the agreement that requires other countries to do what we have already done; an agreement that constrains Russia and China, India and Pakistan from developing more dangerous nuclear weapons; that helps to keep other countries out of the nuclear weapons business altogether; that improves our ability to monitor dangerous weapons activities in other countries....They ignored the advice of our top military leaders, our most distinguished scientists, our closest allies. They brushed aside the views of the American people and betrayed the vision of Presidents Eisenhower and Kennedy, who set us on the road to this treaty so many years ago.[86]

The president subsequently characterized the move by the Senate as "[partisan] politics, pure and simple," and he warned of a "new isolationism" in U.S. foreign policy.[87] Senate Minority Leader Daschle concluded, "No constitutional obligation has been treated so cavalierly, so casually, than this treaty on this day. This is a terrible, terrible mistake. If politics don't stop at the water's edge, nothing does."[88]

This case study does seem to conform with the predictions of neorealism but fails to satisfy the expectations of constructivists. Neorealists predict that a country would be reluctant to sign and ratify an agreement that posed real threats to its security, and critics effectively framed the CTBT as just that. Opponents believed that the treaty would limit U.S. modernization initiatives while at the same time allowing some groups or countries the potential to develop clandestine nuclear weapons programs using only low-yield explosions. Like their counterparts in France, military experts suggested that real-world testing would be essential for future nuclear weapons modernization programs. They worried that the treaty would restrict U.S. security at the very time the international security environment was becoming less predictable. At the same time, the decision to reject the CTBT by the U.S. Senate represents a repudiation of the international nonproliferation norm— the very norm that the United States government had helped to construct over decades.

Domestic conditions offer a critical added dimension of explanation in this case. The Clinton administration devoted few resources to the ratification campaign and only seemed to become engaged when it was too late. The president did not practice a serious program of side payments, synergistic issue linkage, or issue redefinition in efforts to build Senate support for the deal. This is not to discount the press conferences, media events, and official lobbying conducted by the administration, but rather to suggest that the efforts can be categorized as too little, too late. Indeed, one might assert that the administration only truly engaged in an active strategy toward the Senate in the drive to postpone the final vote on the treaty.

Executive–legislative relations and the power of the Senate to block treaty ratification stand out as a very important factor in this case. The administration relied upon a vote by two-thirds of the Senate in favor of the CTBT, and from the beginning it appeared that this threshold might be hard to achieve. Yet instead of lobbying the Senate in a serious way in the fall of 1997, the administration instead submitted the treaty to the Senate then redirected its focus to other issues. Meanwhile, Senate opponents of the treaty were much more active and deliberate regarding its fate. Senate Foreign Relations Committee Chairman Helms stood firm in opposition to any committee hearings on the treaty while others worked to block forward progress on related nonproliferation initiatives. The environment became poisoned, however, with revelations in the Lewinsky scandal. Senate opponents of the CTBT and other administration initiatives effectively held the Clinton legacy hostage as it reviewed the potential for impeachment of the president.

The proposition regarding the relationship between interest groups opposition and treaty ratification appears to be supported by this case study. Opponents mobilized quickly to challenge the treaty, and interest groups worked in close collaboration with Congressional opponents. Right-wing policy institutes launched a public information campaign designed to highlight problems with the treaty, devoting special attention to national security implications of the deal. Finally, the proposition regarding public attitudes and treaty ratification was not upheld by this case study. Public attitudes strongly supported nonproliferation initiatives including the CTBT, yet the government chose a different course.

NOTES

1. Clinton, as quoted in Terry Deibel, "The Death of a Treaty," *Foreign Affairs*, vol. 81, no. 5 (September/October 2002), p. 143.
2. The United States had detonated nuclear test explosions since the end of World War II in the South Pacific. The first incident that helped publicize health concerns regarding radiation occurred in March 1954 when Japanese fishermen on the "Lucky Dragon" trawler were coated by radioactive fallout and fell ill.

3. Parliament of the Commonwealth of Australia, Joint Standing Committee on Treaties, Report #15 (Canberra: Government Printing Office, June 1998), p. 30.

4. For more historical context on the development of test ban treaties and international law, see Egon Schweib, "The Nuclear Test Ban Treaty and International Law," *The American Journal of International Law*, vol. 58, no. 3 (July 1964), pp. 642–70; Eric Stein, "Legal Restraints in Modern Arms Control Agreements," *The American Journal of International Law*, vol. 66, no. 6 (April 1972), pp. 255–89; Thomas Graham Jr. and Damien J. La Vera, "Nuclear Weapons: The Comprehensive Test Ban Treaty and National Missile Defense," in Stewart Patrick and Shepard Forman, eds., *Multilateralism and U.S. Foreign Policy: Ambivalent Engagement* (Boulder, CO: Lynne Rienner, 2002).

5. "Text of the Comprehensive Nuclear Test-Ban Treaty," U.S. Department of State, www.state.gov/t/np/trty/16513.htm (accessed May 18, 2004).

6. Deibel, "Death of a Treaty," p. 144.

7. Today, Australia holds the world's largest known reserves of uranium and operates a significant network of mines in the Northern Territory and South Australia; "Uranium Mining, Processing, and Nuclear Energy—Opportunities for Australia?" (Canberra: Government Printing Office, 2006), pp. 23–4; see also Wayne Reynolds, "Rethinking the Joint Project: Australia's Bid for Nuclear Weapons 1945–1960," *Historical Journal*, vol. 41, no. 3 (1998), pp. 853–73.

8. Sadly, the tests were later linked to severe illnesses in Aboriginal communities located near the test sites. In the late 1950s British scientists conducted nuclear tests at Maralinga in South Australia. Once again, Aboriginal inhabitants in the region experienced severe health effects from the testing; Wayne Reynolds, "Menzies and the Proposal for Atomic Weapons," in Frank Cain, ed., *Menzies in War and Peace* (St. Leonards, NSW, Australia: Allen & Unwin, 1997).

9. "Chronology: Australia's Nuclear Political History," Four Corners, Australian Broadcasting Corporation, www.abc.net.au/4corners/content/2005/20050822_nuclear/nuclear-chronology.htm (accessed April 28, 2007).

10. Jim Walsh, "Surprise Down Under: The Secret History of Australia's Nuclear Ambitions," *The Nonproliferation Review*, no. 5 (Fall 1997), pp. 1–20.

11. Jacques E.C. Hymans, *The Psychology of Nuclear Proliferation: Identity, Emotions, and Foreign Policy* (Cambridge: Cambridge University Press, 2006), p. 114.

12. For a good discussion of Australia's reluctance to sign the NPT, see Richard Broinowski, *Fact or Fission? The Truth About Australia's Nuclear Ambitions* (Carlton North, Victoria, Australia: Scribe Publications, 2003); Glenn T. Seaborg, *Stemming the Tide* (Lexington, MA: Lexington Press, 1987).

13. "Chronology: Australia's Nuclear Political History," Four Corners.

14. Ian Bellany, *Australia in the Nuclear Age* (Sydney: Sydney University Press, 1972); Pilita Clark, "PM's Story: Very Much Alive…and Unfazed," *Sydney Morning Herald* (January 1, 1999), p. 1.

15. J.D.B. Miller, "Australian Foreign Policy: Constraints and Opportunities," *International Affairs*, vol. 50, no. 2 (April 1974), pp. 229–41.

16. Toshiki Mogami, "The South Pacific Nuclear Free Zone: A Fettered Leap Forward," *Journal of Peace Research*, vol. 25, no. 4 (December 1988), pp. 411–30.

17. Richard Broinowski, *Fact or Fission? The Truth About Australia's Nuclear Ambitions* (Carlton North, Victoria, Australia: Scribe Publications, 2003), p. 202.

18. National Interest Analysis: Comprehensive Nuclear-Test-Ban Treaty, Government of the Commonwealth of Australia, www.austlii.edu.au/au/other/dfat/nia/1998/17.html (accessed March 2, 2006).

19. Broinowski, *Fact or Fission?*, p. 206.

20. Paul Keating (memoirs), *Engagement: Australia Faces the Asia-Pacific* (Sydney: Pan Macmillan Australia Pty. Limited, 2000), pp. 221–34.

21. Duane Bratt, "Canada's Nuclear Schizophrenia," *Bulletin of the Atomic Scientists*, vol. 58, no. 2 (March/April 2002), pp. 45–50.

22. Indeed, the Great Bear Lake in the Northwest Territories was one of only two known sources of uranium outside of Nazi-controlled Europe during World War II; see Duane Bratt, "Canada's Nuclear Schizophrenia," *Bulletin of the Atomic Scientists*, vol. 58, no. 2 (March/April 2002), pp. 45–50, p. 45.

23. Joel J. Sokolsky, "A Seat at the Table: Canada and Its Alliances," in Cynthia A. Cannizzo, Ed., *Canadian Defense Policy: Challenges and Continuities, Special Issue of Armed Forces and Society*, vol. 16, no. 1 (Fall 1989), pp. 11–36, p. 12; see also Richard Rhodes, *The Making of the Atomic Bomb*, New York: Simon & Schuster, 1986; Dennis Smith, Diplomacy of Fear: Canada and the Cold War, 1941–1948 (Toronto: University of Toronto Press, 1988).

24. Interview with Author, Canberra, Australia (May 17, 2007).

25. See Brian Buckley, *Canada's Early Nuclear Policy: Fate, Chance, and Character* (Montreal and Kingston: McGill-Queens, 2000), p. 3.

26. See Erika Simpson, *NATO and the Bomb: Canadian Defenders Confront Critics* (Montreal and Kingston: McGill-Queen's, 2001), pp. 224–5; Richard Rhodes, *The Making of the Atomic Bomb* (New York: Simon & Schuster, 1986); Dennis Smith, *Diplomacy of Fear: Canada and the Cold War, 1941–1948* (Toronto: University of Toronto Press, 1988).

27. Jon B. McLin, *Canada's Changing Defense Policy, 1957–1963: The Problems of a Middle Power in Alliance* (Baltimore, MD: Johns Hopkins University Press, 1967), p. 136; see also Sokolsky, "A Seat at the Table."

28. John Clearwater, *Canadian Nuclear Weapons: The Untold Story of Canada's Cold War Arsenal* (Toronto: Dundurn, 1998), p. 23; Duane Bratt, "Canada's Nuclear Schizophrenia," *Bulletin of the Atomic Scientists*, vol. 58, no. 2 (March/April 2002), p. 46.

29. Canada, Department of National Defence (DND), *White Paper on Defence* (Ottawa: Queen's Printer for Canada, 1964), p. 13.

30. See Joseph Levitt, *Pearson and Canada's Role in Nuclear Disarmament and Arms Control Negotiations, 1945–1957* (Montreal: McGill-Queen's University Press, 1993).

31. Department of Foreign Affairs and International Trade, "Government State-ment: Nuclear Disarmament and Non-Proliferation: Advancing Canadian Objectives, April 1999" (Ottawa: Queen's Printer, 1999).
32. SCAIT Report, p. 2.
33. As quoted in Bratt, "Canada's Nuclear Schizophrenia," p. 49.
34. SCAIT Report 1998, p. 4.
35. As quoted in Bratt, "Canada's Nuclear Schizophrenia," p. 46.
36. For broader perspective on this theme, see Erika Simpson, *NATO and the Bomb: Canadian Defenders Confront Critics* (Montreal and Kingston: McGill-Queen's, 2001), pp. 224–5.
37. Xinhua News Agency, "Canadian Prime Minister to Advance International Security Agenda" (December 15, 1998).
38. Lisa Schlein, "Canada Takes Cost-Control Message to UN Test-Ban Body," Canadian Press Newswire (March 6, 1997), CBCA-ACC No. 3805562.
39. "La TN75 un 'saut technologique,'" *Le Figaro* (October 3, 1995), p. 1.
40. See Diego Ruiz Palmer, "French Strategic Options in the 1990s," Adelphi Paper 260 (London: International Institute for Strategic Studies, Summer 1991); see also Avery Goldstein, *Deterrence and Security in the 21st Century: China, Britain, France, and the Enduring Legacy of the Nuclear Revolution* (Stanford, CA: Stanford University Press, 2000).
41. Keith Suter, "Paradise Lost," *Bulletin of the Atomic Scientists* (September/October 1995), pp. 13–14.
42. Hymans, *The Psychology of Nuclear Proliferation*, p. 84.
43. Philip H. Gordon, *A Certain Idea of France: French Security Policy and the Gaullist Legacy* (Princeton, NJ: Princeton University Press, 1993); see also K. Schubert, "France," in Regina Cowen Karp, ed., *Security With Nuclear Weapons: Different Perspectives on National Security* (Oxford: Oxford University Press, 1991), pp. 162–88; Beatrice Heuser, *Nuclear Mentalities? Strategies and Beliefs in Britain, France, and the Federal Republic of Germany* (London: Macmillan, 1998).
44. D. Garraud, "Nuclear Weapons: the Strategic Quarrel Behind the Tests," *Liberation* (October 29, 1993), p. 8.
45. Mitterrand, as quoted in "Coquerico!" *The Economist* (June 17, 1995), p. 53.
46. There was another reason for the tests. The French military was in the process of refining new warhead designs for deployment on submarine-launched ballistic missile (SLBM) systems. They also claim that the TN-75 warhead for the M-45 (that is a new missile system for SSBNs) should be tested so that they would be certified; see Marie-Helene Labbé, "France," in Eric Arnett, ed., *Nuclear Weapons After the Comprehensive Test Ban: Implications for Modernization and Proliferation* (SIPRI: Oxford University Press, 1996), pp. 31–40.
47. Chirac, as quoted in Coquerico! p. 53; see also Stuart Croft, "European Integration, Nuclear Deterrence and Franco-British Nuclear Cooperation," *International Affairs*, vol. 72, no. 4 (October 1996), pp. 771–87.

48. Croft, "European Integration, Nuclear Deterrence and Franco-British Nuclear Cooperation," p. 776.

49. Quoted in *Nuclear Proliferation News*, no. 32 (September 8, 1995).

50. British Broadcasting Corporation, "French Cabinet Gives Go-Ahead to ratify Nuclear Test Ban Treaty" (January 21, 1998).

51. Jacques Chirac, Tony Blair, and Gerhard Schroeder, "A Treaty We All Need," *New York Times* (October 8, 1999), p. A31.

52. David S. Yost, "Nuclear Debates in France," *Survival*, vol. 36, no. 4 (Winter 1994–5), pp. 113–39.

53. "Thousands Demonstrate Against Nuclear Tests," FBIS-WEU-95-119 (June 21, 1995), p. 24.

54. *The Economist*, "France: Plummeteers" (September 30, 1995), p. 40.

55. Croft, "European Integration, Nuclear Deterrence, and Franco-British Nuclear Cooperation," p. 781; *The Economist*, "Nuclear Testing: Not So Pacific" (June 24, 1995), pp. 34–5.

56. "President Chirac Holds News Conference in Paris," Paris France-2 Television Network, FBIS-WEU-95-136 (July 17, 1995), p. 14.

57. British Broadcasting Corporation, "French Cabinet Gives Go-Ahead to Ratify Nuclear Test Ban Treaty" (January 21, 1998).

58. France's Foreign Minister Urges States Crucial to Nuclear-Test-Ban Treaty Success to Ratify It Without Delay, United Nations Press Release DC 2819, Conference on Facilitating Entry into Force of the Comprehensive Nuclear-Test-Ban Treaty (December 11, 2001).

59. As quoted in *Nuclear Proliferation News* (September 8, 1995).

60. Quoted in *Nuclear Proliferation News*, no. 32 (September 8, 1995), www.csf. colorado.edu/dfax/npn/npn32.htm (accessed May 28, 2004); for a broader perspective on this, see Philip H. Gordon, *A Certain Idea of France: French Security Policy and the Gaullist Legacy* (Princeton, NJ: Princeton University Press, 1993).

61. Germany's renunciation was by Konrad Adenauer at the London Nine-Power Conference in October 1954 stating Germany would not produce atomic, biological, or chemical weapons on its territory; reprinted in *Dokumentation zur Abrüstung und Sicherheit* (Documentation on Disarmament and Security), vol. 1 (Bonn: Siegler, 1966), p. 79.

62. Karl-Heinz Kamp, "Germany and the Future of Nuclear Weapons in Europe," *Security Dialogue*, vol. 26, no. 3 (1995), p. 279.

63. Kamp, "Germany and the Future of Nuclear Weapons in Europe," p. 281.

64. See Mathias Küntzel, *Bonn & the Bomb* (London: Pluto Press, 1995), p. 123.

65. Harald Mueller, Alexander Kelle, Katja Frank, Sylvia Meier, and Annette Schaper, "The German Debate on Nuclear Weapons and Disarmament," *The Washington Quarterly*, vol. 20, no. 3 (Summer 1997), pp. 115–16.

66. See William Walker, "International Nuclear Relations After the Indian and Pakistani Test Explosions," *International Affairs*, vol. 74, no. 3 (1998), pp. 505–28;

draft text, as quoted in Mueller et al., "The German Debate on Nuclear Weapons and Disarmament," p. 116.

67. Kamp, "Germany and the Future of Nuclear Weapons in Europe," p. 278.

68. Mueller et al., "The German Debate," p. 118.

69. Ibid, p. 122.

70. "American RAND Corporation Poll in Germany," *Wall Street Journal* (February 16, 1993), p. 21.

71. Kamp, "Germany and the Future of Nuclear Weapons in Europe," p. 278.

72. The United States had detonated nuclear test explosions since the end of World War II in the South Pacific. The first incident that helped publicize health concerns regarding radiation occurred in March 1954 when Japanese fishermen on the "Lucky Dragon" trawler were coated by radioactive fallout and fell ill.

73. Parliament of the Commonwealth of Australia, Joint Standing Committee on Treaties, Report #15 (Canberra: Government Printing Office, June 1998), p. 30.

74. Thomas Graham Jr. and Damien J. La Vera, "Nuclear Weapons: The Comprehensive Test Ban Treaty and National Missile Defense," in Stewart Patrick and Shepard Forman, eds., *Multilateralism and U.S. Foreign Policy: Ambivalent Engagement* (Boulder, CO: Lynne Rienner, 2002), p. 225.

75. Stephen I. Schwartz, "Outmaneuvered, Outgunned, and Out of View," *The Bulletin of Atomic Scientists*, vol. 56, no. 7 (January/February 2000), p. 4.

76. "Senate Inaction on Test Ban Undercuts Effort to Address South Asia Crisis," *Issue* Brief, vol. 4 (June 1998), p. 1.

77. See Helen Dewar and Roberto Suro, "Senate Conservatives to Demand Vote on Test Ban Treaty," *Washington Post* (October 7, 1999), p. A9. Also see Charles Babington, "Clinton Campaigns for Senate Passage of Test Ban Treaty," *Washington Post* (October 5, 1999), p. A5.

78. James M. Jeffords, "Senate Should Ratify Test Ban Treaty," *Boston Globe* (October 11, 1999), p. A19.

79. Tom Z. Collina and Christopher Paine, "Test Ban Treaty: Let's Finish the Job," *Bulletin of the Atomic Scientists* (July/August 1999), p. 33–5.

80. See Kathleen C. Bailey, "The Comprehensive Test Ban Treaty: The Costs Outweigh the Benefits," Policy Analysis No. 330, Cato Institute (January 15, 1999).

81. See Richard L. Berke and Katharine Q. Seelye, "Treaty Ricochets Into Presidential Fray," *New York Times* (October 15, 1999), p. A11; Eric Schmitt, "Why Clinton Plea on Pact Left Lott Unmoved," *New York Times* (October 15, 1999), p. A11.

82. Senator Richard Lugar, "Lugar Opposes Comprehensive Test Ban Treaty," *News Release*, no. 7 (October 1999), p. 2.

83. "32 Nobel Laureates in Physics Back Atomic Test Ban," *New York Times* (October 6, 1999), p. A1.

84. Coalition to Reduce Nuclear Dangers, "Eight in Ten Americans Support Test Ban Treaty," *News Release* (July 20, 1999).

85. Eric Schmitt, "Senate Kills Test Ban Treaty in Crushing Loss for Clinton; Evokes Versailles Pact Defeat," *New York Times* (October 14, 1999), p. A1; R.W.

Apple, Jr., "The G.O.P. Torpedo," *New York Times* (October 14, 1999), p. A1; *Congressional Record* (October 13, 1999), p. S12548.

86. Transcript of President Clinton's Address, "Clinton at News Conference: 'Troubling Signs of New Isolationism,'" *New York Times* (October 15, 1999), p. A14.
87. Ibid.
88. Office of the Press Secretary, The White House, *Statement of the President* (October 13, 1999); Senator Trent Lott, "Response to President Clinton's Remarks," *Federal News Service Transcript*, 14 October 1999.

7

The Australia–United States
Free Trade Agreement

I. HISTORY OF THE AUSTRALIA–UNITED STATES
FREE TRADE AGREEMENT (AUSFTA)

In June 2002, President George W. Bush and Prime Minister John Howard announced their intention to negotiate a free trade pact between Australia and the United States. The leaders hailed a possible agreement as a "milestone" in the history of the alliance.[1] Supporters believed it would be a "win–win" deal for the two advanced industrialized nations, building on an already-strong bilateral trade relationship. In 2002, the United States was the second largest export market for Australian goods, representing some 11–15 per cent of annual Australian export revenues. Australia was the twenty-fourth largest trading partner of the United States, providing 2 per cent of U.S. export revenues. The bilateral trade relationship, already valued at over $20 billion, was primed for expansion.[2]

Given the significance of the deal, some observers expected it to be completed quickly and sail through each home government in noncontroversial ratification processes. Prime Minister Howard enjoyed executive authority to negotiate a trade deal with the United States and a majority coalition government. President Bush also had a Republican majority in Congress and easily secured Trade Promotion Authority to negotiate the agreement. Furthermore, many economists believed that the free trade agreement represented a significant economic opportunity. Early reports predicted that the treaty could boost the Australian economy by as much as $6 billion a year. AUSFTA would build on significant momentum in liberalization and join Australia to one of the largest economies in the world. Negotiations officially began in Canberra in March 2003.[3]

AUSFTA became highly controversial in its progression from promise to reality, however. The negotiation process was surprisingly contentious at times. Furthermore, the complexities of the treaty and implications for specific sectors of the economy awakened key constituencies in both countries to action.[4] Far from viewing the deal as a potential "win–win", critics in Australia began to calculate potential losses even before the ink on the treaty was dry. For example, some farm groups in Australia became irate when they learned that tariffs on products like sugar, beef, and dairy would not be removed immediately. Others warned that the treaty would wreck the Australian public health system by undermining the pharmaceutical benefits program. To some Australians the treaty represented a bitter reminder of the "democratic deficit" in international treaty-making. In the United States, the agreement encountered resistance from some members of the U.S. Congress and the farm lobby. Nevertheless, a draft version of the treaty was completed in February 2004, duly ratified by both countries, and came into effect on January 1, 2005. This chapter outlines the difficult road to AUSFTA in a broader climate of globalization.

II. AUSTRALIA AND THE AUSFTA

The AUSFTA was the most controversial trade agreement in Australia's history. To some, it represented an unprecedented opportunity: Australia's economy would blossom through links to one of the largest and most powerful economies in the world. The treaty would strengthen an already-warm friendship between allies. Yet prospects of the treaty also awakened a latent trade protectionism in Australia, provoked anger on the part of some interest groups, and fueled a spate of anti-Americanism in the polity. In the end, the treaty generated a surprising amount of heat (if not fire) in Australia, and debates over the merits of the deal continue to this day.

International Pressure

The signature by Australia's Trade Minister Mark Vaile and U.S. Trade Representative Robert Zoellick of a draft version of the treaty in February 2004 effectively marked the beginning of the post-commitment politics phase in Australia. Supporters of the AUSFTA argued that it offered tremendous benefits for Australian farmers and producers through the elimination of tariff barriers to trade. The government said that this bilateral deal would "compliment and reinforce" multilateral agreements and "deliver substantial gains to Australia."[5] More broadly, Australian officials perceived a strong national security imperative embedded in the deal. However, critics charged that Australia would actually have to sacrifice much more than it might gain by opening its market to the U.S. economy.

Australia was also greatly influenced by normative pressure to ratify the agreement, although the direction of this pressure was unclear. Australia had actively participated in multilateral trade deals in the past, including through rounds of the General Agreement of Tariffs and Trade (GATT) regime. Economic liberalization had begun to produce real gains for Australia starting in the 1980s. Prime Minister Howard's government also may have felt a sense of obligation to ratify the agreement with the United States. That said, however, there were also contending normative pressures regarding liberalization in a bilateral context. Australia had been actively involved in multilateral trade regimes and had eschewed bilateral arrangements in the past. Indeed, when representatives of the Clinton administration first broached the topic of a free trade deal with Australia in 1997, the Howard government had expressed disinterest.

Executive Strategy

News of Prime Minister Howard's plans to negotiate a free trade pact with the United States came as a surprise to some in the Australian government. In the tradition of executive dominance of foreign affairs, Howard and top Cabinet ministers had secretly discussed the outlines of a potential agreement with the Clinton administration in the late 1990s. The first time that some officials even heard about plans for a treaty was in a speech by the Australian ambassador to the United States in December 2000. Almost two years passed before the prime minister announced his formal intentions to negotiate the deal during a state visit to Washington in June 2002.

The prime minister had both political and economic motivations to seek a free trade pact. Politically, the announcement showed Howard's determination to build on an already-strong relationship with the United States. Howard claimed that Australia stood to gain a great deal by linking the two economies. The prime minister was enthusiastic about prospects for the deal, saying that it would "add enormous long term benefits to the Australian economy."[6] Howard maintained that his coalition Liberal/National government, and not the opposition Labor Party led by Mark Latham, was the true steward of the country's economic growth.

Howard directed Vaile, the Minister for Trade and leader of the National Party, to manage Australia's negotiating team. Vaile outlined his government's objectives in the negotiations through a series of remarks to the parliament and media. First and foremost, he argued, Australia would deepen its ties to one of the most powerful economies in the world. The new deal would dramatically improve market access for Australia in the United States, promote economic growth, and create jobs in Australia. The government also promised protection for Australian industry and farmers, warning that an agreement that did not eliminate tariffs for agricultural products would be unacceptable.[7]

The Australian government appeared determined to achieve key objectives through the negotiation process. Department of Foreign Affairs and Trade (DFAT) officials focused on access for Australian agricultural products (especially beef, dairy, sugar), high-speed catamaran ferries, telecommunications, and intellectual property.[8] The treaty also could have implications for public health policy, rules for foreign investment, and cultural sovereignty (such as local media-content rules). Perhaps the most visible issue of concern was the Pharmaceutical Benefits Scheme (PBS), a cornerstone of the Australian public health system that many feared would be directly threatened by the agreement. The PBS subsidizes hundreds of popular prescription drugs (some 90 per cent of all drugs) for Australian citizens. To regulate the PBS, the government maintains a strict list of pharmaceuticals eligible for this benefit and helps guarantee access for millions of consumers. Howard and key negotiators claimed that the PBS would remain untouched by the treaty.

The prime minister trumpeted the very optimistic results of studies on the potential trade agreement before, during, and after the negotiations. For example, a 2001 Centre for International Economics (CIE) study, sponsored by the DFAT, claimed that Australia would see "net economic welfare gains over 20 years of about U.S. $20 billion, shared evenly between the two countries." The study predicted a 4 per cent increase in Australian GDP by 2010, and greater investment in Australian mining and agriculture.[9] A 2004 CIE study predicted that the GDP would rise by approximately $6 billion AUD over the decade to come and would not have serious costs for Australia's economy nor threaten its public health system. Ironically, the report also concluded that the treaty would "not prevent Australia from meeting its international environment obligations."[10]

Executive strategy to build popular support for the treaty was challenged in early 2004, however, when it became clear that the United States would refuse to make key concessions in the negotiations. In fact, by early February, Vaile had concluded that *the deal would best satisfy the trade policy objectives of the United States.*[11] AUSTFA would eliminate barriers in Australia for all U.S. agriculture and 99 per cent of manufactured goods. But it would not immediately eliminate U.S. protections on beef and dairy products, and the deal totally excluded Australian sugar. Moreover, the treaty included the potential for changes in the PBS. While the Howard government claimed that it had kept negotiations related to the PBS "off the table," Australian negotiators actually had been under pressure to allow changes in the system. For example, the draft treaty established a new Medicines Working Group, meant to "promote discussion and mutual understanding of the issues...including the importance of pharmaceutical research and development."[12] The deal effectively made the Australian PBS more transparent and created opportunities for companies to seek reviews of decisions on which drugs would make the Australian list.

On February 7, 2004, Vaile phoned Prime Minister Howard and raised the issue of walking away from the negotiating table for AUSFTA. Howard was deeply opposed to allowing the agreement to fall apart, however, and ordered Vaile to complete the best possible agreement even with obvious limitations.[13] With this move the prime minister signaled the degree to which he believed that completion of the treaty was in the long-term best interests of his government. The prime minister already had invested heavily in the process, and he believed that major government agencies and interest groups were aligned in support of the deal. On February 8, Vaile duly signed a draft AUSFTA with U.S. Trade Representative Robert Zoellick.[14] While the prime minister hailed the treaty as a "once-in-a-generation opportunity," Vaile later privately admitted that for Australia the deal was "a disappointment."[15]

Thus, even before the ink on the treaty was dry, it seemed that the government would have a hard road of treaty ratification. Later that month, Howard attempted to widen his win-set through a direct discussion with President Bush on the matter. In February 2004 the prime minister appealed for increased market access for beef (an extra 30,000 tons) as well as an accelerated phase-in period for sugar exports. Australian leaders were "stunned," however, when the president rejected any additional concessions. One senior DFAT official commenting on the exchange said, "It caught us off-guard that the relationship wasn't worth 30,000 tonnes of beef. If the Yanks weren't prepared to do that, it really soured our view."[16]

Howard ramped up the government campaign to build support for ratification once the treaty was finalized in May 2004. Vaile conceded that while the treaty did not eliminate the quota for Australian beef exports to the United States, it did promise a (slow) phaseout of tariffs on beef exports over a span of 18 years. Sugar, 1.2 billion AUD-industry in Australia, was even more controversial. Howard was concerned about his government's failure to enforce Downer's promise that no deal would be completed that did not serve the best interest of Australia's farmers.[17] The government put forward legislation to establish a $440 million compensation package for sugar farmers, or the "equivalent of about $70,000 for each of Australia's 6,500 sugar farmers."[18] This plan, along with other promises to key constituencies, represented the prime minister's deep conviction that the treaty should be ratified at all costs.

Regime Type: Executive–Legislative Relations

Ultimately, Prime Minister Howard knew that guaranteeing the implementation of the treaty would require passage of enabling legislation through parliament. In the past, this had not been difficult for Australian governments. Prime ministers had enjoyed strong bipartisan support for international trade agreements post-1945. One expert contends:

Since the end of World War II, there have been no instances of the opposition parties blocking Australia's participation in multilateral or bilateral trade agreements. This was true even in the case of agreements where there was strong parliamentary opposition—for example, Australia's decision to become a contracting party to the General Agreement on Tariffs and Trade in 1947 and the 1957 Commercial Treaty with Japan. During this period parliamentarians did not express major concerns with their lack of involvement with the trade negotiation process or lack of opportunities for community participation and discussion of these agreements and their implications for Australia.[19]

By the 1990s, however, the political climate had changed. Australia experienced a period of debate over the "democratic deficit"—the limited public role in treaty-making. And while Howard enjoyed a majority of support in the House, the Senate had been dominated by the opposition Labor Party for more than a decade. Indeed, with an election imminent, the Senate soon became the battleground for significant political struggles.

The Australian parliament has no constitutional role in the ratification process, but the government was well aware that it needed to pass enabling legislation and build popular legitimacy for the treaty. Ironically, the parliamentary "review process" for AUSFTA actually began *during* the negotiation process when Labor Party leaders in the Senate called for a special inquiry on the treaty led by members of the Senate Foreign Affairs, Defence, and Trade References Committee. Unlike the Joint Standing Committee on Treaties (JSCOT), which was run by a majority of legislators from the governing coalition, the Senate committee was stacked in favor of the opposition. The Senate committee accepted hundreds of inquiry submissions and held public hearings in which opponents claimed that the treaty would harm the Australian economy irrevocably. Senators also sponsored several roundtable gatherings of experts to comment on the implications of the treaty for Australian policy.[20]

The Senate review process included a number of high-profile hearings that generated media attention. Senators heard from a number of conservative economists who had developed a career on protectionist leanings for the broader good of the Australian economy. One of the reasons for this controversy was Australia's tradition of trade protectionism. For decades after World War II, Australia had lagged behind other advanced industrialized nations in terms of economic growth, partly due to protectionism. When the government began to lower capital controls and tariff barriers and confront the dynamics of the global economy in the 1980s, the moves yielded immediate results.[21] Australia experienced positive growth trends in the 1990s and gained significant momentum by keeping pace with advances in information technology and global communications. In 1996, the Organization for Economic Cooperation and Development (OECD) rated Australia as having one of the lowest levels of tariff barriers to trade and investment in the world.[22] The Senate committee's final report, "Voting on Trade" challenged the lack of consultation on the treaty and called for significant changes to the text before ratification.[23]

JSCOT also conducted an official inquiry on AUSFTA once the treaty was tabled in parliament on March 8, 2004. JSCOT conducted inquiries in Canberra and then went on a "listening tour," holding hearings in the capital cities of all states for a period of two weeks. Hundreds of petitions were recorded by the committee, and a select number were invited to give testimony at the public meetings.[24] JSCOT's final report under Chair Andrew Southcott concluded that AUSFTA could benefit the Australian economy significantly.[25] The committee did register concerns about transparency and communication between the federal and state governments, but they concluded that ratification was firmly in Australia's national interest.[26]

Building on the momentum of opposition generated through the special committee hearings, the Labor Party majority in the Senate attempted to derail ratification of the agreement by proposing significant amendments. Labor leaders zeroed-in on the potential damage the treaty would cause to Australia's national health care system.[27] At issue was the possible dismantling of the PBS. For decades, Australia's national health-care system had included a close working relationship with pharmaceutical manufacturers, and Australian drug prices remained consistently much lower than in the United States. But a draft version of AUSFTA circulated to the public included concessions to the U.S. pharmaceutical industry that might extend patents on drugs to prevent the production of generic versions. Critics believed that this would lead to a significant increase in drug prices in Australia.[28]

As time passed, criticism of the AUSFTA in parliament grew in scope and intensity. Parliamentary opponents seized on the results of a new study, authored by prominent economist Professor Ross Garnaut, which concluded that over the long-term the treaty could hurt Australian farms and the economy in general.[29] Parliamentary critics also charged that the United States would gain greater leverage over Australia's strict quarantine laws, that the treaty would allow a greater influx of American-made products into the country, and it would undermine the local automobile industry. Environmental regulations that interfered with liberalized trade could be threatened. Finally, the very heart of Australian culture would be challenged by the loss of protection of local content rules in the media.

Labor Senators seized on this opposition and proposed amendments to the enabling legislation for AUSFTA with a special emphasis on protection of the price of subsidized medicines. Senate opposition leaders demanded that AUSFTA implementing legislation contain within it amendments or conditions that would create fines for drug companies that delayed the introduction of generic medicines in Australia. They feared that U.S. companies would attempt to use their comparative advantage by extending patents on drugs to prevent the production of generic versions. Labor party leader Mark Latham effectively portrayed the prime minister as siding with large pharmaceutical companies and threatened to block the treaty if the amendments were not accepted.[30]

Labor's resolve on the issue presented the prime minister with a conundrum: either he accept the treaty with the amendments and risk U.S. rejection of the new language or his government faced the possibility of a failure to ratify and implement the treaty. At a deeper level, this represented a challenge to the power of the executive in Australian foreign affairs. Howard's immediate reaction was to reject the call for amendments as unnecessary and warned the clauses would kill the treaty. Meanwhile, Labor Party leader Mark Latham held out, arguing: "We see no reason to alter our amendments whatsoever, so we're proceeding with them, standing by them 100 per cent. They're consistent with the text of the FTA. They're good laws. They're good proposals."[31]

After weeks of deadlock, the prime minister did finally agree to allow the amendments to save the agreement. Even in accepting the amendments, though, Howard reiterated his warning that the treaty could fail if the United States refused to accept the modifications. "The government has decided that the common sense thing to do is support the amendments but warn that the enabling legislation could be construed by the Americans as inconsistent with the free trade agreement," Howard told reporters. "If that were to occur, then it would be entirely the fault of the Labor Party," he added. Meanwhile, Labor leader Mark Latham praised the concessions, noting: "it's a good result for the Australian people and the prime minister should have the decency of facing up to the truth of the matter instead of trying to walk both sides of the street."[32]

On August 12, 2004, the Senate voted in support of implementing legislation for the treaty.

Interest Groups

The Australian government traditionally enjoyed support for trade agreements from major corporations. Many business groups saw the advantages that flowed from embracing the global economy beginning in the 1980s. Australian-based corporations flourished in this new environment, profiting from a wider network of trade and increased foreign investment. It is also noteworthy that the government routinely consulted with key corporations and interest groups in the course of negotiations on international agreements. From the 1980s onward, the governing coalition communicated with leaders of trade unions, farm groups, and manufacturers in the process of negotiations. Records on AUSFTA show that the government had been working to build relations with interest groups as long as eighteen months *before* negotiations even began. According to one expert,

[T]he Minister for Trade and senior DFAT officials had been involved in regular consultations with peak industry groups and major companies, seeking their views and specific aims and objectives. In addition, the proposed trade agreement had been a regular agenda item for the meetings of the former consultative groups, established by the Trade Minister and coordinated by DFAT. These groups were overwhelmingly dominated by business and industry interests including the Agricultural Trade Consultative Group representing the export oriented agricultural industries; the Automotive Industry Council representing auto manufacturers, and the WTO Advisory Group representing business and industry organizations.[33]

Interest groups were also well aware that Australia's constitutional system bolstered the power of the executive in international negotiations and limited public involvement in trade agreements. Indeed, the constitution provides exclusive powers for the executive in foreign affairs and defense. Furthermore, statutes provided that Australia's negotiating strategy for international agreements was to be kept secret for the duration of negotiations.

Key interest groups that supported the treaty included big business and agriculture. The Business Council of Australia (BCA), a consortium of chief executives of prominent Australian companies, believed the deal would greatly facilitate trade relations with the United States and help to make Australia more competitive on the world market.[34] The BCA lauded the treaty as a "significant step towards providing Australia with the benefits of global economic integration by providing close economic links with the largest economy in the world," describing the impact on Australia's economy as "far ranging, touching most aspects of economic activity and providing dynamic and long-term benefits."[35] Especially significant to the BCA was the increased ease of foreign direct investment and capital flows, as well as greater access to markets.

The Howard government garnered the support of the largest agricultural group in Australia, the National Farmers' Federation (NFF), through extensive concessions. The NFF's objection to the total exclusion of sugar from the deal, as well as the eighteen-year phase-out period for beef tariffs, helped to nudge the Howard government toward side payments. By the summer of 2004, the Federation was on record supporting the treaty.[36] A similar pattern occurred for dairy. In its submission to JSCOT, dairy representatives said "While the Industry is disappointed that the FTA did not ultimately include free trade in dairy products, the agreement does lead to an immediate three fold increase in Australia's quota access for dairy products to the U.S.A. that new access will also grow at an average compound 5% per year."[37]

As the negotiations for AUSFTA wore on, however, the government faced opposition from agricultural groups including Meat and Livestock Australia and the Cattle Council, who believed that a phased-out elimination of tariffs on beef exports unfairly penalized them. In addition, the Australian Manufacturing Workers Union (AMWU), representing more than 150,000 manufacturing workers, expressed deep concerns about the treaty. AMWU sponsored a 2004 study that predicted AUSFTA would damage the Australian economy and lead to the loss of 200,000 jobs. The study was especially critical of the blow to Australia's competitiveness in technology and information services.[38] Meanwhile, noted economists joined forces with Ross Garnaut, arguing that AUSFTA would limit economic prosperity for Australia and potentially undermine national security.[39]

Medical professionals were deeply concerned about the implications of the agreement in relation to the Pharmaceutical Benefits Scheme. Experts worried aloud that the AUSFTA would provide U.S. pharmaceutical manufacturers with some leverage to challenge the Australian health-care system. The treaty did include provisions for U.S. manufacturers to request independent reviews of decisions by the Australian Pharmaceutical Benefits Advisory Committee (PBAC), a statutory committee of independent experts, regarding decisions on the drug registry. The treaty also included plans for the creation of the Medicines Working Group, a board of health officials from both countries, to discuss progress on pharmaceutical research and development, and the treaty included some new provisions on Australian patent laws. Critics challenged these agreements as providing potential leverage for U.S. companies in decisions about Australia's public health system—such as by delaying the introduction of generic drug equivalents to prescription medicines.

The Doctors Reform Society argued that the AUSFTA would not guarantee Australian health-care policies and they warned of linking Australia to "the nation with arguably the most inefficient and inequitable health and phar- maceuticals system of developed nations."[40] In a similar vein, critics argued that greater liberalization of trade relations with the United States would have adverse effects on the health and prosperity of indigenous groups in Australia.[41]

The PBS became an emotional rallying point for critics of the AUSFTA. Some experts argued that the government had deceived the public on this issue. In submissions to the JSCOT inquiry, critics Richard Dennis and Clive Hamilton argued that the government had not kept its word regarding the integrity of the PBS or other initiatives. They quoted Trade Minister Vaile as saying early in the negotiations that the United States was "in no way going after the PBS."[42] Yet, Australia's chief negotiator, Stephen Deady, reportedly confirmed that "Australian negotiators were under significant and continuous pressure from US negotiators to make significant changes to the PBS from the start of the negotiations."[43] They concluded that "the Commonwealth Government misled the Australian public" on health care and was not worthy of the public's trust on the agreement. Meanwhile, some university academics expressed concerns about the "democratic deficit" and ways that Australian sovereignty might be undermined through international agreements taken without real public consultation.

Public Opinion

Once the outlines of the free trade deal became public, polls showed diffuse support coupled with general disinterest. Most Australians supported the negotiation of free trade agreements (88 per cent of respondents). And in the context of U.S.–Australian relations, more than 70 per cent of Australians believed that the treaty was important. Yet at the same time there was a surprising amount of ambivalence regarding the agreement itself. In a July 2004 poll, 45 per cent of respondents favored the agreement, with 29 per cent opposed, and a full 26 per cent undecided.[44]

Outcome and Analysis

The government passed implementing legislation (with the Senate amend- ments) and ratified the treaty in August 2004. Prime Minister Howard cele- brated the achievement, and later that month called for national elections to be held in October. The Liberal/National coalition cited the trade deal as proof of their stewardship of the economy and their close ties with the United States. In the October elections, the Liberals took over the Senate by a narrow margin. Prime Minister Howard's government now controlled the majority in both the House and Senate for the first time in more than two decades.

The proposition that states are more likely to support treaties that represent a maximization of national interests does not account for Australia's decision to ratify the AUSFTA. A neorealist perspective focused on absolute gains would contend that Australia would actually be disadvantaged in the agreement with the United States. Indeed, there were serious internal debates at the time (especially inside the Trade Ministry and the Prime Minister's Office) about potential costs and benefits. Critics argued that the treaty would hurt the regime by liberalizing trade with an economic powerhouse—effectively allowing U.S. dominance of the Australia economy in exchange for only limited gains. Meanwhile, the constructivist approach emphasizing the power of norms in shaping Australian ratification of the treaty offers some measure of explanation in this case. Australia had pursued more liberal economic policies and engaged in multilateral negotiations to lower tariff barriers to trade since the 1980s, and it was in this context that the country approached a new set of negotiations. This theory also helps to explain how the prime minister could authorize signature on an agreement that he knew was *not* in the best interests of Australia. Rather, there would be serious questions about its completion at the time and beyond.

This study suggests that three of four scope conditions at Level II may have influenced the outcome of the ratification struggle. Executive strategies clearly had an impact on ratification success. From the beginning, Prime Minister Howard sought to sell the deal as beneficial for the Australian economy and a deepening of ties with the United States. He embarked on a sophisticated strategy to build domestic support for this program, including side payments to farmers affected by the deal. He offered an indirect interpretation of the conflict as a national security concern and attempted synergistic issue linkages as well.

Executive–legislative relations were critical in shaping the ratification struggle. Liberal/National leaders knew that they could overcome opposition expressed in the House but they were stymied by efforts in the Senate to challenge their plans. The Senate's move to create its own treaty review committee represented a fairly dramatic challenge to authority. They were well aware that they possessed constitutional authority of key areas of implementation of the protocol and did not hesitate to threaten to block the treaty. At the same time the administration failed to effectively manage relations with provincial leaders and establish consensus on implementation plans.

Interest groups were actively involved in influencing government negotiating strategy and in the ratification debate, yet the proposition that a mobilized opposition could stop ratification was not upheld by this case. One expert characterizes the AUSFTA treaty process as "business as usual," in that "industry and business interests were privileged above other community interests."[45] Some interest groups did oppose the treaty, especially those that focused on its potential impact on key sectors of agriculture, medical care, and culture. Finally, public opinion had little if any measurable impact on the ratification outcome. Most Australians offered diffuse support for the trade deal with the United States. Public ambivalence toward the treaty was an extension of general public disinterest in trade negotiations in the past.[46] It may also have been a product of a flurry of competing projections of the impact of the treaty. Some reports saw a potential boost in the Australian economy by as much as $6 billion a year; others projected billions of dollars in losses to key sectors. In summary, the ratification game model highlights the importance of executive strategy, executive–legislative relations, interest groups, and diffuse public support in completion of the treaty.

III. THE UNITED STATES AND THE AUSFTA

The AUSFTA did not generate significant political controversy in the United States. The Bush administration worked with its Republican majorities in the Senate and House of Representatives to secure support for the deal. The treaty faced minor resistance from members of Congress and key lobby groups, but not enough to much interest on the part of the public or the media. Instead, arguments about ratification of the treaty in the United States remained largely academic.

International Pressure

Generally speaking, elite attitudes in the United States towards the AUSFTA were positive, and government leaders and experts shared the belief that the trade pact would significantly enhance their economy. The government did acknowledge potential costs in the agricultural sector, but the treaty was articulated as promoting future prosperity. It should also be noted that many in the Bush administration viewed the Australia FTA as a way to broaden the already-strong relationship between the two countries. Australia had stood firm in its alliance with the United States in the war on terrorism, and Bush appears to have sought to reward Howard for his support. In addition, the United

States had supported multilateral trade agreements for some time, including through rounds of GATT negotiations. The U.S.–Canada FTA and the NAFTA also served as precedents for bilateral trade deals like the one to be negotiated with Australia. These and other initiatives effectively may have created a policy space that supported greater liberalization.

Executive Strategy

Pre-negotiations with the Howard government on a free trade deal began during the Clinton era. President Bush moved ahead on the plan in 2002 by requesting trade promotion authority to negotiate a treaty. In a letter to Congressional leaders, United States Trade Representative Robert Zoellick argued that the treaty would greatly benefit the United States. They framed the initiative within the larger bounds of the relationship, arguing that the United States would enjoy a greatly strengthened security alliance that would "facilitate the building of new networks that enhance our Pacific democracies' mutual interests, shared experiences, and promotion of common values so that we can work together more effectively with third countries."[47] Specifically, the treaty would "boost trade in both goods and services" and promote "employment opportunities in both countries." The administration also emphasized the special nature of this agreement as the first bilateral trade deal since the 1988 Canada–U.S. Free Trade Agreement.

The Bush administration approached negotiations on the treaty with a measure of confidence. Zoellick and his team recognized from the outset that they were negotiating from a position of strength. Australia was much more dependent on U.S. trade than the reverse. In 2001, only 2 per cent of U.S. exports went to Australia, but Australian producers exported 11 per cent of all goods and commodities to the United States. Furthermore, the trade balance clearly favored the United States.[48] Australia was one of the few advanced industrialized countries in the world that purchased more goods from the United States than it sold to that market.

U.S. trade negotiators had several objectives. In general, administration officials were interested in creating new opportunities for American agricultural products while at the same time guarding the vulnerability of its own sectors. Sugar was one of the commodities that the administration sought to protect in the negotiations, for example. The sugar lobby was highly influential in Washington, having secured large government subsidies and price protections for decades. Sugar was also highly vulnerable to international competition, meaning that liberalization of the sugar trade could carry dramatic economic costs. Other U.S. objectives in the negotiations included addressing lax Australian policies on patents, copyright, and protection of intellectual property, and the public health subsidy of the PBS system. In a 2003 USTR *National Trade Estimates* document, the administration said that it would focus negotiations on the Australian PBS as related to larger goals for liberalizing trade. From the U.S. perspective, the PBS was a protective subsidy program for pharmaceuticals and an unfair advantage for Australian consumers in the global market. Australians typically paid as little as one-third the price of drugs as compared to U.S. citizens.

Once the treaty was finalized in May 2004, President Bush began promoting his diplomatic team's achievements to Congress and the American public. Not only did the agreement lower 99 per cent of tariff barriers to trade for exports to Australia, the administration argued, negotiators even had achieved success on more sensitive issues. The draft treaty called for the creation of a new bilateral Medicines Working Group devoted to public health issues and an avenue of appeal for decisions on pharmaceuticals by Australia's PBAC management board. In a March 2004 Senate hearing, Zoellick said that the United States had established an inroad on this aspect of Australia's public health system and predicted that drug costs would change.

The Bush administration also sold the deal in terms of maintaining protections for key agricultural concerns. While the treaty called for the elimination of tariff barriers to trade for most agricultural products, key sectors including beef, sugar, and dairy were shaded by protections. Specifically, U.S. negotiators allowed the elimination of tariffs on the importation of Australian beef, but to be phased-out over an 18-year period. Dairy farmers also received a reprieve in the form of a waning protective tariffs plan (by raising the quota on dairy product imports by 5 per cent per annum). And the sugar industry was ecstatic: it was singled out for exclusion from the AUSFTA. Some farmers could expect to continue to enjoy billions of dollars in subsidies for the foreseeable future.

In a signing ceremony in the Rose Garden of the White House, President Bush hailed the virtues of the agreement. He said:

The U.S.-Australia free trade agreement is a milestone in the history of our alliance. It expands our security and political alliance by creating a true economic partnership. It will create jobs and opportunities in both nations.... The United States and Australia have never been closer. We're allies in the war on terror. We're partners in the effort to help democracy take root in Afghanistan and Iraq and throughout the world. We understand that free societies will be peaceful societies. We long for peace.... This trade agreement serves the interests of our countries. It serves the interests of the United States and Australia. It serves the interests of citizens with ambitions and initiative and entrepreneurial instincts in both our countries. It advances the principle of free and fair trade.[49]

Regime Type: Executive–Legislative Relations

President Bush expected Congressional support for the deal. Indeed, the timing and nature of this FTA were ideal from the administration's standpoint. Australia emerged as one of the most steadfast and vocal allies of the United States in the war on terror. Prime Minister Howard was actually in Washington DC, on September 11, 2001. Government officials claim that this shared experience between the leaders of the two countries further deepened the alliance. Indeed, some experts have characterized U.S. willingness to enter into a free trade pact with Australia as a *quid pro quo* for Australian support in the war on terror.

AUSFTA was also likely to be popular in Congress for what it was *not*: it was not a free trade agreement with a less developed country in Latin American, Africa, or Asia. AUSFTA brought together two, like-minded advanced industrialized economies. The completion of AUSFTA came during the same month that Zoellick announced the outlines of new trade deals with Peru and Ecuador, negotiations with Colombia, and the opening of talks on trade with five southern African nations.[50] A potential Central American Free Trade Agreement (CAFTA) had already prompted some in Congress to express their opposition. By contrast, AUSFTA was seen as a "natural" arrangement even by some who traditionally opposed trade liberalization.[51]

The Republican Party controlled majorities in both the U.S. House of Representatives and the Senate during the period for consideration of AUSFTA. House Republicans favored a strong alliance with Australia, and a majority of members viewed liberalized trade relations as simply broadening the avenue of this relationship. House Speaker Dennis Hastert (R-IL) did briefly delay consideration of the treaty in the spring based on concerns that the government had not worked hard enough to gain access to the Australian public health system. But this matter was quickly resolved in consultations with the White House, which promised that it would press for greater access to other such systems in ongoing free trade negotiations in Central and South America. Even some House Democrats expressed support of the deal, including Charles Rangel (D-NY), a ranking member of the House Ways and Means Committee. Others opposed the agreement based on concerns about the potential impact on U.S. health-care policy and other sectoral issues.[52] A Congressional Budget Office report at the time touted the potential benefits of the deal, claiming implementation "would cost less than $500,000 each year."[53]

The Senate did become the stage for political theater related to AUSFTA for a brief period. According to fast-track legislation, the Senate Ways and Means Committee and the Finance Committee were assigned to hold "informal non-markup markups" sessions on the treaty and then to report them on to the

Senate floor for final up-or-down votes.[54] But when the treaty was referred to the Senate Finance Committee for initial review in June 2004, Senator Kent Conrad (D-ND) led a minor revolt, arguing that the treaty language failed to protect U.S. beef producers and agriculture. Conrad was concerned about the eventual elimination of protections for the beef industry—and he challenged a clause in the treaty that would allow the U.S. Trade Representative to waive safeguard protections for the industry if domestic beef prices dropped too low.[55] Conrad joined with ten other members of the committee to pass an amendment that called for the committee to require approval for the waiver of safeguards. Effectively this would have given the Senate a voice in regulating the level of Australian beef imports to the United States. In response, Senator Charles Grassley (R-IA), the chairman of the committee, sharply opposed the amendment and called it unconstitutional. Ultimately, members of the committee agreed to disagree—voting not to recommend the amended bill to the president and effectively rendering no official opinion on the treaty unto the Senate.[56]

Interest Groups

The Bush administration enjoyed support for the treaty from major interest groups. Like their counterparts in Australia, administration officials consulted leaders from the relevant sectors during the negotiation process. Zoellick's Advisory Committee for Trade Policy and Negotiations (ACTPN) included representatives of major businesses, labor groups, agriculture, retailers, and the service sector. In the group's March 2004 report on the treaty, ACTPN praised the agreement as a "state-of-the-art" deal that would "not only will benefit the United States and Australian economies and employment opportunities, but also will provide a strong base on which to construct additional bilateral or regional agreements."[57]

More than 200 U.S. corporations joined a newly established American–Australian Free Trade Agreement Coalition (AAFTAC) in support of completion of the deal. Executives from companies including Caterpillar, Colgate-Palmolive, and 3M believed that greater access to the Australian market would significantly boost exports.[58] Other groups exhibited a change of heart toward the treaty over time. For example, the U.S.-based Pharmaceutical Research and Manufacturers of America (PhRMA) was an extremely influential lobbying organization in Washington that expressed real concern over the deal in 2003. PhRMA lobbyists pressured the government to address the PBS in negotiations, and they were pleased by the achievements that appeared in the draft treaty. While pharmaceutical companies had not achieved the complete eradication of the PBS and related protections, they believed the Bush administration had gotten its nose under the tent of the restrictive program. USTR Zoellick told a Senate committee in March 2004 that the cost of drugs would change as a result of the agreement. Indeed, he claimed that the trade agreement with Australia was the "first important step" in a broader effort to bring equity to drug prices around the world.[59]

Farm groups adopted a range of positions on the treaty. Representatives of some dairy, sugar, and beef producers testified to Congress that the deal would do irreparable harm to U.S. agriculture and force thousands of farmers out of business. At the same time, the chairman of the United States Wheat Farmers Association (USW) said that the FTA left "intact the trade distorting monopoly practices exercised by Australian wheat interests."[60] Meanwhile, other groups strategically chose *not* to press this fight against the government in anticipation of a struggle over CAFTA. A spokesman for the American Farm Bureau Federation chose a middle ground, saying "It doesn't appear agriculture will play a role in trying to get this agreement passed."[61] Labor unions including the AFL-CIO saw the larger struggle on the horizon over Central America, and lobbyists expressed concern but not alarm about the pending AUSFTA.[62]

Outcome and Analysis

The debate in the United States over ratification of AUSFTA was somewhat muted. In accordance with Trade Promotion Authority, the U.S. House of Representatives voted in favor of the treaty by a vote of 314–109 on July 13, 2004. One day later, the Senate voted overwhelmingly in favor of the deal. The treaty went into effect on January 1, 2005, leading to reductions of tariffs on a wide range of goods. Other provisions of the treaty regarding phase-in periods for beef importation and technical restrictions were also implemented.

Neorealism would predict that the U.S. government would avoid agreements that undermine its economic sovereignty. Nevertheless, strong material considerations provided incentives for the Bush administration to follow through with implementation of the program. Top trade advisors to the president argued that the treaty offered a range of economic benefits to the United States at very little cost. Indeed, even Australian trade negotiators privately conceded that the United States had gotten much more out of the deal than it had given away. Thus, the government calculated that the benefits outweighed the costs of cooperation. There were also strong normative reasons for the United States to proceed with this bilateral agreement with Australia. The U.S. government traditionally supported trade liberalization, having cooperated in a succession of rounds of GATT negotiations for example. More directly, the Bush administration felt a sense of obligation to reward the Australian government for its century of close friendship with the United States.

Three of the four domestic-level considerations affected the outcome of the treaty program. President Bush and USTR Zoellick conducted a sophisticated strategy to move the treaty from idea to reality. This included a fairly aggressive stance in negotiations on the specifics of the deal followed by a steady press on Congress to support the treaty. When Kent Conrad attempted to hold up Finance Committee review of the treaty, for example, the White House worked closely with the chairman of the committee, Senator Grassley, to maneuver around the opposition. The White House also effectively co-opted key interest groups through the advisory council construct. In addition, propositions regarding interest group activism and public support were upheld by this case study. There were surprisingly few vocal opponents of the treaty at the grassroots level, again partly due to the executive strategy. There was also diffuse public support for the U.S. relationship with Australia in general and the AUSFTA. Indeed, the treaty passed steadily through the channels of review and on to full implementation with barely any public dialogue on the matter. In summary, a mix of international and domestic political conditions helped to shape the successful outcome of this case study of ratification.

NOTES

1. Statements by President George W. Bush, *Weekly Compilation of Presidential Documents*, The White House (August 3, 2004), pp. 1429–31.
2. Andrew L. Stoler, "Australia-US Free Trade: Benefits and Costs of an Agreement," Paper presented at the Conference on Free Trade Agreements and U.S. Trade Policy (Washington DC: Institute for International Economics, May 7, 2003), p. 11; see also Australian Bureau of Statistics Report 5422 (Canberra: December Quarter, 2002).
3. Stoler, "Australia-U.S. Free Trade," p. 12.
4. Peter Dawkins and Paul Kelly, eds., *Hard Heads, Soft Hearts: A New Reform Agenda for Australia* (Crows Nest, NSW, Australia: Allen & Unwin, 2003), p. 49.
5. Department of Foreign Affairs and Trade, *Free Trade Agreements* (2005), www.dfat.gov.au/trade/ftas.html (accessed November 1, 2006).
6. Ann Capling, "Can the Democratic Deficit in Treaty-Making Be Overcome? Parliament and the Australia-United States Free Trade Agreement," in Hilary Charlesworth, Madelaine Chiam, Devika Hovell, and George Williams, eds., *The Fluid State: International Law and National Legal Systems* (Sydney: The Federation Press, 2005), p. 71.

7. Stoler, "Australia-US Free Trade," p. 12.
8. Minister for Trade Mark Vail, Department of Foreign Affairs and Trade, *Submission 54*, Joint Standing Committee on Treaties (Canberra: Department of Foreign Affairs and Trade, March 3, 2003), pp. 37–8. These issues are discussed in greater detail in Linda Weiss, Elizabeth Thurbon, and John Mathews, *How to Kill a Country—Australia's Devastating Trade Deal with the United States* (Sydney: Allen & Unwin, 2004).
9. Center for International Economics, "Economic Impacts of an Australia-United States Free Trade Area" (Canberra: June 2001), p. 91; Australian APEC Study Center, "An Australia-USA Free Trade Agreement: Issues and Implications," Monash University, August 2001; "A Bridge Too Far? An Australian Agricultural Perspective on the Australia/United States Free Trade Idea," ACIL Consulting for Australian Rural Industries Research and Development Corporation (February 2003).
10. Centre for International Economics, *Economic Analysis of AUSFTA: Impact of the Bilateral Free Trade Agreement with the United States*, Report Prepared for the Department of Foreign Affairs and Trade (Canberra: Centre for International Economics, April 2004), pp. vii and xiii.
11. Interview with Author, Canberra (March 21, 2007).
12. Ann Capling, *All the Way with the USA: Australia, the US and Free Trade* (Sydney: UNSW Press, 2005).
13. Capling, *All the Way with the USA*, p. 57; see also Interviews with Author, Sydney (February 22, 2007) and Canberra (March 21, 2007).
14. Stoler, "Australia-US Free Trade," p. 57.
15. As quoted in Capling, *All the Way with the USA*, p. 42.
16. Christine Wallace, "Bush Rebuff Stunned Negotiators," *The Australian* (February 25, 2004), p. 6.
17. Patrick Barta, "Sugar Sours Australian Deal," *The Wall Street Journal* (April 29, 2004), p. B15.
18. Stoler, "Australia-US Free Trade," p. 67.
19. Capling, "Can the Democratic Deficit in Treaty-Making Be Overcome?", p. 62.
20. Commonwealth of Australia, Senate Committee Report, www.aph.gov.au/senate/committee/freetrade_ctte/index.htm (accessed February 19, 2007); see also Capling, "Can the Democratic Deficit in Treaty-Making Be Overcome?", pp. 57–79.
21. See Peter Kriesler, ed., *The Australian Economy*, 3rd edition (St. Leonards NSW: Allen & Unwin, 1999).
22. Peter Dawkins and Paul Kelly, eds., *Hard Heads, Soft Hearts: A New Reform Agenda for Australia*, p. 44.
23. Senate Foreign Affairs, Defence and Trade References Committee, Parliament of Australia, Voting on Trade: The General Agreement on Trade in Services and an Australia-US Free Trade Agreement (Canberra: Government Printing Office, 2003), p. 36; for a broader discussion, see Charlesworth, Chiam, Hovell, and Williams, eds., *The Fluid State*.

24. Joint Standing Committee on Treaties, "Treaty Scrutiny: A 10-Year Review," Joint Standing Committee on Treaties, Proof Committee *Hansard*, Commonwealth of Australia (Canberra: Government Printing Office, March 31, 2006); see, for example, Department of Foreign Affairs and Trade, "Submission to the Senate Foreign Affairs, Defence and Trade Committee Inquiry into the General Agreement on Trade in Services and Australia/US Free Trade Agreement."

25. AAP Newsfeed, "Fed: Costello calls on Labor to clarify FTA position" (June 23, 2004).

26. Joint Standing Committee on Treaties, Australia-United States Free Trade Agreement (Canberra, 2004), p. 275; see also Interview with Author, Sydney (February 22, 2007).

27. This is perhaps imprecise. In truth, Labor leaders were quietly searching for all possible reasons to oppose the treaty; Interview with Author, Canberra (June 1, 2007).

28. Rod McGuirk, Associated Press, "Prime Minister Agrees to Amendments to Australia-US Free Trade Deal" (August 12, 2004).

29. See Stoler, "Australia-US Free Trade".

30. "Australian Prime Minister Accepts Opposition Amendment to US Trade Deal," BBC Monitoring, ACC # A20040812D-8E6B-GNW (August 12, 2004).

31. Ibid.

32. "Australian PM Accepts Political Compromise to Save US Free Trade Deal," Channel News Asia, www.channelnewsasia.com/stories/afp_asiapacific_business/view/100439/1/.html (accessed August 12, 2004).

33. Capling, "Can the Democratic Deficit in Treaty-Making Be Overcome?", p. 64.

34. Katie Lahey, "BCA Backs Free Trade Talks," *The Australian Financial Review* (March 24, 2003), p. 8.

35. Business Council of Australia, "Submission to the Joint Standing Committee on Treaties Inquiry into the Australia US Free Trade Agreement (USFTA)," AUSFTA Submission #132 (April 19, 2004).

36. Tasmanian Country Newswire, "NFF Backs FTA Draft" (April 23, 2004).

37. Australian Dairy Industry Council Inc., "Submission to the Joint Standing Committee on Treaties Inquiry into the Australia US Free Trade Agreement (USFTA)," AUSFTA Submission #19 (April 8, 2004).

38. Financial News, "FTA Will Cost Australia $50 Bln/Thousands of Jobs; Study Says," Australian Associated Press Newsfeed (June 7, 2004).

39. ACIL Consulting Pty. Ltd., "A Bridge too Far? An Australian Agricultural Perspective on the Australia/United States Free Trade Area Idea" (Canberra: ACIL Consulting and Australian Rural Industries Research and Development Corporation, 2003).

40. Doctors Reform Society, "Submission to the Joint Standing Committee on Treaties Inquiry into the Australia US Free Trade Agreement (USFTA)" (April 2004).

41. Larissa Behrendt and Megan Davis, "Adverse Effects of Free-Trade Deal Will Hit Indigenous Groups Hard," *Sydney Morning Herald* (March 8, 2004), p. 1.

42. House of Representatives, *Hansard* (May 26, 2003), p. 14869.

43. Department of Health and Ageing FTA Briefings (March 8, 2004); Richard Denniss, Dr. Clive Hamilton, The Australia Institute, Patricia Ranald and Louise Southalan, Australian Fair Trade and Investment Network, "Submission to the Joint Standing Committee on Treaties Inquiry into the Australia US Free Trade Agreement (USFTA)" (April 2004).

44. Ivan Cook, "Australians Speak 2005: Public Opinion and Foreign Policy," Lowy Institute Poll (2005).

45. Capling, "Can the Democratic Deficit in Treaty-Making Be Overcome?", p. 72.

46. Ibid., p. 63.

47. USTR's Zoellick November 13, 2002, letters to Hastert and Byrd, and Stoler, p. 6.

48. Australian Bureau of Statistics Report 5422 (December Quarter, 2002); see also Senator Grassley, Committee on Finance, "United States-Australia Free Trade Agreement Implementation Act," 108th Congress, Report of the Senate, 2nd Session #108-316 (August 25, 2004).

49. Comments by Bush at Rose Garden Signing of Treaty: Statements by President George W. Bush, *Weekly Compilation of Presidential Documents*, The White House (August 3, 2004), pp. 1429–31.

50. Jeffrey Sparshott, "U.S., Australia to Sign Free Trade Deal; Congress Will Vote on Agreement as Bush Pursues Pacts Worldwide," *The Washington Times* (May 4, 2004), p. 9.

51. Elizabeth Becker, "U.S.-Australia Trade Pact Faces Divided Congress; Distracted by Iraq, Bush Hasn't Sold Deal," *New York Times* (May 20, 2004), p. A16.

52. Jim Abrams, "Congress Approves Australia Free Trade Agreement with Senate Vote," *San Diego Union-Tribune* (July 15, 2004), p. 6.

53. "Congressional Budget Office Cost Estimate" (Washington DC: Congressional Budget Office, July 30, 2004), http://thomas.loc.gov/cgi-bin/cpquery/ T?&report=sr316&dbname=108&.htm (accessed December 7, 2005).

54. "Senate Finance Committee Action Could Delay Australia FTA," *Washington Tariff and Trade Letter*, vol. 24, no. 26 (June 28, 2004), p. 2.

55. John Godfrey, "US House Clears US Australia Trade Agreement," Dow Jones Newswires (July 15, 2004).

56. Senator Grassley, Committee on Finance, "United States-Australia Free Trade Agreement Implementation Act," 108th Congress, Report of the Senate, 2nd Session #108-316 (August 25, 2004); "Additional Views of Chairman Grassley," http://thomas.loc.gov/cgi-bin/cpquery/T?&report=sr316&dbname=108&.htm (Washington DC: July 30, 2004; accessed December 7, 2005); see also "Snowe Opposes Trade Agreement," Press Herald Online http://snowe.senate.gov/ articles/art062404_1.htm (June 24, 2004); "Senate Finance Committee Action Could Delay Australia FTA," *Washington Tariff and Trade Letter*, vol. 24, no. 26 (June 28, 2004), p. 2.

57. The advisory board was a creation of legislation from the Trade Acts of 2002 and 1974, which calls for the group to provide "an advisory opinion as to

whether and to what extent the agreement promotes the economic interests of the United States and achieves objectives of Trade Act of 2002" within thirty days of the finalization of an agreement; see "Report to the President, the Congress, and the United States Trade Representative on the U.S.-Australian Free Trade Agreement," Report by the Advisory Committee for Trade Policy and Negotiations (ACTPN) on the US-Australia Free Trade Agreement (March 12, 2004).

58. Elizabeth Becker, "U.S.-Australia Trade Pact Faces Divided Congress; Distracted by Iraq, Bush Hasn't Sold Deal," *New York Times* (May 20, 2004), p. A16.
59. Capling, *All the Way with the USA*, p. 51.
60. U.S. Wheat Associates, "News & Policy: Wheat Letter" (February 19, 2004), www.uswheat.org/wheatLetter/doc/0C4D6AE43A107D1F852.
61. Becker, "U.S.-Australia Trade Pact Faces Divided Congress," p. A16.
62. Martin Vaughan, "Labor to Give Australia Deal a Pass, But Target CAFTA," *Congress Daily* (May 26, 2004), p. 4; see also Sparshott, "U.S., Australia to Sign Free Trade Deal," p. 9.

8

The European Constitution

I. HISTORY OF THE TREATY

The Treaty Establishing a Constitution for Europe (or European Constitution) provided a plan for deepening European integration with the centralization of power in Brussels. Supporters believed that it offered the promise of greater political, economic, and social unity for Europe in the twenty-first century. French and German government leaders joined with others to hail the advent of the treaty as a "moment of destiny" for the continent.

The European Constitution proposed dramatic reforms of the EU decision-making process, with special attention to challenges brought on by expansion of the institution. The treaty was also designed to address problems with transparency and popular legitimacy in the integration process. Indeed, the passage of the TEU by razor-thin majorities served as a wake-up call to many governments. Each round of growth added complexity to the already-cumbersome institutional structure. An organization that started with only six member states in the 1950s expanded to nine in 1973; another six countries joined the community in the 1980s and 1990s. In 2004, the EU nearly doubled in size again with the accession of ten states (many of them from Eastern Europe and former satellites of the Soviet Union), and in 2007 it grew to encompass twenty-seven countries.

Progress toward a European Constitution began with an Intergovernmental Conference (IGC) in February 2000. France played a significant role in fostering follow-on negotiations during its control of the Council presidency in late 2000. From the beginning, diplomats discussed a wide range of issues that they would like to see in a revised organizational structure, including the qualified majority voting in the European Council, a greater role for the European Parliament, and clearer delineation of mandates for the European Commission.

The 2001 Treaty of Nice included a detailed plan for deepening European integration, including the extension of qualified majority voting and the role of the European Commission and greater work in common foreign and security policy. Specifically, member states proposed an apportionment plan for voting powers in the European Council that would move away from the old system whereby states could veto major initiatives in the EU. The new "Nice formula" called for the four member states with the largest populations—France, Germany, Italy, and the United Kingdom—to be granted a larger portion of votes than medium-sized countries like Poland and Spain. Using a double-trigger or dual-threshold system, decisions in Europe would be taken by a simple majority of votes, with a total representing 60 per cent or more of EU population. Changes in the structure of the European Commission were designed to complement the power of the new President and help order the enlargement process.

In December 2001, the European Council called for the elements of the Treaty of Nice to be expanded into a larger program of EU reforms. Valery Giscard d'Estaing, former president of France (1974–81), was appointed head of the EU convention on reform initiatives that began work in February 2002. d'Estaing and others soon pushed the group to move beyond its mandate and develop plans for a draft constitution.[1] Particularly controversial were issues including voting procedures in the European Council, the right of member states to veto major regional or foreign policy initiatives, religious references, and criteria for the expansion of membership. In spite of significant disagreements, the Convention produced a draft treaty on the constitution in July 2003.

In October 2004 leaders gathered in Rome to sign the European Constitution. The treaty was a monumental achievement: 341 pages laden with 448 articles describing all manner of integration mechanisms. One of its central features was the plan for weighted voting in European Council decision-making. The new voting plan represented a philosophical shift in the dreams of a united Europe run by consensus to a more practical arrangement for a weighted majority to determine European policy. Existentially, some claimed, this allowed an opportunity for the European Union to find greater unity in potential divisions and "speak with one voice."[2] The Constitution would also create new posts for political leadership of the integrated body. Europe would have a new president of the European Council, a new foreign minister, and a European diplomatic corps. Framers believed that these changes would greatly improve the administration of EU regional and foreign policy. Of course, these mechanisms would also have profound implications for future decisions on the expansion of membership and the deepening of integration structures.

Finally, EU leaders agreed that a unanimous vote of support from all member governments would be required for the Constitution to enter into force. In 2005, European member states set about ratification in earnest. In some cases, parliamentary governments chose to ratify it through a simple majority vote of the legislature; in others, leaders chose the path of referendum to provide citizens a larger say in the process.[3] The treaty was ratified in a succession of member states, beginning with Lithuania in November 2004 and continuing through eight more capitals. One of these ratifications, the Spanish referendum in early 2005, generated a striking 77 per cent majority in support of the treaty. All eyes turned to the larger countries to make a firm commitment to Europe; experts warned that any wavering on the part of these major players might permanently sink the agreement.

II. FRANCE AND THE EUROPEAN CONSTITUTION: THE DEMOCRATIC CHASM?

The French government expressed strong support for the European Constitution. President Jacques Chirac launched a bipartisan campaign for ratification. Indeed, he was so confident of the treaty's popularity that he ordered a referendum to be held on June 1, 2005. Voter turnout was high, but the majority chose to reject the European Constitution. The outcome represented a serious blow to European integration as well as a rebuke of the leadership of Chirac. Ultimately, the vote was much more than a referendum on the European Constitution: it was an opportunity for the public to register their discontent on issues ranging from Chirac's leadership to the country's poor economic performance, immigration policy, sovereignty, and the costs of integration. This case examines the troubled road to the referendum and the democratic chasm that seemed to open between elite and public opinion toward the treaty.

International Pressure

The French government faced a great deal of international pressure to ratify the European Constitution. Supporters believed that the treaty would offer material benefits to the nation and guarantee regional economic and political stability. The treaty proposed a streamlined decision-making mechanism designed to be more democratic than past arrangements. More broadly, the treaty would help address concerns about management of the enlarged institution. Operating as a political and economic unit, supporters maintained, would greatly strengthen the EU to deal with twenty-first-century challenges. Yet the treaty also represented a fundamental sacrifice of sovereignty to centralized EU authority in Brussels. At the same time, France was also subject to normative pressure to ratify the agreement. France had been a steadfast supporter of past European integration efforts, and Chirac and others became personally involved in the negotiation of the Constitution.

Executive Strategy

The Constitution of the French Fifth Republic grants the president significant political authority. Jacques Chirac was first elected president in May 1995 as a leader of the *Union pour un Mouvement Populaire* (UMP), a coalition of conservative Gaullist parties. His election marked a turnover of government after years of Socialist control under President François Mitterrand. Ironically, one of the issues on which Chirac found resonance in the campaign was a challenge to the "monarchical drift" of the office under Mitterrand. Chirac's pledge of a more constrained leadership style, however, soon gave way to a determined exercise of executive authority.[4] In his bid for reelection in 2002, Chirac received a large percentage of the popular vote (82 per cent), but within months his government faced criticism for its handling of controversial issues.[5] His prime minister, Jean-Pierre Raffarin, also became a magnet for negative press.

Following the signature of the EU Constitution in Rome in October 2004, Chirac had two options for ratification: take the matter to parliament for a majority vote or gauge popular support for the treaty through a referendum. Chirac formally announced in March 2005 that a national referendum would be held two months later. The president appears to have made this fateful choice for several reasons. First and foremost, he believed that the referendum would be successful. After all, the president had personally negotiated with other European leaders to ensure that the new EU decision-making process would allow a strong role for France and other large member states in the Union. Chirac and his government sorely needed a "win" after years of public frustration with problems including unemployment and economic stagnation. Screening polls at the time showed that more than 65 per cent of French citizens favored the treaty.[6] Second, the president was pressured to order a referendum by members of the ruling council of the UMP, including Finance Minister Nicholas Sarkozy, as early as six months before the Constitution was signed.[7] Finally, other European leaders pushed Chirac to consider a referendum as a way to restore popular legitimacy to the European integration process. For example, British Prime Minister Tony Blair announced that the United Kingdom would hold a referendum on the Constitution, and other leaders soon followed suit.

The referendum campaign in France quickly got out of hand, however. Within weeks of Chirac's announcement it became clear that the public interpreted the vote as about much more than the European Constitution itself; it would be a referendum on the economic situation in France and presidential leadership. Supporters of the Constitution believed that deepened integration with Europe represented the only road forward for the French economy. Economists predicted that liberalization would allow macroeconomic forces to help redress labor and economic problems in France. They contended that it would promote efficiency both within France and in the larger setting of the EU governing structure. Opponents expressed serious concern that it would effectively cause a loss of national identity, further decrease sovereignty, and promote a problem with the influx of cheap labor in the face of serious unemployment problems in France.

The French campaign on the referendum began in February 2005, with the president and top government officials playing an active role. One of the first major initiatives was to try to head off criticism about the complexity of the Constitution. The government distributed more than five million copies of a booklet explaining the Constitution and extolling its virtues. The government also announced the establishment of an information hotline on the Constitution (that reportedly received thousands of calls per day). French leaders also held a series of public forums on the treaty in venues across the country. Chirac, his Foreign Minister Michael Barnier, and the Minister for Europe Claudie Haigneré all appeared in meetings promoting ratification of the Constitution. In April, for example, Chirac made a high-profile appearance in a televised town meeting in which he debated the virtues of the Constitution with dozens of French young people (aged 18–30). The Constitution, he argued, was essential "to help build a stronger Europe in the face of other rising powers in the world.... If we block the process, if the no vote wins the May referendum, we will not be strong and Europe will not be strong enough against the big powers."[8]

By May 2005, however, public opinion clearly had swung against the treaty. To further magnify the problem for the government, polls seemed to reflect broad frustrations brought on by strikes by public unions and mass demonstrations.[9] Political observers also noted that Chirac began to distance himself from the outcome by deflecting some of the potential negative sentiment toward Prime Minister Raffarin. Chirac also noted on several occasions that he recognized that European integration was not the only issue at hand. But the president pledged not to resign in the face of a negative outcome. In his final address before the referendum, Chirac offered a solemn case for voters not to reject the Constitution. He said,

Do not be afraid [of the European Constitution]. Only our political power today within Europe will allow us to defend our interests; if tomorrow we have voted "no" we will no longer have that power.... In the face of a growing world power that worries the French and which is carried by an ultra-liberal current, facing the United States and the large emerging markets such as China, India, Brazil, and South America and Russia, the European Union has to equip itself with useful rules.... These powers, we will not face them individually, France does not have that capability. That is why Europe must be strong and organized in order to oppose that evolution.... On Sunday, each of us will have a part of France's destiny in their hands.... What a responsibility if France, a founder nation of Europe, took the risk of breaking the union of our continent.[10]

Regime Type: Executive–Legislative Relations

The French National Assembly also provided a forum for debate about the future of the EU Constitution.[11] The president crafted a coalition in favor of the agreement that included both conservative Gaullist parties (the UMP and the *Union pour la Démocratie Française*, or UDF, established by Giscard d'Estaing the the late 1970s) and the Socialist Party. In past years, Mitterrand and the Socialists had spearheaded the movement for the TEU, and other party leaders including former European Commission President Jacques Delors were vocal champions of the initiative. In late 2004, an internal survey of Socialist Party members showed 58 per cent in support of the treaty. In early 2005, the French legislature took a series of formal actions to set the stage for a referendum. The National Assembly and the Senate held a joint session in February in which they voted to amend the French Constitution for compatibility with the proposed EU Constitution and hold the referendum on May 29, 2005. They also voted to require that all future issues of enlargement of membership of the EU be addressed through a popular referendum.[12]

In spite of the unified stand by the major parties, there were reports of internal divisions during the referendum campaign. Some conservatives in the UMP were reluctant to work closely with the Socialists, and they occasionally made public statements that seemed to undermine Chirac's leadership. Finance Minister Nicholas Sarkozy (a political rival of Chirac's inside the conservative coalition) seemed particularly adept at issuing barbed statements that supported the Constitution but challenged the president himself. As the volume of criticism of Chirac grew in 2005, one observer warned, "the party of the president is no longer behind him."[13] The Socialists were also divided over the treaty. The party's deputy leader (and former prime minister), Laurent Fabius, openly split with his organization's leadership and issued a series of public statements against the Constitution.[14] Other Socialists followed suit and warned that the opposition should not cozy up to the conservatives on such a thorny issue. Jacque Delors reportedly grew so disheartened that he said publicly he was considering leaving the party altogether.[15]

Political opponents of the treaty were able to seize on a wide range of issues to challenge it. For example, the state of the economy was a persistent problem in the Chirac presidency. The general unemployment rate in France in 2005 was 10.2 per cent, with more than 20 per cent of those under 25 years of age out of work. Concerns about unemployment dovetailed with another issue embedded in European integration: reforms of service industry regulations. Proposed reforms would make it possible for service providers such as architects, plumbers, and accountants to run businesses in any member state. Opponents argued that it would lead to "social dumping," as businesses and jobs relocated to the low-cost economies of eastern Europe. Chirac was left with little room to maneuver on this issue while opponents like Fabius called the issue a "foretaste of the European Constitution."

Political opponents also gained some advantage in the debate by tapping into French nationalism, concerns about an influx of immigrants, and other factors. Especially controversial was a concurrent discussion regarding the potential entry of Turkey into the European Union. In October 2004, the European Commission formally recommended the opening of entry negotiations between the EU and the government of Turkey. Not only did this raise questions about economic inequalities across Europe, but it also stirred the cauldron of religious identity. Turkey, a predominantly Muslim country, represented a new type of would-be EU member state. France had experienced its own turmoil over issues like students wearing religious symbols in public schools (such as head scarves for Muslim women). Devoutly religious citizens believed that the EU was, after all, a political organization crafted in the Christian tradition and that expansion of the Union to a Muslim country was against the intended spirit of the framers. One expert argued that the way that the government handled the larger EU negotiations with Turkey allowed the issues to become conflated, allowing more voters more excuses to consider rejecting the treaty.[16]

It is important to note that President Chirac did little to address the challenges to the Constitution from leaders of minor parties on the political left and right. On the left, the Communist Party and leaders of a few minor parties opposed it on the grounds that it challenged socialist values and French sovereignty. Jean-Pierre Chevenement, a former Socialist Party Interior Minister (who had fought against the TEU a decade earlier), was a leading critic of the Constitution. He quoted Napoleon as saying, "that a good constitution should be 'short and obscure.'" "With this one," Chevenement added, "we have only obscurity." Right-wing political parties including the National Front and the *Mouvement Pour la France* (MPF) warned of the loss of sovereignty and the challenge to French national identity. Chirac openly challenged the nationalist statements of leaders like Le Pen while maintaining that the mainstream of French voters recognized the broader potential in supporting the treaty.

Interest Groups

Interest groups historically have played an important role in French politics, often aligning with party organizations on issues. In this case, however, groups found their traditional loyalties divided by fissures within the parties themselves and, more broadly, by the larger ideological, economic, and political implications of the European Constitution. Interest groups' mobilization was due to the broader interpretation of dissatisfaction with current economic and social conditions and Chirac's leadership.

French business organizations mobilized both for and against the treaty. Conservative government leaders sought allies within the network of corporations arguing that the treaty would ultimately advantage big businesses through greater liberalization. Leaders of major businesses joined with economists and prominent cultural figures to champion the Constitution. Mainstream media coverage was also overwhelmingly favorable. These groups cooperated in a well-financed government campaign in favor of the Constitution. The government distributed millions of copies of brochures to voters explaining the value of the Constitution. They targeted families as well, producing a children's book entitled, *Explain the European Constitution to Me*, with a preface by former President d'Estaing.

Other business groups like the National Council of French Employers mobilized against the Constitution. Labor groups were also deeply divided over potential implications of the deal. One of France's largest labor unions, the Confédération Générale du Travail, adopted a position against the Constitution. Some linked planned reforms to the services sector with the European Constitution and came out strongly against ratification. They warned that skilled workers from other EU member states might take advantage of liberal transfer laws and take jobs away from French citizens. Other Labor leaders who traditionally looked to their allies in the Socialist Party found only mixed signals. Farm groups also came out in opposition to the Constitution, expressing suspicion that an empowered EU bureaucracy would lead to diminished protections for farm interests. One poll conducted in spring 2005 showed almost 75 per cent of farmers opposed to the plan.[17] In sum, interest groups were divided in their opinions on the European Constitution and appear to have played only a supporting role in the outcome of the referendum.[18]

Public Opinion

Public attitudes had a profound effect on the ratification outcome through the vehicle of the national referendum. Chirac had called for a referendum with confidence that his government would secure victory. Indeed, in late 2004, polls showed popular support for the Constitution as high as 68 per cent.[19] Yet surveys soon showed that the referendum had become an opportunity for French citizens to voice frustration over government policies. One analysis suggested that, "There's a tradition of France of answering a referendum question, not answering the question but saying something else."[20] In this case, voters seemed to link concerns about the Constitution to problems with unemployment in France, flaws in Chirac's own leadership style, and regional economic stagnation. Polls showed that public confidence in government was very low, with just 28 per cent of voters saying that they trusted controversial Prime Minister Raffarin to tackle the key challenges facing France.[21] The winter of 2004–5 also saw a series of antigovernment strikes and demonstrations, and government reports showed that incomes had fallen in many sectors of the economy.[22]

Things went from bad to worse in March, as polls began to indicate that the referendum could fail. A survey published that month in *Le Parisien* showed that 51 per cent of French voters were opposed to the EU Constitution. While the Socialist party leadership continued to support the treaty, some 59 per cent of party members were opposed. At the same time, the EU moved forward with its plan to reform European service industry regulations—a plan that might allow a massive shift in employment patterns to lower-expense economies in eastern Europe. The "no" campaign gained real momentum in April 2005 when prominent voices began to link anti-Constitutional rhetoric to anti-immigration and antiglobalization programs. By May a negative outcome seemed likely. While the "yes" campaign enjoyed a slight increase in support in the wake of television appearances by Chirac and former Socialist Prime Minister Lionel Jospin on behalf of the Constitution, polls by the middle of the month showed trouble. By the end of May, ten national polls in a row indicated that the Constitution would likely fail.[23]

Outcome and Analysis

The European Constitution was rejected by French voters by a wide margin, 54.87 per cent to 45.13 per cent. The outcome of the referendum was a major defeat for the European Constitution and for Chirac. In a nationally televised address afterward, the president said that he accepted the will of the voters on the treaty, but added, "let's not be mistaken. The decision of France inevitably creates a difficult context for the defense of our interests in Europe."[24] Days later, Chirac accepted the resignation of Prime Minister Raffarin and named Dominique de Villepin in his place.

Chirac's warning regarding the outcome of the French referendum was no understatement; the "no" vote represented a significant blow to European integration. While one can argue that the defeat of the treaty reflects the prediction of neorealism, it is not well accounted for by constructivism. Neo-realists would predict the rejection of the treaty based on concerns regarding a sacrifice of French sovereignty and national interests. Indeed, the EU Constitution was a remarkable plan for the transfer of decision-making power away from states and to more centralized authority structures in Brussels. At an individual level, reforms in the services sector legislation for the European Union also threatened to liberalize labor flows on the continent. French citizens feared an "invasion by Polish plumbers" and others who might take away French jobs through the social services reform package.[25] At the same time, the rejection of the treaty appears to disconfirm constructivist models. French voters appeared to ignore or even reject the notion of France's obligation to other member states to support a treaty that they believed threatened their national interests.

Two domestic-level explanations appear helpful in deciphering the outcome of this puzzling case. Chirac was actively involved in lobbying voters for passage of the Constitution via public referendum, and he and other leaders ran a bipartisan campaign in support of the treaty. In the end, however, it was Chirac's decision to take the issue to a referendum that effectively neutered executive and legislative control of the issue. Once the referendum had been announced, the president witnessed a redefinition of the issues at hand through interest group activism and public opposition. He saw what he believed to be a sure bet devolve into a losing proposition. Interest groups and public opponents in France played a significant role in ending the dream of a European Constitution in 2005.

III. GERMANY AND THE EUROPEAN CONSTITUTION

Germany's experience with the European Constitution was fundamentally different than that of France. Generally speaking, many Germans interpreted the treaty as a significant step forward in the European Union. Deepening integration in Europe remained entirely consistent with Germany's own political identity. Stronger EU institutions promised regional order, better legislative processes, and economic growth. In June 2004, German Chancellor Gerhard Schröder (SPD) and Foreign Minister Joschka Fischer (Greens) participated in final negotiations for the treaty, signed it, and returned home determined to ratify it within a year. As the final votes in the parliament approached in 2005, leaders seemed so assured of the outcome that they became actively involved in the referendum campaigns in France and the Netherlands. What they had not anticipated, however, was that the treaty would spark a surprisingly intense debate over constitutional reform and the democratic deficit in international treaty-making.

International Pressure

Germany was under a great deal of regional pressure to ratify the European Constitution. Its leaders had themselves been instrumental in the creation of the treaty and establishment of blueprints for legislative reforms. Put simply, Germany was the most powerful country in Europe following unification, and its fate was tied to that of the regional enterprise. The treaty also addressed issues of economic security for Germany in relation to the future prosperity of the region and more transparency and democracy in decisions about monetary and fiscal policy. However, the treaty represented a significant sacrifice of sovereignty at an uncertain time in global politics. Germany would essentially be transferring policymaking authority to Brussels by ratifying the agreement. It would lose its veto in the Council and, potentially, see a diminished influence in regional affairs.

If Germany faced concerns about material interests related to the treaty, it faced a potential tsunami of normative and institutional pressures for cooperation. Following in the footsteps of their predecessors, Schröder and Fischer were heavily invested in Europe. Government officials believed that deepening European integration by creating greater supranational authority was entirely consistent with their own national political identity.[26] Indeed, German leaders referred to international norms and institutions as important influences on European integration. In one high-profile speech, Schröder said, "The Constitution we are voting on today is the result of a democratic process that is without precedent in the history of European integration. . . . [It] is as much a document of self-assurance as an expression of the self-image of a unified Europe at the beginning of the 21st century."[27] Thus, German leaders had helped to establish the expectations and norms of behavior in the EU to which they would be held in the ratification process. It is also important to note that European integration established an intricate network of legal standards and processes that fostered continued cooperation.

Executive Strategies

Chancellor Schröder and Foreign Minister Fischer were shrewd advocates for the European Constitution. They began championing the treaty almost as soon as initial negotiations had gotten underway. While some members of their parties, the Social Democratic Party (SPD) and the Alliance '90/Greens, respectively, had been skeptical of European integration initiatives in the past, many factors contributed to a new political wind in the SPD–Green coalition government (1998–2006). Cabinet leaders determined that the European Constitution initiative would be vital to the further development of the organization. They also endorsed a plan that would allow weighted voting and greater influence for the larger and more prosperous members of the EU. They believed that the Constitution would help reform the existing legislative processes and provide a foundation for controlled expansion of the EU in the future.[28]

As early as 2000, Foreign Minister Fischer began urging Europe ahead toward more intensified integration. Fischer called for progress on the finalization of the politics of European integration, saying the EU faced the "parallel task" of enlargement and institutional changes for deepening integration. Fischer boldly called for a new "European federation" composed of a "European parliament and a European government which really do exercise legislative and executive power within the federation."[29] To achieve this goal, a European Constitution would be formulated that specified clear divisions of sovereignty between the central federation authority and member states.

From 2000 to 2004, German officials participated actively in negotiations to advance the concept of a Constitution. Fischer and Schröder were instrumental in the design of the 2001 Treaty of Nice and its subsequent ratification by parliament. The Nice formula gave France, Germany, Italy, and the United Kingdom a larger portion of Council votes than medium-sized countries like Poland and Spain. German representatives participated in the constitutional planning meetings led by d'Estaing beginning in early 2002 and engaged in negotiations over voting procedures in the European Council, the right of member states to veto major regional or foreign policy initiatives, and criteria for the expansion of membership. In July 2003, the Convention produced the Draft Treaty establishing the Constitution for Europe, which Fischer hailed as "historic." When consensus on the weighted voting plan collapsed in December 2003, German leaders were again instrumental in follow-on negotiations to achieve specific goals in the final draft Constitution. Notably, they helped steer French President Chirac back toward a more unified vision of the Constitution when he threatened to break away and create a "two-speed Europe."

German leaders signed the Constitutional Treaty for European Union in June 2004 and returned home to pursue ratification of the treaty. In this critical period from mid-2004 to mid-2005, the chancellor devoted significant time and resources to the promotion of ratification. Cabinet ministers were caught by surprise, however, by the intensity of debates in the fall of 2004 regarding the democratic deficit. Grassroots organizations, academics, the media, and even German party officials became involved in a fascinating debate about reforms of the treaty-making process. The democratic deficit discussion also led to philosophical disputes over the degree to which the government would be willing to sacrifice sovereignty to a larger federation of Europe.

The chancellor acknowledged the importance of the debates but largely dispensed with the issue in connection to the EU Constitution by announcing his intention for ratification by parliament in the spring of 2005. With Schröder's blessing, parliamentary leader Wolfgang Thierse negotiated an agreement with his counterpart in France, Jean-Louis Debré, that would schedule the German parliamentary vote earlier than the French referendum. Under Schröder's directive, the cabinet submitted implementing legislation to the *Bundestag* and *Bundesrat* for review in February 2005. Cabinet leaders worked to ensure support for the Constitution among their parliamentary groups, but there was never a question that the government could achieve the two-thirds majorities needed for ratification. Schröder even worked closely with CDU leader Angela Merkel in garnering support for the treaty from opposition Conservatives.

Assured of victory at home, Schröder and Fischer turned their attention to building support for the Constitution across Europe. In a joint appearance at the Sorbonne in Paris in April 2005, Schröder and French President Chirac praised the Constitution. The chancellor said, "If we want to have influence in the world and keep our European society, then it will only happen through, in, and with a strong and united Europe. And for that we need the European Constitution."[30] Well aware of the declining support for the treaty in France, he opined that ratification would ensure that Europe could "find its unity again, as well as prosperity and lasting peace." A month later, Fischer appeared alongside French government officials and EU parliamentarians in a pro-Constitution rally in Paris. Schröder also wrote an editorial for *Le Figaro*, a leading French newspaper, that appeared in print just one day before their referendum, arguing: "If we want to play our role in the world, if we want to take decisions and not see them imposed by others, if we want to keep our European social model, we can only do so with a strong and united Europe. The European Constitution lays the foundation."[31]

Regime Type: Executive–Legislative Relations

According to the new Article 23 of the German Basic Law, any treaty commitment that required a change in the Basic Law would require a two-thirds majority vote by both houses of parliament.[32] Schröder's coalition government enjoyed support for deepening European integration from a cross-section of the legislature. SPD leaders who gained power in 1998 endorsed major steps toward deepening integration. Members of the junior party in the coalition, the Alliance '90/Greens, generally supported integration as well (even as a few continued to express discomfort with aspects of European integration). The CDU and its sister party, the Christian Socialist Union (CSU), also endorsed the treaty. Those parties had controlled government from 1982 to 1998 in coalition with the Free Democratic Party (FDP) and had been responsible for a number of major EU initiatives. It was under Helmut Kohl's leadership as chancellor that Germany had helped to design and implement the Single European Act and the Maastricht Treaty on European Union. Kohl had been at the helm when the outlines of what would become the European Constitution were crafted.

Tensions did arise in the legislature, however, over *how* the treaty should be ratified. A fascinating debate emerged during which potential opponents (and even some supporters) of the Constitution began to call for Germany to adopt a referendum instrument for ratification of international treaties. Early on, leaders of the Party of Democratic Socialism (PDS) introduced a bill in the *Bundestag* calling for a constitutional amendment to allow referendums. They contended that Article 20 of the Basic Law, which stated, "All state authority is derived from the people through elections and other votes," was open for interpretation to allow national referendums on major policy initiatives. The response from the SPD was immediate and firm, however. Leaders countered that the Basic Law did not provide a mechanism for public referendums on foreign policy initiatives. While Article 20 mentioned the importance of a popular voice through elections and "other votes," legal scholars contended that other articles clarified that the term only really applied to postwar territorial adjustments.[33]

Pressures for referendums translated into a very interesting public dialogue over the openness of the German treaty ratification process.[34] Some party officials joined with policy research institutes and nongovernmental organizations in a mini campaign for the government to amend the Basic Law and then allow a referendum on the Constitution. FDP leaders proposed an amendment for referendums targeted specifically at approval of major European integration initiatives. This approach had a much larger base of popular support, with some 70 per cent of Germans saying that they wanted to have a public voice in European integration initiatives, especially a European Constitution.[35] They argued that the German political system already allowed for referendums at the local and *Länder* levels, and that such initiatives had provided a strong voice for the public in policy development. After some hesitation, the position of the SPD and the Greens evolved to support an amendment to the Basic Law for referendums in specific circumstances but argued that the question of the EU Constitution should be kept entirely separate. On ratification of the Constitution, Schröder argued, the "Basic Law does not allow for a referendum. We will have a parliamentary process."[36] However, the initiative fell short of the necessary two-thirds majority because of opposition from the CDU/CSU and the FDP.[37] Finally, after more rancorous debate SPD leaders decided in January 2005 to eschew the referendum initiative and move forward definitively on EU ratification by parliament.[38]

Interest Groups

The position of key interest groups in Germany on the European Constitution was relatively unfocused. While there were a number of groups with interests in EU policy in general, they did not appear to become actively engaged on the Constitution. There were at least three factors at work that may have minimized the role of interest groups in this case study. First, the legislature was fairly unified in its position in favor of the treaty, providing few points of access for interest group opposition to the deal. Second, interest group inactivity may have been a function of the nature of the treaty which focused on macro-level political institutional reforms as opposed to economic adjustments by member states. Reform of the Council voting procedures and parliamentary powers were issues that did not translate easily to concerns about domestic distribution of costs. Third, the Schröder government, like the conservative coalition governments before it, had effectively co-opted most German interests on matters of European integration. By the 1990s, many areas of German public policy were intertwined with EU initiatives Academic debates about the democratic deficit were significant, however. Grassroots lobbies did mobilize in the fight in 2004 over the democratic deficit. Organizations including the group *Mehr Demokratie* lobbied for the introduction of direct democratic elements in the Basic Law. As noted earlier, these groups had some success in generating public interest. A poll conducted in the summer of 2004 found that 86 per cent supported the concept of national referendums on major foreign policy issues.[39] But in the end the government was successful in keeping the issue separate from support of the actual Constitution.

Public Support

Public attitudes provided diffuse support for the European Constitution even while questioning the legitimacy of the current government through regional elections. Surveys showed steady support for the European Union at about 50–60 per cent. A poll published in early May 2005, for example, found some 59 per cent of Germans in favor of the treaty.[40] As noted earlier, however, many Germans said that they also wanted a greater say in foreign policy initiatives, especially those tied to Europe. A poll published in July 2004 in the *Stern* magazine found that 70 per cent of Germans wanted to have a say in the EU Constitution.[41] This sentiment expressed a growing concern for how and when the EU might expand to include potential member states like Turkey.

A view of support for the Constitution in Germany is magnified when contrasted with broader political trends at the time. The spring of 2005 actually saw a significant decline in public support for the SPD–Green coalition government. Many Germans were pessimistic about the economic and social situation in their country at the time, with special concerns about immigration. Germany also had a high rate of unemployment, some 11.8 per cent nationwide. In the very weeks that the German parliament was endorsing the European Constitution by wide margins, voters were sending strong signals to the government that it was time for a change.

Outcome and Analysis

The German parliament ratified the European Constitution by an overwhelming majority. The *Bundestag* held its final vote on May 12, endorsing the treaty by a vote of 569/23.[42] The final *Bundesrat* vote on May 27 offered a chance to celebrate not only the German achievement in ratification but mark the larger process underway in Europe. The chancellor used the occasion to try to build momentum for ratification in France by inviting former French President Giscard d'Estaing to address the chamber. D'Estaing called the German vote "historic," and said, "[r]atification by Germany and France would mark an historic step forward for the future of the constitution and for Europe." The treaty passed by a wide margin, with only representatives from Mecklenburg-Vorpommern abstaining.[43]

There are several important postscripts to this story. On May 22, 2005, just days before the final *Bundesrat* vote on the treaty, the SPD lost control of North-Rhine Westphalia for the first time in forty years in a regional election. The dramatic defeat for the Schröder government led the chancellor to call early national elections for September. The CDU/CSU won the largest percentage of votes and formed a grand coalition with the SPD under new Chancellor Angela Merkel.[44]

The French rejection of the Constitution came only days after the final German vote. European Commission President Jose Manuel Barroso tried to hold out hope in the aftermath of the veto, claiming, "We cannot say that the treaty is dead."[45] Others were more pessimistic. British Prime Minister Tony Blair announced a suspension of plans to hold a referendum in his country on the treaty, calling instead for a "time of reflection" in the wake of developments in France. That same day, the *euro* traded sharply downward in international currency markets, and foreign ministers and heads of states scrambled to find new solutions. Voters in the Netherlands also rejected the European Constitution. As if giving a benediction at a graveside ceremony for the treaty, one editorial in *The Economist* said that the rejections signaled "that the dream of 'ever closer union' is over."[46]

The proposition that states are more likely to ratify treaties that represent maximization of national interests does not appear to explain the German study. While the European Constitution enjoyed broad political support, opponents in Germany argued that the treaty would produce significant costs in terms of influence in the regional organization. The government's assessment of costs and benefits likely recognized the short-term disadvantages of participation in the Constitutional arrangement. Conversely, the constructivist argument that the stronger the international normative pressure, the more likely it is that the state will successfully ratify an international agreement does help to explain this case outcome. The European Constitution was the extension of decades of progress in the EU. German diplomats had been leading and progressive voices in the negotiations to develop the Constitution. And in many ways, German identity was synonymous with cooperation in the European Union. Thus, cooperation with the norm of integration was consistent with constructivist interpretations.

All four domestic political conditions seem relevant to this case. German diplomats had a strong role in defining the new weighted voting scheme for the Council. Chancellor Schröder adopted a proactive stance toward negotiations and ratification of the treaty, reaching out across the political aisle to build bipartisan support for the initiative. The parliament, in turn, played an important role in ratifying the treaty. Interest group mobilization against the treaty was relatively limited, allowing a broad and permissive public consensus to shape discourse. In sum, both normative pressures and domestic political conditions favored the positive outcome in Germany.

NOTES

1. "Treaty of Nice: A Comprehensive Guide," www.europa.eu/scadplus/nice_treaty/introduction_en.htm (accessed April 4, 2007).
2. This is clearly an optimistic assessment. Some areas of the Constitution were left purposefully vague, such as those governing security commitments and ties to other organizations including NATO.
3. "The Great Constitutional Debate Begins," *The Economist* (February 10, 2005), p. 16.
4. John T.S. Keller and Martin A. Schain, "Presidents, Premiers, and Models of Democracy in France," in John T.S. Keller and Martin A. Schain, eds., *Chirac's Challenge: Liberalization, Europeanization, and Malaise in France* (New York: St. Martins, 1996), p. 23.
5. D.S. Bell and B. Criddle, "Presidentialism Restored: The French Elections of April–May and June 2002," *Parliamentary Affairs*, October 2002.
6. Philip Gordon, Senior Fellow at Brookings, Director of the Center on the United States and Europe, "The French Vote and Europe's Future," Brookings Institution Briefing, Washington DC, May 27, 2005 (transcript from tape recording).
7. Jon Henley, "Chirac Isolated After His Own Party Votes in Favour of EU Referendum," *The Guardian* (May 11, 2004), p. 15.
8. Chirac Town Meeting and the Yes Campaign: Claude Salhani, "Analysis: Chirac: To the Ballots, Citizens," UPI Report (April 15, 2005).
9. Hugh Schofield, "EU Constitution Opposition Surges," *Washington Times* (March 19, 2005), p. 1; see also Nicolas de Boisgrollier, "Will the EU Constitution Survive a Referendum in France?" U.S.–Europe Analysis Series, Brooking Institution Center on the United States and Europe (March 2005).
10. "French Territories Begin EU Voting," CNN.com, May 28, 2005, http://edition.cnn.com/2005/WORLD/europe/05/28/france.eu/index.html (accessed April 2, 2007).
11. See John T.S. Keller, "Executive Power and Policy-Making Patterns in France: Gauging the Impact of Fifth Republic Institutions," *West European Politics*, vol. 16, no. 4 (October 1993), pp. 518–44.
12. Nicolas de Boisgrollier, "Will the EU Constitution Survive a Referendum in France?".
13. Katrin Bennhold, "Chirac and Socialists Reel After a Debate on Europe," *International Herald Tribune* (May 29, 2005), p. 4.
14. Colin Randall, "French Rift over EU Vote," *The Daily Telegraph* (September 14, 2004), p. 11.

15. Katrin Bennhold, "Chirac and Socialists Reel After a Debate on Europe," p. 4.
16. See discussion in Nicolas de Boisgrollier, "Will the EU Constitution Survive a Referendum in France?".
17. Harry De Quetteville, "French Farmers Dig in Against Chirac," *Sunday Telegraph* (April 17, 2005), p. 29.
18. S. Marthaler, "The French Referendum on Ratification of the Constitutional Treaty, European Parties Elections and Referendum Network, Sussex European Institute (May 29, 2005).
19. Philip Gordon, "The French Vote and Europe's Future".
20. Ibid.
21. Jon Henley and Patrick Wintour, "French Non a Disaster for World Says EU Chief," *The Guardian* (May 26, 2005), p. 2.
22. Gordon, "The French Vote and Europe's Future".
23. Henley and Wintour, "French Non a Disaster for World says EU Chief," p. 2.
24. As quoted in "Chirac Reacts to EU 'Non'," BBC.com, May 29, 2005, http://news.bbc.co.uk/2/hi/europe/4592393.stm (accessed April 2, 2007).
25. Paul Hainsworth, "France Says No: The 24 May 2005 Referendum on the European Constitution," *Parliamentary Affairs*, vol. 59, no. 1 (2006), p. 102.
26. For a broader discussion of these issues, see Thomas Banchoff, "Germany Identity and European Integration," *European Journal of International Relations*, vol. 5, no. 3 (1999), pp. 259–89.
27. "Parliament Says 'Yes' To European Constitution," German Information Center, http://www.germany.info/relaunch/politics/new/pol_EU_Constition.html (accessed October 12, 2006).
28. Regina Karp, "The New German Foreign Policy Consensus," *Washington Quarterly*, vol. 29, no. 1 (Winter 2005–6), p. 68.
29. "Fischer fordert Entscheidungen ueber die Zukunft der EU," *Süddeutsche Zeitung* (July 7, 2000), p. 1.
30. "Roundup: Schröder and Chirac Pitch for EU Constitution," Deutsche Presse-Agentur (April 26, 2005).
31. Ibid.
32. Ingolf Pernice, "The Role of National Parliaments in the European Union," Walter Hallstein-Institut für Europeaisches Verfassunsrecht, Humbolt-Universtaet zu Berlin, WHI Paper 5/01 (July 2001).
33. Indeed, the very idea of national referendums in Germany was politically charged. The Weimar Constitution had allowed referendums on key policy initiatives, and the National Socialist Party leadership manipulated the instrument to gain popular endorsement of two aggressive actions in the Rhineland and Austria in the late 1930s.
34. For an interesting debate about legal interpretation of the Basic Law and the referendum question, see Wissenschaftliche Dienste des Deutschen Bundestages, "Die Ratifikation des Vertrags über eine Verfassung für Europa," no. 36 (November 12, 2004).

35. "Mehrheit der Deutschen für Volksentscheide und EU-Referendum," *Die Welt* (September 1, 2004), p. 1.
36. "Schröder will EU-Verfassung noch 2004 ratifizieren," *Der Spiegel* (July 15, 2004), p. 51.
37. It should be noted, however, that some Conservatives expressed an interest in future referendums on issues related to European integration such as Turkey's potential membership in the EU; "Ein Traum ist jetzt Wirklichkeit," *Der Spiegel* (October 29, 2004), p. 26.
38. "SPD-Fraktion lehnt Volksabstimmung zur EU-Verfassung ab," *Der Spiegel* (January 14, 2005), p. 31.
39. "Mehrheit der Deutschen für Volksentscheide und EU-Referendum," *Die Welt* (September 1, 2004), p. 4.
40. www.unizar.es/euroconstitucion/Treatties/Treaty_Const_Rat_germany.htm (accessed September 25, 2006).
41. "Mehrheit der Deutschen für Volksentscheide und EU-Referendum," p. 1.
42. Deutscher Bundestag, *Stenografischer Bericht*, 175. Sitzung, Berlin, Donnerstag, den 12. Mai 2005, Plenarprotokoll 15/175, pp. 16347–98.
43. It is important to note that signature of the treaty by Germany's president and the deposit of the instrument of ratification of the treaty in Brussels was delayed by a legal challenge to the Constitution. Some two dozen conservative leaders opposed the Constitution as too great a sacrifice of sovereignty, and they challenged the legality of not holding a referendum on ratification of the treaty in the country's highest court. This matter would soon be settled in favor of the government. Assured of ultimate victory in late May, however, all eyes had turned to France and the Netherlands where crucial referendum votes would be held only days later; "Germany Ratifies the EU Constitution," BBC News Online, May 27, 2005, news.bbc.co.uk/2/hi/Europe/4585265.stm (accessed June 5, 2007); "EU-Verfassung: Politiker aller Fraktionen für die EU-Verfassung," *Frankfurter Allgemeine Zeitung* (February 24, 2005), p. 1.
44. Judy Dempsey, "Christian Democrats Name Challenger to Schröder in Elections," *New York Times* (May 31, 2005), p. A8.
45. As quoted in Craig Whitlock, "France Rejects European Constitution," *Washington Post* (May 30, 2005), p. A1.
46. Hainsworth, "France Says No," p. 99; "The Europe that Died," *The Economist* (June 2, 2005), p. 31.

9

Analysis and Conclusions

This study highlights the significance of ratification processes in shaping outcomes of international cooperation or conflict. It also addresses the delicate balance between democratic openness and international commitments by focusing on the legislative phase of international relations. Cases explored in this book demonstrate how leaders of democracies must engage in post-commitment politics to win ratification by their domestic constituencies. The study has also explored the historical record on international treaty ratification as well as legal and political requirements for ratification of an international agreement across democratic systems.

I. RESULTS

The broad lessons of this study are that the ratification process can be highly controversial, produce a significant amount of political exchange, and alter state behavior. Indeed, eleven out of eighteen case studies appear to show signs of moderate or high amounts of political controversy during the ratification stage. In some cases, politicians have made or lost their careers over the fate of international treaties, groups have struggled for government protection, and voters have repudiated the wishes of their leaders. This evidence, coupled with the observations of dozens of experts and policymakers, illustrates the complexity of the international treaty ratification process.

This study also provides insights on the puzzle of treaty near-failures and failures in democratic systems, illuminating the importance of system pressures, executive strategies for ratification, interest group mobilization, and regime type (manifest in executive–legislative relations). For example, the study highlights the constitutive tensions between international normative pressures and the treaty ratification process and outcomes, as well as the dynamic relationship between system structure and state behavior. During the ratification stage, actors often mobilize for or against international agreements in relation to their particular roles, interests, and identities. Discrete perspectives on the distribution of costs and benefits of a treaty seem especially important. In seeking a workable solution to ratification dilemmas this distribution may sometimes matter more than the nature of the problem itself.[1]

Cases also highlight the unusual combination of actors that may align for or against an international treaty. The prospect of a European Constitution created deep fissures in the French polity, for instance. Conservative government leaders sought out support for the treaty from young voters and large corporations. Labor groups who traditionally looked to their allies in the Socialist Party for direction found the party leadership itself seriously divided. The "no" campaign included defectors from Chirac's own Gaullist party working hand in hand with agricultural groups. At the same time, prospects for an Australian–United States Free Trade Agreement (AUSFTA) brought together an unusually strong group of backers in Australia including business leaders, trade unions, and even peanut farmers. Yet other agricultural groups joined with medical professionals to argue that the treaty did not represent the national interest. Time and again, the old adage "politics makes strange bedfellows" has been sharply illustrated during ratification struggles in these countries, sometimes pitting traditional allies against one another in debates about state commitments and sovereignty.

Finally, it is clear that ratification struggles have altered state behaviors in profound ways. While there have always been controversies over treaties, one could argue that in the past they rarely seemed to upset the political balance and undermine international commitments. The United States maintained a strong record of support for nonproliferation initiatives in the Cold War, for example, and European leaders could count on a general commitment to integration initiatives. Today, dynamics appear to have shifted, however. Treaty failures in the post-commitment phase may be on the rise. This study shows that the broad bipartisan support in many democracies for international treaties during the Cold War has given way to something qualitatively different in the past two decades. In the course of my research, for example, Australian diplomats told me they looked back wistfully at the days when there was near universal support in their country for trade agreements. Canadian diplomats wondered aloud about the implications of a democratized treaty review process. Pessimists warn that we have entered an era in which countries are more reluctant to endorse formalized international agreements due to a variety of contending forces.[2] This chapter provides a more detailed analysis of the results of the study and an exploration of the theoretical implications, and discusses additional avenues for investigation.

II. ANALYSIS

This study was based on the assumption that cooperation is the product of a sequential policy process in liberal democracies—not a simultaneous alignment of domestic and international conditions, as Putnam argued. A leader's initial commitment to cooperate with other states often mobilizes domestic political actors and conditions in a liberal democracy. Executive preferences may be buffeted by international pressures and developments as well. What follows is a survey of the outcome of the exploratory propositions.

International Pressures

The first proposition explored in this study suggested that the more a treaty maximized state power and national interests, the more likely a government would be to ratify it. As illustrated in Table 9.1, however, the balance of benefits versus costs of international cooperation appear positively associated with ratification outcomes in only seven of the eighteen cases.[3]

The case of the CTBT suggests the strongest alignment between security concerns and ratification outcomes. Nonnuclear weapons states, including Germany, Australia, and Canada, tended to view the CTBT through the lens of their own assessment of capabilities and interests. Germany, a nonnuclear weapons state, believed the CTBT provided tangible security benefits by constraining the clandestine development of nuclear weapons. The Australian and Canadian cases demonstrate the importance of national interest calculations, but with an interesting twist. In both countries, past governments had pursued the acquisition or development of nuclear weapons. The Australian government tried but failed to obtain nuclear weapons from its allies, and only a

Table 9.1. Conditions shaping ratification: systemic pressures*

Kyoto Protocol	**CTBT**	NAFTA	TEU	AUSFTA	European Constitution
System pressures					
Australia: Y	Australia: Y	Canada: N	France: N	Australia: N	France: Y
Canada: N	Canada: Y	USA: N	Germany: N	USA: N	Germany: N
France: N	France: N				
Germany: N	Germany: Y				
USA: Y	USA: Y				

* Y = Yes, there appears to be a positive association between national interests and the ratification outcome in each case study. This coding *does not* indicate whether the ratification vote itself was positive or negative. N = No, there appears to be no alignment between national interest calculations and the ratification outcome in the case study.

change in party control of the government in the early 1970s effectively ended its drive for weapons. The Canadian government co-owned nuclear warheads with the United States during the Cold War. By the 1990s, however, international security conditions had changed markedly, and both governments could make rather simple calculations that the CTBT would enhance future security.

The U.S. and French position on the CTBT were somewhat different. The United States possessed one of the largest nuclear arsenals in the world in the 1990s. Critics inside and outside the government argued that the treaty might undermine the integrity of the U.S. nuclear deterrent, limit modernization, and yet still allow rogue states to test low-yield weapons in secret. Neorealists would predict U.S. rejection of the treaty. At the same time, the French government took a circuitous path toward ratification of the CTBT by first announcing that they would complete a series of underground tests in the South Pacific before they could endorse the Agreement. While the move by new President Jacques Chirac was highly inflammatory, his government did follow through on its commitment to end testing and sign the CTBT in 1996. France was one of the first nuclear weapons states to ratify the agreement. In neither case would rational calculation of national security concerns suggest that the CTBT would be signed or ratified by these nuclear weapons states.

The Kyoto Protocol posed a very different set of questions for advanced industrialized countries, and national interest calculations appear to be positively associated only with rejections of the treaty. For example, both France and Germany agreed with the Kyoto pledge to reduce greenhouse gas (GHG) emissions by about 8 per cent by 2012 (from 1990 baseline levels) in spite of the fact that this was a costly venture with an uncertain outcome. The governments of Canada, Australia, and the United States adopted a very different posture toward the Kyoto Protocol. Throughout the 1990s, all three participated in the Umbrella Group, a bloc of advanced industrialized states demanding concessions, flexibility mechanisms, and cooperation from developing countries in order to achieve a comprehensive solution to climate change. Building on promises for concessions, the Canadian government pledged to reduce its GHG emissions in line with long-term interests concerning climate change. Yet ratification of the treaty came only five years later, with little support from the prime minister. Left in its wake was significant debate among provincial legislatures over policy implementation. In the same spirit, the U.S. repudiation of the Kyoto Protocol after six years of consideration can be interpreted as an expected outcome based on calculations of benefits and costs. The Clinton administration pledged U.S. support for the treaty but chose to never submit the treaty for advice and consent by the Senate. One of George W. Bush's first foreign policy acts in office was to announce the withdrawal of U.S. support for the plan. U.S. government officials can be said to have calculated that the costs of compliance with the new protocol would outweigh the potential benefits.

Other case studies appear to underscore the limitations of structural realist predictions on ratification outcomes. Both the North American Free Trade Agreement (NAFTA) and the AUSFTA offered challenges to state sovereignty. While government leaders cast these as winning commitments, evidence debated during all four ratification stages showed high costs and uncertain benefits. NAFTA was a treaty that threatened to undermine job security in the United States and have high associated costs. The Canadian government recognized serious costs associated with liberalization. In a similar vein, both the Australian and U.S. governments knew there would be costs associated with the completion of the AUSFTA (although there remains significant debate about whether the gains would favor one player or the other). In this case, however, most experts inside the negotiations recognized that the United States stood to benefit from the treaty.

International Norms

Normative pressures appear to have played a significant role in shaping state commitments and influencing ratification processes over time. The second proposition explored in this study was that the greater the level of international normative pressure to cooperate, the more likely that governments would ratify an agreement. In fourteen of eighteen cases examined here, actors involved in the ratification process referenced their country's institutional commitments and obligation to come through on the agreement (see Table 9.2). Executives most often recommended cooperation with existing norms in relation to agreements on the environment and security. Less direct references to normative commitments were made in relation to trade agreements, although there was clearly a role for institutions in these cases as well.

Table 9.2. Conditions shaping ratification: norms

Kyoto Protocol		CTBT	NAFTA	TEU	AUSFTA	European Constitution
Norms						
Australia:	N	Australia: Y	Canada: Y	France: Y	Australia: Y	France: N
Canada:	Y	Canada: Y	USA: Y	Germany: Y	USA: Y	Germany: Y
France:	Y	France: Y				
Germany:	Y	Germany: Y				
USA:	N	USA: N				

The strongest links between normative pressures and ratification outcomes appeared in cases where there were already strong institutional networks for cooperation in place. For example, European diplomats were able to exchange ideas regularly through existing EU institutions and built upon decades of international cooperation to achieve new initiatives (that would themselves reinforce and expand the norm of integration). French and German governments were highly committed to the two European integration programs explored in this study. In the case of the Treaty on European Union (TEU), government officials had been instrumental in negotiating the agreements that would achieve the lofty goal of economic union but include convergence criteria in line with their own national interests. There was strong normative, legal, and institutional pressure for ratification and compliance, and this dynamic appears to have contributed to a positive debate in both countries. However, these dynamics were also present in French consideration of the European Constitution, yet they failed to determine the final outcome. In this case, normative pressure was not sufficient to overcome resistance to the initiative among French voters.

Ratification debates over trade deals examined for this study were influenced by decades of cooperation toward a positive normative outcome. The NAFTA, for example, represented an extension of the U.S.–Canada FTA. While Canadian Prime Minister Mulroney may have been personally predisposed not to negotiate an expanded trade network, it is clear that the Canadian government was influenced by strong normative, institutional, and material pressures to join the talks. In the case of the AUSFTA, most officials on both sides of the Pacific Ocean saw the agreement as more than a simple trade deal—it was an affirmation of the strong economic and political relationship between the two countries. Over time Australian government officials came to view completion of the deal as essential to deepen ties between the two countries.

Normative pressures appear to have been less significant in influencing ratification debates over the CTBT in the United States and the Kyoto Protocol in Australia and the United States. The rejection of the CTBT by a Senate vote in 1999 seemed to defy existing normative and institutional commitments to nonproliferation. The Australian and U.S. government rejections of the Kyoto Protocol also indicate a lack of alignment between prevailing conditions and outcomes. The Australian government was quite conscious of normative pressures for cooperation on climate change for a decade before its rejection of the treaty. Indeed, to some degree Australian and U.S. diplomats had played important roles in negotiation of a workable framework for GHG emissions cuts that would include both ambitious goals and more practical (and flexible) compliance mechanisms. By these actions, these governments set themselves apart from institutional advancement in key issue areas and appeared to be unmoved by prevailing norms. Questions remain as to whether these acts of defiance will themselves force a change in prevailing norms.

Executive Strategies

In fourteen of eighteen cases, data suggest that the strategies of presidents and prime ministers influenced the process of ratification and the ultimate outcome of government decisions. The relationship between executive strategies and ratification outcome could be either positive or negative, depending on the intended outcome of the individual leaders and their level of commitment to the cause. In some cases, ratification success was the direct product of leadership strategies; in others, failure resulted when a leader consciously chose not to actively pursue treaty ratification or devote significant political capital to the enterprise. Thus, as illustrated in Table 9.3, the centrality of executive strategies in ratification processes seems to represent a compelling interpretation of many of the cases.

Elite strategy for ratification was very important in shaping the outcome of trade agreements. Indeed, were it not for the active engagement of President Clinton in the NAFTA ratification campaign in the United States and Prime Minister Howard in the AUSFTA ratification campaign in Australia, these treaties might never have been realized. President Clinton launched a pro-NAFTA campaign soon after taking office in 1993 in order to secure the necessary votes in Congress for its ratification. His strategies to build support included the implementation of all three executive strategies for action: side payments, synergistic issue linkages, and issue redefinition. In the lead up to the final House vote, Clinton worked the phones and twisted arms to secure a majority for NAFTA. The White House offered undecided Congressional representatives incentives to vote in favor of the trade deal—from promises to seek special protections against import flooding to a federal grant to build a

Table 9.3. Conditions shaping ratification: executive strategy

Kyoto Protocol		CTBT		NAFTA		TEU		AUSFTA		European Constitution	
Executive strategies											
Australia:	Y	Australia:	N	Canada:	Y	France:	Y	Australia:	Y	France:	N
Canada:	N	Canada:	N	USA:	Y	Germany:	Y	USA:	Y	Germany:	Y
France:	Y	France:	Y								
Germany:	Y	Germany:	Y								
USA:	Y	USA:	Y								

bridge in Texas. Ralph Nader, speaking for a group that opposed the NAFTA, condemned Clinton's endgame as a "process of complex sleaze."[4]

Similarly, the AUSFTA generated a surprising amount of domestic political controversy within Australia. Champions of the treaty, including Prime Minister Howard himself, argued that linking Australia's economy to that of the United States offered incredible benefits. Critics of the deal, meanwhile, charged that the treaty was actually most favorable to the United States (by allowing maintenance of subsidies on sugar, for example), and that Australia would be disadvantaged by the deal. The record shows that the prime minister intervened personally in February 2004 to ensure that the draft treaty was signed, and he then exhibited an unusual level of personal engagement in deliberations with opposition leaders in the Senate over the final implementing legislation. Howard actively engaged the opposition, employing side payments, synergistic issue linkages, and issue redefinition to achieve his desired ratification of the treaty.

The story of the two major agreements in European integration over the past two decades—the Maastricht Treaty and the European Constitution—could not be complete without attention to the role of leaders and their efforts to achieve ratification outcomes. In the case of the TEU, both French and German leaders managed the ratification debates in their respective countries (and, in fact, in one another's countries) and offered side payments to groups opposed to the deal. Mitterrand was especially instrumental in achieving French ratification of the TEU through referendum, practicing issue redefinition repeatedly in the "yes" campaign. One case study of EU Constitution ratification underscores the importance of executive strategy—in Schröder's management of the Constitution debate in Germany. However, the French rejection of the EU Constitution in 2005 occurred in part because French President Chirac announced a referendum on the treaty in spite of the fact that he did not have to. But then the president also engaged in a heavy campaign to lobby support for the treaty. Chirac devoted significant time and energy to build popular support for the treaty, but it ultimately failed.

All five rounds of consideration of the Kyoto Protocol examined for this study illustrate the relationship between executive strategies and ratification outcomes. In the United States, for example, Clinton administration strategies for negotiating, signing, and ratifying the Kyoto Protocol were minimal at best. The administration knew that the issue would awaken significant domestic political opposition, including resistance from the U.S. Senate, interest groups, and the energy sector. The president made the crucial decision not to submit the treaty for review by the Republican-controlled Senate, and just three months after taking office President George W. Bush formally withdrew U.S support for the treaty. Similarly, the conservative leadership of Australia opposed the Kyoto Protocol and therefore devoted few resources to its passage in parliament. The Kyoto Protocol had a very different reception in European governments, however. German Chancellors Helmut Kohl and Gerhard Schröder supported the EU GHG emissions cuts targets and managed a strong political base in support of the deal for ratification. At the same time, the French government supported the treaty through to ratification even with the change of government from Mitterrand's Socialist Party control to Chirac's Gaullists. In summary, a majority of the cases examined here suggest that executive strategies are essential components of the drive for successful treaty ratification.

Regime Type: Executive–Legislative Relations

Variation in electoral systems (electoral laws, formally defined institutional relationships between executive and legislative authority structures, and seat distribution in the legislature) also appeared to have influenced ratification outcomes. As illustrated in Table 9.4, the proposition suggesting correspondence between the type of government and levels of ratification success appears confirmed in fourteen of eighteen case studies. Majoritarian parliamentary systems seemed to allow the executive a wide degree of latitude regarding ratification strategies than did presidential separation-of-powers systems. Parliamentary systems based wholly, or in part, on proportional representation created a dynamic in which executives would have to negotiate minimally with legislators in both houses of parliament.

The proposition that regimes with more centralized political power would be more likely to ratify treaties appears to be supported in the majority of cases examined here. The strongest illustrations of the relationship between regime type and ratification outcome occurred in Westminster-style parliamentary democracies. In majoritarian systems, there seemed to be distinct advantages granted to the executive position in controversial ratification debates.

Table 9.4. Conditions shaping ratification: regime type: executive–legislative relations

Kyoto Protocol	**CTBT**	NAFTA	TEU	AUSFTA	European Constitution
Regime type					
Australia: N	Australia: Y	Canada: Y	France: Y	Australia: Y	France: N
Canada: Y	Canada: Y	USA: N	Germany: Y	USA: N	Germany: Y
France: Y	France: Y				
Germany: Y	Germany: Y				
USA: Y	USA: Y				

In both Canada and Australia, leaders were aware that they could essentially force implementing legislation through the parliament to ratify international agreements, and they played this flexibility to their advantage. For example, Prime Minister Chrétien supported the Kyoto Protocol but was content to see the larger political debate play out regarding GHG emissions cuts in many other Annex I countries for several years. The prime minister moved forward on ratification of the treaty at a time of his own choosing—and even then devoted few resources to the ensuing debate over the legislation in 2002.

In two of three Australian case studies it appears that the executive faced much greater resistance on international treaty ratification than anticipated. The prime minister's intentions to pass enabling legislation for the AUSFTA and ratify the treaty smoothly were stymied by significant resistance in the Senate. The nature of the bicameral legislature actually allowed the Labor Party to shape the debate that followed, and there were clear indications that Labor leader Mark Latham would roadblock the agreement without concessions on the terms of the treaty. Prime Minister Howard had to agree to Labor's amendments in order to gain the necessary votes for ratification. Australia's dealings with the Kyoto Protocol also fail to uphold the proposition that the more centralized regime will be more likely to successfully pass the agreement. In this case, the executive actually opposed the treaty and manipulated his own political system to stymie any efforts by supporters of the protocol to make substantial legislative initiatives.

Case studies of parliamentary systems based on proportional representation appeared to uphold the proposition across the board. In all four cases of German ratification of treaties the parliamentary system afforded the executive some advantages. Chancellor Helmut Kohl assembled and maintained parliamentary support for major initiatives including the Maastricht Treaty, and Gerhard Schröder was able to build strong support for the European Constitution. In fact, the chancellors used the strong base of German support for these treaties as leverage in encouraging ratification of the treaties in other countries. It should be noted that in all four of these cases, the German government was composed of a coalition cabinet that spanned a broader ideological grouping than single-party Westminster systems. This may have allowed a greater degree of consensus on support for treaties.

The mixed presidential–parliamentary system of France showed a surprising degree of executive autonomy present in three of four case studies. French President Mitterrand was able to build popular support for the Maastricht Treaty and used the parliamentary system as a wedge to establish a working majority for the agreement. President Chirac was adept at using his parliamentary advantages to achieve key objectives including ratification of the

CTBT and the Kyoto Protocol. Yet on European integration initiatives, both presidents appear to have taken a step too far in attempting to exert authority. Mitterrand and Chirac announced plans for referendums on major European treaties—moves that both would come to regret. The case of the European Constitution was particularly frustrating for both participants and observers. Here, the president chose the route of referendum instead of parliamentary ratification, allowing a window of opportunity for opponents to broadside the deal.

Finally, the presidential system of the United States demonstrates mixed results in relation to the centralization of government proposition. The separation-of-powers system gave the executive authority to negotiate two major free trade agreements, AUSFTA and NAFTA, but authorized Congress to ratify the treaties. The AUSFTA generated little to no public controversy and received Congressional support. NAFTA meanwhile was highly controversial, yet the ratification success occurred in spite of the fact that there were serious rifts and differences inside the polity. The electoral system appears to have operated as predicted in contributing to the dramatic failures of ratification of the Kyoto Protocol and the CTBT. In both cases, the president supported international treaties and sought Senate endorsement of the deals. Also, in both cases, the president faced a divided government in which Republican control of the Senate established a roadblock to ratification of international agreements. In summary, results appear to support the contention that leaders in majoritarian parliamentary systems have an institutional advantage vis-à-vis treaty ratification.

Interest Groups

Cases suggest that the role of interest groups in ratification debates may be important in select conditions. In general the proposition that the less organized the opposition to an international treaty by interest groups, the more likely it would be that the government would successfully ratify a treaty was upheld by case data. As illustrated in Table 9.5, thirteen of eighteen case studies show some relationship between interest group mobilization and ratification outcome. Yet in some of these cases, this relationship is far from clear-cut. Interest groups became mobilized on some issues in predictable ways, but groups also failed to mobilize on others with which they might typically concern themselves. Another common pattern was the mobilization of a large number of interest groups both for and against major international treaties. This pattern neutralizes the measurement device employed for this study (a design concern discussed later in the chapter).

Table 9.5. Conditions shaping ratification: interest groups

Kyoto Protocol	CTBT	NAFTA	TEU	AUSFTA	European Constitution
Interest groups					
Australia: Y	Australia: Y	Canada: N	France: N	Australia: N	France: Y
Canada: N	Canada: Y	USA: N	Germany: Y	USA: Y	Germany: Y
France: Y	France: Y				
Germany: Y	Germany: Y				
USA: Y	USA: Y				

In Europe, democratic leaders who were trying to finalize the Maastricht Treaty faced a tremendous amount of pressure from interest groups. Business, labor, and agricultural groups saw the TEU as a high stakes deal. From the outset, German Chancellor Kohl was quite conscious of building domestic support for ratification of the TEU among key interest groups. The German government became aware of opposition to the TEU from the *Bundesbank* and labor unions in key economic sectors, threatening potential strikes that might cripple the German economy. In the end, however, while the Kohl government acknowledged concerns of key interest groups, it nevertheless forged ahead in its drive to secure domestic support for the deal throughout 1992. The chancellor recognized that vested lobbies would have concerns related to the scope and pace of monetary union as well as social and justice initiatives. These concerns were further magnified by Germany's uncertain economic situation during the unification process.

Free trade treaties awakened numerous interest groups in Australia, the United States, and Canada. But in each case, there emerged groups that strongly supported the treaties and those that opposed them. The Bush and Clinton administrations found support for the NAFTA from the U.S. Chamber of Commerce, the National Association of Manufacturers, agricultural groups, and even some environmental lobbies. But the treaty faced strong opposition from organized labor and environmental groups like the Sierra Club. Ralph Nader joined with Ross Perot to challenge a deal that they believed would harm U.S. interests in the long run. The Canadian debate over NAFTA was less intense, yet policy institutes, labor, and environmental groups aligned both for and against the NAFTA. And in Australia, an unusual coalition of actors lined up on both sides of the free trade deal with the United States. These groups generated significant controversy over the treaty, but ultimately failed to stop it. In summary, thirteen of eighteen cases appear to show that when governments faced less organized interest group opposition to a treaty they were more likely to ratify it.

Table 9.6. Conditions shaping ratification: public opinion

Kyoto Protocol	CTBT	NAFTA	TEU	AUSFTA	European Constitution
Public opinion					
Australia: N	Australia: Y	Canada: N	France: Y	Australia: Y	France: Y
Canada: Y	Canada: Y	USA: N	Germany: Y	USA: Y	Germany: Y
France: Y	France: Y				
Germany: Y	Germany: Y				
USA: N	USA: N				

Public Opinion

Prevailing public attitudes toward international treaties appear positively associated with ratification outcomes in thirteen of eighteen case studies. Overall, however, the evidence suggests that public opinion may have created more of a "permissive consensus" for state action than full endorsement. In some cases, public opinion on the subject of endorsement of treaties favored the international agreement but it was subsequently rejected; in other cases, polls indicated a general ambivalence regarding a treaty, yet the government forged ahead with ratification. Finally, in five of eighteen case studies, public attitudes contrasted government actions on treaties.

As illustrated in Table 9.6, public opinion generally favored ratification success for most treaties examined in this study, but surveys often showed that this was diffuse support. For example, there was diffuse support for a treaty to lower GHG emissions in many advanced industrialized economies in the 1990s. In Canada, polls showed 50–60 per cent of the public in favor of the Kyoto Protocol, but opposition was higher in some provinces that anticipated negative domestic distributional effects. The American public offered diffuse support for action on climate change, but surveys also show that citizens lacked detailed knowledge of the issue. Public support for the Kyoto Protocol increased over time. In the early 1990s, 94 per cent of Germans called climate change either "very serious" or "somewhat serious."

Public opinion toward European integration also tended to be diffuse. Surveys in Germany from the period showed a range of opinions about integration, from general disinterest to steadfast belief in the value of the enterprise, to serious concerns about the economic implications of the treaty. Broadly speaking, European policy was less salient to Germans than some other issues in the 1990s. Most Germans offered their support for the EU in surveys in the 1990s, but there was a gap between those generally favoring integration and those who actually expected positive benefits for Germany from the process. It is also worth noting that the German public felt disconnected from the European integration process. According to polls conducted during the summer and fall of 1992, more than 80 per cent of Germans said that they knew "nothing" or "very little" about the TEU. Public opinion did play a special role in the two cases of French votes on European integration in this study. Decisions by Mitterrand and Chirac to hold referendums on major treaty initiatives vaulted public opinion from the background to center stage. In the buildup to both referendums, polls showed that the idea of advancing European integration enjoyed diffuse support. But this support for the treaties eroded dramatically as more specific concerns began to emerge through a period of public debate.

There were, however, five notable exceptions to the overall pattern of support developed in this study: the U.S. and Australian rejection of the Kyoto Protocol, U.S. rejection of the CTBT, and negative attitudes in Canada and the United States toward the NAFTA treaty. While U.S. public attitudes toward global warming did vary significantly over time, polling data from 2001 found that 72 per cent of respondents believed that immediate steps were necessary to fight global warming. The Australian government's rejection of the protocol seems even more out of step with prevailing public opinion; 80 per cent of Australians supported action on climate change and ratification of the Kyoto Protocol—with or without U.S. participation in the regime. Finally, the very idea of NAFTA generated deep public opposition in both Canada and the United States. In the 1988 Canadian "free trade election," Prime Minister Mulroney won by a narrow plurality of the popular vote (but almost 60 per cent of the public voted against his government's position). According to a poll conducted in April 1992, 66 per cent of Canadians opposed NAFTA. The U.S. public was sharply divided over the treaty as well.

From these cases it appears that government leaders were concerned about diffuse public support for international agreements, but they appear not to have allowed such opposition to constrain their ratification drives. Overall, these results were less robust than those for more proximate variables and seem to offer little additional explanatory power regarding constraints on treaty ratification.

III. CONCLUSIONS

This project set out to explore the politics of international treaty ratification processes in comparative perspective. While Putnam's two-level game theory assumes that chief negotiators are fully aware of domestic political constraints on Level I deals, case data show that the ratification process is sometimes surprisingly difficult. The assumption that the executive can anticipate the preferences of domestic actors and, therefore, would only develop agreements that are ratifiable does not hold. Simultaneous management of Level I and Level II pressures is unrealistic in most modern democracies, and ratification seems anything but preordained.

Life? Treaty Ratification Successes

Five of six propositions regarding the relationship between international and domestic pressures and ratification outcomes seemed to be supported by a majority of case outcomes (see Table 9.7). This suggests that multiple factors are at work in determining ratification success and that a more comprehensive approach to analysis of decision-making on treaties is appropriate. This also recognizes the potential for interactions between the various actors and conditions to shape the process. In all cases, a government's initial commitment to a treaty (often in the form of an executive's signature) was followed by a reflective period in which international system pressures, normative commitments, and domestic constraints were weighed before formulating a ratification program. Sometimes these considerations were quite public: leaders openly discussed the benefits of treaty ratification and lobbied domestic actors to build support for final legislation. In other cases, the ratification "campaign" consisted of little more than a speech by the prime minister and management of the passage of enabling legislation by a majority in parliament.

Treaty ratification seems *most* likely when international conditions are permissive and elites are actively engaged in building support for ratification at home. A comparison of the ratification struggles over NAFTA, the CTBT, and the Kyoto Protocol in the United States underscores this point. All three treaties were controversial and had powerful opponents. For NAFTA, President Clinton crafted a sophisticated strategy to win over necessary support in Congress, among key interest groups, and the public. Clinton lent his own political capital to the enterprise and developed a plan to represent the free trade agreement as a bipartisan, win–win situation. Under pressure to secure Congressional approval of the deal in the fall of 1993, Clinton used targeted side payments to win the necessary votes. This contrasted with the half-hearted attempts of the Clinton administration to build support for the Kyoto Protocol and the CTBT. Some have argued that the president knew full well that the protocol deal signed in Kyoto would be "dead on arrival" in the U.S. Senate and instead chose to postpone serious consideration of the agreement on Capitol Hill until the political winds might change. The CTBT

Table 9.7. Summary of conditions shaping ratification

Kyoto Protocol	CTBT	NAFTA	TEU	AUSFTA	European Constitution
System pressures					
Australia: Y	Australia: Y	Canada: N	France: N	Australia: N	France: Y
Canada: N	Canada: Y	USA: N	Germany: N	USA: N	Germany: N
France: N	France: N				
Germany: N	Germany: Y				
USA: Y	USA: Y				
Norms					
Australia: N	Australia: Y	Canada: Y	France: Y	Australia: Y	France: N
Canada: Y	Canada: Y	USA: Y	Germany: Y	USA: Y	Germany: Y
France: Y	France: Y				
Germany: Y	Germany: Y				
USA: N	USA: N				
Executive strategy					
Australia: Y	Australia: N	Canada: Y	France: Y	Australia: Y	France: N
Canada: N	Canada: N	USA: Y	Germany: Y	USA: Y	Germany: Y
France: Y	France: Y				
Germany: Y	Germany: Y				
USA: Y	USA: Y				
Regime type					
Australia: N	Australia: Y	Canada: Y	France: Y	Australia: Y	France: N
Canada: Y	Canada: Y	USA: N	Germany: Y	USA: N	Germany: Y
France: Y	France: Y				
Germany: Y	Germany: Y				
USA: Y	USA: Y				
Interest groups					
Australia: Y	Australia: Y	Canada: N	France: N	Australia: N	France: Y
Canada: N	Canada: Y	USA: N	Germany: Y	USA: Y	Germany: Y
France: Y	France: Y				
Germany: Y	Germany: Y				
USA: Y	USA: Y				
Public opinion					
Australia: N	Australia: Y	Canada: N	France: Y	Australia: Y	France: Y
Canada: Y	Canada: Y	USA: N	Germany: Y	USA: Y	Germany: Y
France: Y	France: Y				
Germany: Y	Germany: Y				
USA: N	USA: N				

* Y = Yes, there appears to be a positive association between national interests and the ratification outcome in each case study. This coding *does not* indicate whether the ratification vote itself was positive or negative. N = No, there appears to be no alignment between national interest calculations and the ratification outcome in the case study.

also faced strong opposition, but the Clinton administration did very little to attempt to build support for the treaty on Capitol Hill, K Street, or with the general public.

Positive normative pressures seem to be necessary but not sufficient conditions for ratification success. Governments seemed to believe that they were obligated to uphold international commitments and that ratification conformed to international legal and institutional precedents as well. However, in many of these cases constructivism does not account well for the actual timing and process of treaty review. Twelve of fourteen cases of success demonstrated the importance of government centralization of power (through electoral systems) and positive public support for ratification success. Eleven of fourteen cases demonstrated the importance of executive strategies. Nine of fourteen cases had less mobilized opposition groups that enabled a smoother progression toward ratification. More often in centralized systems, institutional dynamics were used in the system to the advantage of treaties favored by government leaders, who also benefited from a permissive consensus among the public.

Instead of simply managing two-level games simultaneously, as Putnam suggests, it is clear that government leaders must sometimes engage in complex interactions with domestic players to ensure ratification. Putnam's discussion of domestic resonance, whereby leaders may use their connections with particular constituencies to help legitimate foreign policy programs, seems particularly relevant in these cases. Executives are more likely to win domestic struggles over ratification when they have the backing of major interest groups. The most efficient way to gain this backing appears to be co-optation of existing groups during the negotiation process. Time and again, cases illustrate how savvy executives invited representatives of interest groups to join advisory councils or panels of experts to help advise the government on treaty development. For example, Australia allowed lobbyists and industry representatives to be part of their official delegations at COPs for development of the Kyoto Protocol. Germany and France regularly consulted advisory groups during their development of EU integration programs. An active elite strategy coupled with interest group co-optation appeared most conducive to successful outcomes.

Life Support? Near-Failures of Ratification

This study also has identified conditions associated with near-failures and failures of international treaty ratification. Six cases of near-failure were identified: (1) Canada and the Kyoto Protocol; (2) France and the CTBT; (3) the

United States and NAFTA; (4) France and the Maastricht Treaty; (5) Germany and the Maastricht Treaty; and (6) Australia and the AUSFTA. According to case data, treaties may nearly fail when international conditions place contending pressures on government leaders. Indeed, in all six cases normative pressures predicted cooperation as the final outcome—yet national security concerns predicted defection. Normative pressures help to get international treaties negotiated and signed, yet they are not sufficient to produce universal ratification. For example, French and German governments were highly committed to the two European integration programs explored in this study. They themselves had helped to fuel strong normative pressure for ratification and compliance, yet in the case the TEU this was almost insufficient in overcoming lingering resistance to the initiative among French voters.

Cooperation in the realm of trade liberalization was not sufficient to guarantee either the outcome in the U.S. debate over NAFTA or the Australian debate over AUSFTA. In a similar vein, the rejection of the CTBT by a Senate vote in 1999 seems to defy all semblance of normative and institutional commitments. By these actions, the governments set themselves apart from institutional advancement in key issue areas and appear to be unmoved by prevailing norms. Questions remain as to whether these acts of defiance will themselves force a change in norms. In summary, while international pressures may appear to explain the ultimate outcome of the ratification, they do not appear to predict near-failures; they certainly fail to capture the drama of the process along the way.

At the domestic level, treaties may be more likely to nearly fail even when executives devote considerable time and resources to promoting of their ratification. In addition, treaties may be more likely to nearly fail regardless of regime type and public attitudes. Data from several of the cases of near-failure, including the French and German consideration of the Maastricht Treaty suggests that regardless of the type of government engaged in the debate, the outcome of the treaty ratification remained uncertain up to the end. Mitterrand's control of French politics could not ensure a positive outcome in the TEU referendum; Kohl's control of the German coalition government could not prevent opposition party leaders from placing significant roadblocks in the way of ratification. Public attitudes in both of these cases were marginally supportive but on their own seem not to have guaranteed a positive outcome.

Interest group activity may be the one key indicator closely associated with near failures of treaty ratification. Interest group mobilization appears not to fit expected positive outcomes in four of six case studies of near-failures. Thus, one could argue that near-failures could be associated with active and mobilized oppositional groups. Their impact on near-failure situations was

increased when the group positions were not in line with executive preferences. In other words, when interest groups mobilized to work hard against
international treaties—and these group positions were not in line with executive preferences—treaties appeared to be more likely to nearly fail.

Death? The Failure of Ratification

Finally, this study has highlighted conditions associated with failures of international treaty ratification. Four cases of ratification failure were examined:
(1) the United States and the Kyoto Protocol; (2) Australia and the Kyoto
Protocol; (3) France and the European Constitution; and (4) the United States
and the CTBT. While each story is different, process tracing suggests prevailing
patterns of conditions that helped contribute to ratification failure.

Strong national security reservations can be positively associated with all
four cases of defection. Actors in the United States pushed to reject the CTBT
and the Kyoto Protocol on the grounds that the costs of the agreements
outweighed the benefits. In the case of the French veto of the European Constitution, realists rejected the sacrifice of sovereignty to supranational authority,
the elimination of veto power in the European Council, and other measures
that might limit French power in the region. The Australian rejection of the
Kyoto Protocol can also be explained as a product of realization that the treaty
would impose significant costs on the government and big businesses.

Conversely, constructivism appears to explain none of the four cases of
decisions to defect from international agreements. Normative and institutional pressures to cooperate did not prevent governments from reneging
on treaties across issue areas. For example, the strong normative pattern of
cooperation on the international environment leading up to the Kyoto Protocol did not ensure that governments of Australia or the United States would
ratify the treaty. Indeed, both Australia and the United States had signed the
UNFCCC and provided support for a binding protocol at subsequent COPs.
The French government had been instrumental in shaping the new European
Constitution, yet the public was not convinced that its longtime allegiance to
the EU should be supported through the new treaty.

Richer explanations of treaty rejection can often be found in the interaction
between external and internal conditions. For example, negative executive
strategies can be associated with outcomes in three of these cases: the United
States' rejections of the CTBT and the Kyoto Protocol, and the Australian
rejection of the Kyoto Protocol. Here, leaders chose *not* to heavily invest in
the international agreements and not to use sophisticated executive strategies
to build support for the treaties. In only one case did a leader commit fully to

a treaty only to see it fail: Chirac's drive for the referendum in France. Once again, interest group mobilization also appears to be significant to failures. It should be noted that interest groups mobilized on both sides of major debates, yet the very existence of a strong anti-ratification grassroots campaign appears to have helped executives overcome resistance from treaty supporters.

One conclusion is that treaty failures appear to be primarily at the hands of the executive, who determines that a treaty is no longer in the national interests of his government and defects from the international agreement. Regardless of systemic and normative pressures, treaties are less likely to be ratified when the executive commits few resources to their passage or opposes their passage and looks for support for this position from strong interest groups and lobbies. International treaties are more likely to be ratified when executive strategies articulate clear reasons why agreements are in the national interest, support prevailing institutional and legal arrangements, and provide a positive domestic distribution of costs. It may very well be that executive strategies become the catalyst for changes in policies in some cases, and that by signaling their disagreement with international treaties, the executive opens the door to interest group and popular opposition to treaties. Leaders who sign an international treaty (or inherit a signed document from a previous administration) seem to play a critical role in carrying the agreement through to ratification and implementation. Finally, these arguments are consistent with foreign policy analysis literature recognizing the role of interest groups in world politics. Studies of the U.S. position toward the Kyoto Protocol, for example, emphasize the degree to which climate change responses would be costly and disruptive. Interest groups that opposed the protocol seized on the government's own Department of Energy report suggesting that the costs of implementation would range anywhere from $91 billion to $311 billion.[5] Industry representatives worked hard to oppose the Kyoto Protocol on the grounds that it would undermine the nation's (and their own) economic security.

Other conditions appear to be slightly less significant in treaty failures. For example, regime type seemed to be important in only two of the four cases of failure. While the rejections of the CTBT and Kyoto Protocol by the U.S. Congress were significant, the more centralized governments of France and Australia did not ensure ratification success. In only one case of ratification failure was there a positive alignment with public attitudes: French voters' rejection of the European Constitution. In all three other cases, the public offered its strong support for international cooperation but the government subsequently rejected the treaty.

In summary, national security concerns can derail international treaty ratification in spite of strong normative pressures. Treaty failure is not necessarily a function of regime type. In only two of four cases was there a presidential separation-of-powers system that led to failure (because of strong Senate opposition to the agreement). In the other two cases, the governments were much more centralized. Treaty failure does seem to have been influenced by interest group mobilization, as more groups mobilized against treaty passage in all four countries. And finally, treaty failure cannot often be blamed on the public. In three of four case studies, the public strongly supported international cooperation, yet the treaty was not forwarded for ratification.

IV. AREAS FOR FURTHER INVESTIGATION

This study yields several additional observations. First, case evidence suggests that federalism can play a hidden role in the ratification process in some democracies. Weaker federal systems sometimes empower states and provinces in some areas of foreign affairs, and they can become involved in international treaty negotiations, ratification, and implementation. Second, this work highlights the need for further comparative study of government efforts to address the "democratic deficit," links between ratification processes and outcomes, and the role of bicameralism in parliamentary review of treaties.

Federalism appears to have played a role in influencing ratification outcomes in several cases (Table 9.8). For example, in Canada the provinces are granted constitutional authority over key elements of environmental policy, dictating a role for them in the policy process. The 1867 Constitution Act of Canada (derived from the British North America Act) states that provincial legislatures "may exclusively make laws in relations to the exploration, development, conservation, and management of non-renewable natural resources." Subsequent reviews of the Canadian constitution have confirmed provincial jurisdiction over natural resources and the need for consultation in areas such

Table 9.8. Comparative political institutions

Australia	Canada	Germany	France	United States
Presidential vs. parliamentary				
Parliamentary (constitutional monarchy)	Parliamentary (constitutional monarchy)	Parliamentary	Mixed: presidential and parliamentary	Presidential
Unitary vs. federal				
Federal (weak)	Federal (strong)	Federal (strong)	Unitary	Federal (strong)

as agricultural policy.[6] As a result of this division of powers, Boileau con-
cludes "the Canadian federal government possesses no institutional recourse
to bind provinces to international agreements relating to the environment,
or any other matters under provincial jurisdiction. Provinces must voluntarily
declare their willingness to be bound by such agreements."[7] The constitutional
power of Canadian provinces in the policymaking process is further bolstered
by their relative economic power (such as Ontario and Quebec).

The Canadian federal government began formal consultations with
provinces on trade policy during the Tokyo Round of GATT negotiations in
the 1970s. This led to expanded consultations between federal and provincial
authorities during the Uruguay rounds as well as the preparation phase of the
FTA. As the free trade agenda expanded, the Canadian government reluctantly
acknowledged that more issues would likely fall under provincial jurisdiction.
The rift between federal and provincial government positions on Kyoto was
particularly salient because of the constitutional arrangement in Canada that
vests the provincial governments with authority over natural resources. The
federal government had negotiated a compromise with provincial leaders in
the buildup to the Kyoto Summit whereby they would only agree to reduce
emissions by 3 per cent. But the protocol actually committed Canada to a 6
per cent reduction, and provincial leaders warned that the deal was politically unacceptable. Nova Scotia Premier John Hamm said that his province's
economy might be "decimated" if Ottawa ratified the Kyoto Protocol without
consideration of provincial and sectoral needs.[8] Ontario's premier, Ernie Eves,
warned that his provincial government would simply refuse to implement
terms of the Kyoto Protocol without federal government compensation for
anticipated job losses and economic damage.

Federalism can also have an indirect effect on state behavior. For example,
the TEU represented one of the most comprehensive and significant reform
programs in the history of the European Community, and Chancellor Kohl
was keenly aware that ratification would require a broad base of support in
Germany. The success of the German delegation in the marathon negotiations
at Maastricht may have assured a German position of leadership in the Community, but it did not translate into significant domestic political clout back
in Bonn. The complexity of the ratification process increased exponentially
when the SPD leadership succeeded in converting consideration of the TEU
from the status of a treaty (requiring a simple majority in the *Bundestag*)
to a constitutional amendment (requiring a two-thirds majority vote in both
houses of parliament). Because the Social Democrats controlled a majority of
seats in the *Bundesrat* and *Länder* concerns dominated discourse in the chamber, the government automatically became dependent upon the opposition
for ratification of the TEU in 1992. Kohl had to modify the treaty to grant the

Länder more control over EU legislation and to grant the parliament a final say over monetary and currency union.

This study has also hinted at ways in which state and provincial actors are establishing more prominent roles in the processes of treaty negotiation and ratification. For example, the Australian government now regularly invites representatives of the states to be part of its official delegations in international negotiations; the U.S. Trade Representative and Department of Commerce engage in more regular dialogue with state legislators; and French provinces are asserting their right to participate in EU affairs.[9] While Australia has experienced fewer transnational linkages to foreign governments (in part because of its geographical isolation), countries like the United States and Germany have seen the dramatic proliferation of these types of exchanges. Duchacek has called this emerging pattern, "perforated sovereignties," in which noncentral governments interact increasingly with the counterparts and even heads of government in foreign countries.[10]

This study also seems to confirm arguments that there is a limited role for the general public in treaty-making processes across all political systems. This lack of engagement in what are often significant political commitments by central governments has led to a widespread perception of a "democratic deficit" in international treaty-making. These concerns have been expressed through civilized public discourse, academic conferences, and government studies over the last several decades. They are also raised in campaigns against treaties in referendums such as the recent Lisbon Treaty debate in Ireland. But at the extreme, concerns about a democratic deficit have fueled civil unrest and even violent protests at events such as the 1999 World Trade Organization talks in Seattle, Washington, and the Group of 8 summit in Germany in 2007.

Debates about a democratic deficit have occurred in all countries examined for this study, but they have been most acute in majoritarian parliamentary systems. Australia represents a fascinating case wherein the democratic deficit debate actually translated into specific treaty-making reforms. In the early 1990s there was a storm of public protest (stoked by academic discourse and media coverage) regarding the perception that the Labor governments had engaged in treaty development without careful public consultation. In 1995, the Senate Legal and Constitutional References Committee conducted a review of the treaty process that recommended a number of reforms.[11] These were quickly embraced by the newly elected Howard government in 1996. Changes included the establishment of a new Joint Standing Committee on Treaties (JSCOT), empowered to conduct inquiries on international treaties negotiated by the executive and to hold public hearings. Treaties also would be tabled in parliament for fifteen sitting days, providing legislators with a longer period for consideration of the issues at hand. In addition, the government would produce treaty impact statements that surveyed potential costs and benefits of the commitment. This revised treaty review process was in force throughout the period under study.

How has the JSCOT process fared? Today there remains a healthy debate about the role of the committee in the treaty development process in Australia. JSCOT has held hearings on dozens of major treaties over the past decade and does an impressive job of gathering serious attention to the process of treaty development. JSCOT allows parliamentarians and the public to have a say in the process by discussing their views of the potential benefits and costs to treaty implementation. However, the committee is also representative of the majoritarian control of committee proceedings and does not represent a fully representative body in terms of wide views on political issues. JSCOT is much more than a tool of the government, but it is far short of an effective, objective instrument in the treaty development process.

The perception of a democratic deficit extends beyond majoritarian systems. The German government confronted an interesting challenge in the buildup to its ratification of the EU constitution in 2005. Prior to the actual debate over the EU Constitution, there was a fascinating pre-debate focused on the instrument of ratification. In the buildup to the May 2005 final vote, opponents (and even some supporters) of the Constitution began to publicly call for Germany to adopt a referendum instrument for ratification of the Constitution. Finally, it should be noted that other democracies have implemented reforms to the treaty-making process. A parliamentary review in New Zealand led to greater democratization in the process, for example. During a national review of Constitutional framework in India, the government pledged to consider development of alternative models of treaty-making that would give a greater voice to the people. And left Liberal Party leaders in Canada made strides to increase the degree of communication between the federal government and the polity regarding international commitments.

Cases suggest that ratification outcomes also may be conditioned by bicameralism and divided government. Contemporary studies have suggested that bicameralism is allowing parliaments to become more active in governance regardless of the type of electoral system. Martin contends, for example, that the so-called 100-years of parliamentary decline thesis is not supported by the empirical evidence.[12] The emphasis on parliamentary passivity, therefore, is misplaced in real studies of active policymakers and processes. Comparative analyses of the Australian and New Zealand parliaments and Canadian parliament show that even in majortarian systems there may be a surprising amount of policy development underway in parliament (among both frontbenchers and backbenchers).[13] Sherman contends that issues like trade policy often divide legislators not according to party lines but rather perceive benefits and costs for their constituencies.[14] At a minimum, these works suggest that traditional distinctions between regime types may be fading as democratic regimes grappled with increasingly complex, intermestic issues.

Finally, the actual nature of the ratification mechanism is a subject worthy of greater scrutiny. Nowhere is this distribution more significant than in parliamentary democracies with referendum requirements for international cooperation. Once seen as exceptional events, referendums have become a normalized component of policymaking in some democracies.[15] For example, the Danish federal constitution provides power to referendums to approve or reject international treaties, and four major referendums have been held in Denmark on themes of European integration in the past two decades. The French model allows the president and prime minister to determine when a referendum may be in the best interests of the country. In some cases, different referendum requirements have made life more complicated for governments, parliaments, and political parties; in other cases they have been useful instruments to solve difficulties that these bodies seem unable or unwilling to tackle. Further empirical study of the relationship between the ratification mechanism and outcomes would be useful.

Looking Ahead: International Treaties in the Twenty-First Century

Ratification represents a crucial stage in international negotiation that is underrepresented in the literature. This study has shown that the ratification process may exhibit more similar than different dynamics around the world. Indeed, generalizations about factors such as regime type often obscure the degree of nuance in any process of ratification and marked similarities in political dynamics. The presidential system, exemplified in this book in the United States (pure form) and France (mixed form) provides multiple avenues for policy influence. In the Westminster systems of Canada and Australia, there remains the potential for differences over key elements of legislation. Australia's bicameral system creates an institutional framework within which leaders of the opposition can gain control of the upper house of parliament, the Senate, and significantly impede legislation. Without careful policy management and openness between the executive and legislature, major international agreements may not receive endorsement in the form of enabling legislation. A similar dynamic exists in the German parliamentary system, where the upper and lower houses of parliament may see different working majorities. Indeed, the proportional representation system enables a degree of strength for the opposition at any given point in the legislative cycle.

Recent controversies raise the question of whether the twenty-first century will see a decline in the use of large-scale international treaties as instruments of diplomacy. This is not idle speculation. For example, a survey by Robyn Eckersley suggests that U.S. leadership on global environmental concerns tends to wane in correlations with the intensity of the problem. The study identifies a growing proportion of environmental treaties that had been signed but not ratified by the United States government. In the period from 1970 to 1991, three of thirteen treaties had not been ratified; but from 1992 to 2007, seven of ten major environmental treaties had not been ratified by the United States. Non-ratified agreements address a range of concerns, from the Kyoto Protocol to the 1972 London Convention on Ocean Dumping to the 2001 Stockholm Convention on Persistent Organic Pollutants. Eckersley argues that it appears the United States "will not enter into an environmental treaty if it is incompatible with domestic regulations or if it is shown that existing domestic regulations cannot easily be changed without significant backlash."[16] In a similar vein, former Vice President Al Gore cautions that "the Kyoto protocol has been so demonized in the United States that it probably cannot be ratified—much in the way the Carter administration was prevented from winning ratification of an expanded strategic arms limitation treaty in 1979."[17]

Global trade policy is also at a crossroads. The hurdle of ratification may be influencing progress in the negotiations of the Doha Round of trade talks sponsored by the World Trade Organization. Government leaders had high hopes for this latest round of international negotiations begun in 2001 to lower tariff barriers to trade. Some called this a "development round" that would focus primarily on narrowing the gap between developed and developing countries around the world. At this writing, however, the WTO talks are on "life support."[18] Negotiations have stalled on significant issues that cut across differences between wealthy countries, between developed and developing states, and even among developing states themselves.

Facing continuing problems with multilateral agreements, some countries have scaled back or watered down treaties to fit existing constraints while others have turned to bilateral deals that they believe can produce more immediate and effective results. For example, the EU Amsterdam Treaty of 1999 was designed to expand coordination of policies in areas including employment, the environment, and justice and home affairs. Experts note that ratification of this treaty "hardly stirred the public's attention in the member states," especially as compared to the process of the Maastricht Treaty. In fact, government negotiators were mindful of potential Level II constraints throughout the negotiating process—circulating draft proposals widely inside and outside governments, approaching the issues in a cautious way through intergovernmental conferences, and paring the list down in the face of serious domestic obstacles. Experts conclude that the ease of ratification of the Amsterdam Treaty was "probably not unrelated to [its] considerably less ambitious nature."[19]

At the same time, governments appear to be turning toward bilateral agreements. For example, Australia completed a significant joint security framework with Indonesia in 2006 as well as bilateral agreements with India and Russia for the export of uranium. France maintains lucrative security framework deals with many North African countries. And under fast-track authority from 2001 to 2007, the Bush administration signed several bilateral trade deals. For example, the 2007 Korean Free Trade Agreement (KFTA) treaty promised $100 million in liberalized trade between the United States and South Korea (ranking it as the second largest free trade deal in U.S. history behind the NAFTA). The administration also negotiated bilateral trade deals with Colombia, Panama, and Peru.

In summary, the future of international treaties is unclear. This study has begun to yield insights into the role of key actors and conditions in ratification processes in advanced industrialized democracies. It has shown that domestic political controversies over treaties have profound implications for international cooperation. Given the imperative of addressing serious global problems such as environmental degradation, economic inequality, weapons proliferation, and human rights abuses, it is hoped that this work will serve as a springboard for further investigations of treaty ratification struggles in comparative perspective.

NOTES

1. See Kal Raustiala, "Domestic Institutions and International Regulatory Cooperation: Comparative Responses to the Convention on Biological Diversity," *World Politics*, vol. 49, no. 4 (1997), p. 487; Detlef Sprinz and Tapani Vaahtoranta, "The Interest-Based Explanation of International Environmental Policy," *International Organization*, vol. 48, no. 1 (Winter 1994).

2. For an interesting discussion of this perspective, see Barbara Crossette, "Washington is Criticized for Growing Reluctance to Sign Treaties," *New York Times* (April 4, 2002), p. A1.

3. Cases in which prevailing conditions and the ratification outcomes were aligned did not necessarily mean that cooperation was the final outcome (e.g., U.S. nonratification of the Kyoto Protocol).

4. Nader, quoted in Helen V. Milner and B. Peter Rosendorff, "Democratic Politics and International Trade Negotiations: Elections and Divided Government as

Constraints on Trade Liberalization," *Journal of Conflict Resolution*, vol. 41, no. 1 (1997), p. 121.

5. Department of Energy, "Comparing the Cost Estimates for the Kyoto Protocol," Report No. SR/OIA/98-03 (1998). http://www.eia.doe.gov/oiaf/kyoto/cost.html (accessed June 2, 2005).

6. The exact opposite pattern has emerged in Australia. There the courts have consistently ruled in favor of the federal government's authority over matters that might traditionally be associated with the states (especially environmental and resource management issues).

7. Guy Boileau, "The Interplay Between Domestic Institutions and International Negotiations: A Case of the North American Agreement on Environmental Cooperation," Master's Thesis (Ottawa: The Norman Paterson School of International Affairs, Carleton University, 2001), p. 32.

8. Hamm, quoted in *National Post* (October 10, 2002), p. A1.

9. In 1992 the Australian prime minister and state premiers established the Council of Australian Governments (COAG), a new forum for intergovernmental policy coordination; see Henry Burmester, "Federalism, the States, and International Affairs: A Legal Perspective," in Brian Galligan, ed., *Australian Federalism* (Melbourne: Longman Cheshire 1989); John Trone, *Federal Constitutions and International Relations* (Brisbane: University of Queensland Press 2001); John Ravenhill, "Australia," in Hans J. Michelmann and Panayotis Soldatos, eds., *Federalism and International Relations* (Oxford: Clarendon Press, 1990).

10. Ivo Duchacek, "Perforated Sovereignties: Towards a Typology of New Actors in International Relations," in Hans J. Michelmann and Panayotis Soldatos, eds., *Federalism and International Relations* (Oxford: Clarendon Press, 1990) pp. 1–33.

11. Commonwealth of Australia, Senate Legal and Constitutional References Committee, Parliament of Australia, *Trick or Treaty? Commonwealth Power to Make and Implement Treaties* (Canberra: Government Printing Office, 1995), pp. 300–5.

12. John Uhr, "Bicameralism," in A.W. Rhodes, Sarah A. Binder, and Bert A. Rockman, eds., *The Oxford Handbook of Political Institutions*, pp. 474–94 (Oxford: Oxford University Press, 2006).

13. See Tapio Raunio and Simon Hix, "Backbenchers Learn to Fight Back: European Integration and Parliamentary Government," *West European Politics* 23 (2001), pp. 142–68; Elizabeth McLeay and John Uhr, "The Australian and New Zealand Parliaments: Context, Response and Capacity," *Australian Journal of Political Science*, vol. 41, no. 2 (June 2006), pp. 257–72.

14. See Alberto Alesina and Howard Rosenthal, *Partisan Politics, Divided Government, and the Economy* (New York: Cambridge University Press, 1995); Michael Bailey, Judith Goldstein, and Barry R. Weingast, "The Institutional Roots of American Trade Policy: Politics, Coalitions, and International Trade," *World Politics*, vol. 49 (1997), pp. 309–38.

15. See David Butler and Austin Ranney, eds., *Referendums: A Comparative Study of Practice and Theory* (Washington DC: American Enterprise Institute, 1994).

16. Robyn Eckersley, "The Environment," in Michael Cox and Douglas Stokes, ed., *American Foreign Policy* (Oxford: Oxford University Press, 2008), p. 20.

17. Al Gore, "Moving Beyond Kyoto," *New York Times* (July 1, 2007), p. 13.

18. Steven R. Weisman, "After Six Years, the Global Trade Talks Are Just That: Talk," *New York Times* (July 21, 2007), p. B1.

19. Simon Hug and Thomas Koenig, "In View of Ratification: Governmental Preferences and Domestic Constraints at the Amsterdam Intergovernmental Conference," *International Organization*, vol. 56, no. 2 (2002), pp. 447–76.

Bibliography

Government Documents

Bundesministerium für Umwelt, Naturschutz und Reaktorsicherheit. 1990. "Bericht des Bundesministers für Umwelt, Naturschutz und Reaktorsicherheit zur Reduzierung der CO_2-Emissionen in der bundesrepublik Deutschland zum jahr 2005: Erster Bericht auf der Grundlage des Beschlusses der Bundesregierung zu Zielvorstellungen fuer eine erreichbare Reduktion der CO_2 Emissionen." Bonn: Federal Environment Ministry (June 13).

Commonwealth of Australia. 1995. Senate Legal and Constitutional References Committee. "Trick or Treaty? Commonwealth Power to Make and Implement Treaties." Canberra: Government Printing Office.

—— 1998. "National Interest Analysis: Comprehensive Nuclear Test-ban Treaty." www.austlii.edu.au/au/other/dfat/nia/1998/17.html (accessed March 2, 2006).

—— 1998. Parliament. Joint Standing Committee on Treaties. "Report #15." Canberra: Government Printing Office (June).

—— 2002. "Australian Bureau of Statistics Report 5422" (December Quarter).

—— 2002. Prime Minister John Howard. *Hansard: Commonwealth Parliament Debates* (June 5): 3163.

—— 2003. Department of Foreign Affairs and Trade. "Submission to the Senate Foreign Affairs, Defence and Trade Committee Inquiry into the General Agreement on Trade in Services and Australia/US Free Trade Agreement." Canberra: Government Printing Office.

—— 2003. Minister for Trade Mark Vaile, Department of Foreign Affairs and Trade, Submission 54. Joint Standing Committee on Treaties. Canberra: Department of Foreign Affairs and Trade (March 3).

—— 2003. Senate Foreign Affairs, Defence and Trade References Committee. "Voting on Trade: The General Agreement on Trade in Services and an Australia-US Free Trade Agreement." Canberra: Government Printing Office.

—— 2004. Australian Dairy Industry Council Inc. "Submission to the Joint Standing Committee on Treaties Inquiry into the Australia US Free Trade Agreement (USFTA)." #19 (April 8).

—— 2004. Business Council of Australia, "Submission to the Joint Standing Committee on Treaties Inquiry into the Australia US Free Trade Agreement (USFTA)." #132 (April 19).

—— 2004. Parliament. "Report 61: The Australia-United States Free Trade Agreement." Canberra: Government Printing Office (June).

—— 2004. Richard Denniss and Dr. Clive Hamilton, The Australia Institute, Patricia Ranald and Louise Southalan, Australian Fair Trade and Investment Network.

"Submission to the Joint Standing Committee on Treaties Inquiry into the Australia US Free Trade Agreement (USFTA)" (April).

—— 2006. "Uranium Mining, Processing, and Nuclear Energy—Opportunities for Australia?" Canberra: Government Printing Office.

—— 2006. Department of Foreign Affairs and Trade. *Free Trade Agreements.* www.dfat.gov.au/trade/ftas.html (accessed November 1, 2006).

—— 2006. Joint Standing Committee on Treaties. "Treaty Scrutiny: A 10-Year Review," Joint Standing Committee on Treaties. Proof Committee *Hansard.* Canberra: Government Printing Office (March 31).

—— 2006. Parliament. Joint Standing Committee on Treaties. "Treaty Scrutiny: A Ten Year Review, Report #78." Canberra: Government Printing Office.

Department of Foreign Affairs and Trade, *Free Trade Agreements* (2005), www.dfat.gov.au/trade/ftas.html (accessed November 1, 2006).

Deutscher Bundestag. 2005. *Stenografischer Bericht.* 175. Sitzung, Berlin (Donnerstag, den 12. Mai 2005). Plenarprotokoll 15/175:16347–98.

European Commission. 1994. *Eurobarometer: Trends, 1974–1994.* Luxembourg: European Communities.

—— 1995. "Conclusions of the Presidency, Madrid, December 15–16, 1995," *Bulletin of the European Union*, no. 12. Luxembourg: European Communities.

—— 1995. "Conclusions of the Presidency." *Bulletin of the European Union*, no. 12 (15–16 December). Luxembourg: European Communities.

—— 1995. *Intergovernmental Conference 1996: Commission Report for the Reflection Group.* Brussels, Belgium: European Communities.

—— 1996. *Eurobarometer: Top Decision Makers Survey: Summary Report.* Brussels.

European Parliament. 2002. "Report on the Proposal for a Council Decision Concerning the Conclusion, on Behalf of the European Community, of the Kyoto Protocol to the United Nations Framework Convention on Climate Change and the Joint Fulfillment of Commitments Thereunder." A5-0025/2002.

Government of Canada. 1964. Department of National Defence (DND). *White Paper on Defence.* Ottawa: Queen's Printer for Canada.

—— 1983. "Department of External Affairs, A Review of Canadian Trade Policy and Canadian Trade Policy for the 1980s: A Discussion Paper." Ottawa: Supply and Services.

—— 1985. Ministry of Industry, Trade and Technology, Government of Ontario. "Background Paper: Assessment of Direct Employment Effects of Freer Trade for Ontario's Manufacturing Industries; Annual First Ministers' Conference, Halifax, Nova Scotia" (November 28–9).

—— 1999. Department of Foreign Affairs and International Trade. "Government Statement: Nuclear Disarmament and Non-Proliferation: Advancing Canadian Objectives, April 1999." Ottawa: Queen's Printer.

The White House. 1999. Office of the Press Secretary. *Statement of the President* (October 13).

—— 2004. President George W. Bush. *Weekly Compilation of Presidential Documents* (August 3): 1429–31.

United States Congress. 2001. Congressional Research Service. "Treaties and Other International Agreements: The Role of the U.S. Senate." Washington DC: Library of Congress.

United States Department of Energy. 1998. "Comparing the Cost Estimates for the Kyoto Protocol." Report #SR/OIA/98-03. http://www.eia.doe.gov/oiaf/kyoto/cost.html (accessed February 18, 2005).

United States Department of State. 1998. "Text of the Comprehensive Nuclear Test-Ban Treaty." www.state.gov/t/np/trty/16513.htm (accessed May 18, 2004).

United States House of Representatives. 1992. Committee on Small Business. "The North American Free Trade Agreement." Y4.SM1:102–190 (September 18).

—— 1993. Committee on Energy and Commerce, Subcommittee on Commerce, Consumer Protection and Competitiveness. "North American Free Trade Agreement." Y4.En2/3:103–10 (February 18).

—— 1998. "Oversight Hearing on the Kyoto Protocol: The Undermining of American Prosperity: Hearing before the Committee on Small Business." House of Representatives. 105th Congress (June 4). Washington DC: U.S. Government Printing Office.

—— 1998. The Kyoto Protocol and its Economic Implications: Hearing before the Subcommittee on Energy and Power of the Committee on Commerce, House of Representatives, 105th Congress, 4 March. Washington DC: U.S. Government Printing Office.

—— 1999. "Road from Kyoto." Hearing before the Committee on Science. U.S. House of Representatives. 105th Congress. Washington DC: U.S. Government Printing Office.

—— 1999. "The Kyoto Protocol: Is the Clinton–Gore Administration Selling Out Americans?" Parts I–VI. Hearing before the Subcommittee on National Economic Growth, Natural Resources, and Regulatory Affairs of the Committee on Government Reform and Oversight. 105th Congress (April 23, May 19, May 20, May 24, June 24, July 15, September 16). Washington DC: U.S. Government Printing Office.

United States Senate. 1997. "Senate Resolution 98—Expressing the Sense of the Senate Regarding the United Nations Framework Convention on Climate Change." *Congressional Record* (June 12).

—— 1999. Economic Impacts of the Kyoto Protocol: Hearing before the Committee on Energy and Natural Resources, United States Senate. 106th Congress. 25 March. Washington DC: U.S. Government Printing Office.

—— 2004. Committee on Finance. "United States-Australia Free Trade Agreement Implementation Act." 108th Congress. 2nd Session #108-316 (August 25, 2004).

Wissenschaftliche Dienste des Deutschen Bundestages. 2004. "Die Ratifikation des Vertrags über eine Verfassung für Europa." 36 (November 12).

Interviews

Michael Bliss
Anthony Burke

Ann Capling
Hilary Charlesworth
Madelaine Chiam
Allastair Cox
Michael Dawson
Mark Diesendorf
Bruce Doern
George Dracoulis
Robyn Eckersley
Trevor Findlay
Chad Gaffield
Brian Galligan
David Goetz
Clive Hamilton
Michael Hart
Mark Hibbs
Greg Hunt
William Jarvis
Karl-Heinz Kamp
Karl Kaiser
Joachim Krause
Robert Lawson
Ian Lowe
David Mason
Bryan Mercurio
Christine Milne
Kathy Morton
Henry Molot
Maureen Appel Molot
Brendan O'Connor
James Reese
James Reiskind
Jean Riopel
Don Rothwell
Jacek Rulkowski
Stephan Schott
Stephen Smith
Andrew Southcott
Ziggy Switkowski
Brian Tomlin
Anne Twomey
John Uhr
Kim Wilkie

Secondary Sources

ACIL Consulting Pty. Ltd. 2003. *A Bridge Too Far? An Australian Agricultural Perspective on the Australia/United States Free Trade Area Idea*. Canberra: ACIL Consulting and Australian Rural Industries Research and Development Corporation.

Aeschimann, Eric and Pascal Riché. 1996. *La guerre de sept ans: Histoire secrete du franc fort, 1989–1996*. Paris: Calmann-Lévy.

Alesina, Alberto and Howard Rosenthal. 1995. *Partisan Politics, Divided Government, and the Economy*. New York: Cambridge University Press.

Allen Consulting. 2000. *Greenhouse Emissions Trading*. Melbourne, Australia.

Alston, Philip and Madelaine Chiam. 1995. *Treaty-Making and Australia: Globalisation Versus Sovereignty*. Canberra: Federation Press.

Andersen, Mikael Shou and Duncan Liefferink, eds. 1997. *European Environmental Policy: The Pioneers, Issues in Environmental Politics*. Manchester: Manchester University Press.

Andrews, William G. 1982. *Presidential Government in Gaullist France*. Albany: SUNY Press.

Appleton, Andrew. 2000. "The New Social Movement Phenomenon: Placing France in Comparative Perspective." In *The Changing French Political System*, ed. Robert Elgie. London: Frank Cass, 57–75.

Audley, John J. 1997. *Green Politics and Global Trade: NAFTA and the Future of Environmental Politics*. Washington DC: Georgetown University Press.

Auerswald, David. 2002. *Policymaking Through Advice and Consent: Treaty Consideration by the United States Senate*. New Orleans, LA: Annual Meeting of the International Studies Association (March 25).

Australian Broadcasting Corporation. "Australian Government Forces Its Position at Climate Summit." www.abc.net.au/news/features/kyoto/default.htm (accessed March 28, 2007).

—— "Chronology: Australia's Nuclear Political History." www.abc.net.au/4corners/content/2005/20050822_nuclear/nuclear-chronology.htm (accessed April 28, 2007).

—— "The Greenhouse Mafia." www.abc.net.au/4corners/content/2006/s1566257.htm (accessed April 26, 2007).

Australian APEC Study Center. 2001. *An Australia-USA Free Trade Agreement: Issues and Implications*. Melbourne: Monash University.

Avery, William P. 1998. "Domestic Interests in NAFTA Bargaining." *Political Science Quarterly* 113(2): 281–305.

Bailey, Kathleen C. 1999. "The Comprehensive Test Ban Treaty: The Costs Outweigh the Benefits." Policy Analysis No. 330. Washington DC: Cato Institute (January 15).

Bailey, Michael, Judith Goldstein, and Barry R. Weingast. 1997. "The Institutional Roots of American Trade Policy: Politics, Coalitions, and International Trade," *World Politics* 49(3): 309–38.

Banchoff, Thomas. 1999. "Germany Identity and European Integration." *European Journal of International Relations* 5(3): 259–89.

Barrett, Scott. 1998. "Political Economy of the Kyoto Protocol." *Oxford Review of Economic Policy* 14(4): 20–39.

Baun, Michael J. 1995. "The Maastricht Treaty as High Politics: Germany, France, and European Integration." *Political Science Quarterly* 110(4): 605–24.

Bell, David S. and Byron Criddle. 2002. "Presidentialism Restored: The French Elections of April-May and June 2002." *Parliamentary Affairs* 55(4): 643–63.

Bellany, Ian. 1972. *Australia in the Nuclear Age.* Sydney: Sydney University Press.

Bergman, Brian. 2002. "The Cost of Kyoto: How Far Are Canadians Willing to Go to Help Prevent Global Warming?" *Maclean's* 115: 38–9.

Bernstein, Steven. 2002. "International Institutions and the Framing of Domestic Policies: The Kyoto Protocol and Canada's Response to Climate Change." *Policy Sciences* 35(2): 203–36.

—— 2001. *The Compromise of Liberal Environmentalism.* New York: Columbia University Press.

Beuermann, Christiane and Jill Jäger. 1996. "Climate Change Politics in Germany: How Long Will Any Double Dividend Last?" In *The Politics of Climate Change: A European Perspective*, eds. Timothy O'Riordan and Jill Jager. New York: Routledge, 186–227.

Beuter, Rita. 1994. "Germany and the Ratification of the Maastricht Treaty." In *The Ratification of the Maastricht Treaty: Issues, Debates, and Future Implications*, eds. Finn Laursen and Sophie Vanhoonacker. London: Martinus Nijhoff Publishers, 87–112.

Body, A.H. "Australian Treaty Making Practice and Procedure," in D.P. O'Connell, ed., *International Law in Australia* (Sydney: Law Book Co., 1965).

Boileau, Guy. 2001. "The Interplay Between Domestic Institutions and International Negotiations: A Case of the North American Agreement on Environmental Cooperation." Master's Thesis. Ottawa, Ontario: The Norman Paterson School of International Affairs, Carleton University.

Bratt, Duane. 2002. "Canada's Nuclear Schizophrenia." *Bulletin of the Atomic Scientists* 58(2): 45–50.

Brechen, Steven R. 2003. "Comparative Public Opinion and Knowledge on Global Climate Change and the Kyoto Protocol: The U.S. Versus the World?" *International Journal of Sociology and Social Policy* 23(10): 106–43.

Breidenrich, Claire, Daniel Magraw, Anne Rowley, and James W. Rubin. 1998. "The Kyoto Protocol to the United Nations Framework Convention on Climate Change." *American Journal of International Law* 92(2): 315–31.

Britton, Andrew and David Mayes. 1992. *Achieving Monetary Union in Europe.* London: National Institute of Economic and Social Research.

Broadhead, Lee-Anne. 2001. "Canada as a Rogue State: Its Shameful Performance on Climate Change." *International Journal* 56(3): 461–80.

Broinowski, Richard. 2003. *Fact or Fission? The Truth About Australia's Nuclear Ambitions.* Carlton North, Victoria, Australia: Scribe Publications.

Buckley, Brian. 2000. *Canada's Early Nuclear Policy: Fate, Chance, and Character*. Montreal and Kingston: McGill-Queens.

Bulkeley, Harriet. 2000. "The Formation of Australian Climate Change Policy: 1985–1995." In *Climate Change in the South Pacific*, eds. Alexander Gillespie and William C. G. Burns. Boston: Kluwer Academic Publishers, 33–50.

Burmester, Henry. 1989. "Federalism, the States, and International Affairs: A Legal Perspective." In *Australian Federalism*, ed. Brian Galligan. Melbourne: Longman Cheshire.

Butler, David and Austin Ranney, eds. 1978. *Referendums: A Comparative Study of Practice and Theory*. Washington DC: American Enterprise Institute.

Caldwell, Lynton Keith. 1996. *International Environmental Policy: From the 20th Century to the 21st Century*. Durham, NC: Duke University Press.

Cameron, David R. 1996. "National Interests, the Dilemmas of European Integration, and Malaise." In *Chirac's Challenge: Liberalization, Europeanization, and Malaise*, eds. John T. S. Keller and Martin A. Schain. New York: St. Martin's Press, 325–82.

—— 1992. "The 1992 Initiative: Causes and Consequences." In *Euro-Politics: Institutions and Policymaking in the "New" European Community*, ed. Alberta M. Sbragia. Washington DC: The Brookings Institution, 23–74.

Cameron, Maxwell and Brian W. Tomlin. 2000. *The Making of NAFTA: How the Deal Was Done*. London: Cornell University Press.

Cameron, Peter D. and Donald Zillman, eds. 2001. *Kyoto: From Principles to Practice*. The Hague: Kluwer Law International.

Campbell, Edwina S. 1994. "United Germany in a Uniting Europe." In *Germany in a New Era*, ed., Gary L. Geipel. Indianapolis, IN: Hudson Institute, 81–110.

Capling, Ann. 2005. "Can the Democratic Deficit in Treaty-Making Be Overcome? Parliament and the Australia-United States Free Trade Agreement." In *The Fluid State: International Law and National Legal Systems*, eds. Hilary Charlesworth, Madelaine Chiam, Devika Hovell, and George Williams. Sydney: Federation Press, 70–94.

—— 2005. *All the Way with the USA: Australia, the US and Free Trade*. Sydney: UNSW Press.

—— and Kim Richard Nossal. 2003. "Parliament and the Democratization of Foreign Policy: The Case of Australia's Joint Standing Committee on Treaties." *Canadian Journal of Political Science* 36(4): 835–55.

Carter, Ralph G. 1998. "Congress and Post-Cold War U.S. Foreign Policy." In *After the End: Making U.S. Foreign Policy in the Post-Cold War World*, ed. James M. Scott. Durham, NC: Duke University Press, 108–37.

Cass, Loren Ray. 2001. "The Politics of Climate Change: The Origins and Development of Climate Policy in the United Kingdom, Germany, and the United States." Doctoral Dissertation. Brandeis University.

Centre for International Economics. 2004. *Economic Analysis of AUSFTA: Impact of the Bilateral Free Trade Agreement with the United States*. Report Prepared for the Department of Foreign Affairs and Trade. Canberra: Centre for International Economics (April).

Charlesworth, Hilary, Madelaine Chiam, Devika Hovell, and George Williams. 2003. "Deep Anxieties: Australia and the International Legal Order." *Sydney Law Review* 25(4): 424–65.

———————— 2006. *No Country Is an Island: Australia and International Law.* Sydney: University of New South Wales Press.

Chasek, Pamela S. 2001. *Earth Negotiations: Analyzing Thirty Years of Environmental Diplomacy.* New York: United Nations University Press.

Checkel, Jeffrey T. 1998. "Norms, Institutions and National Identity in Contemporary Europe." Arena Working Paper 98/16. Oslo: Advanced Research on the Europeanisation of the Nation-State. Oslo, Norway: University of Oslo.

——— 1999. "Norms, Institutions, and National Identity in Contemporary Europe." *International Studies Quarterly* 43(1): 83–114.

Ching-Cheng, Chang, Robert Mendelsohn, and Daigee Shaw. 2003. *Global Warming and the Asian Pacific.* Cheltenham, UK: Edward Elgar.

Clearwater, John. 1998. *Canadian Nuclear Weapons: The Untold Story of Canada's Cold War Arsenal.* Toronto: Dundurn.

Climate Action Network Europe. 2003. Brussels, Belgium. www.climnet.org/EUenergy/ratification/calendar.htm (accessed July 14, 2003).

——— 2006. "European Climate Change Programme," www.climnet.org/euenergy/ECCP.html (accessed October 20, 2006).

Collina, Tom Z. and Christopher Paine. 1999. "Test Ban Treaty: Let's Finish the Job." *Bulletin of the Atomic Scientists* 55(4): 24–7.

Collins, Hugh. 1983. "Political Factors." In *Australia's External Relations in the 1980s: The Interaction of Economic, Political and Strategic Factors*, ed. Paul Dibb. Canberra: Croom Helm.

Cooper, Andrew F. 2000. "Waiting at the Perimeter: Making US Policy in Canada." In *Canada Among Nations 2000: Vanishing Borders*, eds. Maureen Appel Molot and Fen Osler Hampson. Don Mills, Ontario: Oxford University Press.

Craven, Greg. 1993. "Federal Constitutions and External Relations." In *Foreign Relations and Federal States*, ed. Brian Hocking. New York: Leicester University Press.

Croft, Stuart. 1996. "European Integration, Nuclear Deterrence and Franco-British Nuclear Cooperation." *International Affairs* 72(4): 771–87.

Davies, Peter G.G. 2001. "Climate Change and the European Community." In *Kyoto: From Principles to Practice, International Environmental Law and Policy Series*, eds. Peter D. Cameron and Donald Zillman. The Hague: Kluwer Law International, 27–38.

Dawkins, Peter and Paul Kelly, eds. 2003. *Hard Heads, Soft Hearts: A New Reform Agenda for Australia.* Crows Nest, NSW: Allen & Unwin.

"Debatte des Deutschen Bundestages am 8. Oktober 1992 ueber die Ratifizierung des Maastrichter Vertrages." 1992. *Das Parlament* 44 (October 23).

Deibel, Terry. 2002. "The Death of a Treaty." *Foreign Affairs* 81(5): 142–61.

Delaet, James C., Charles M. Rowling, and James M. Scott. 2005. "Politics Past the Edge: Partisanship and Arms Control Treaties in the U.S. Senate." *Journal of Political and Military Sociology* 33(2): 179–207.

Department of Justice Canada. 2001. *A Consolidation of The Constitutional Acts, 1867–1982* (January 1).

DeSombre, Elizabeth R. 2000. *Domestic Sources of International Environmental Policy: Industry, Environmentalists, and U.S. Power.* Cambridge, MA: MIT Press.

Destler, Irving M. 1992. *American Trade Politics*, Second edition. Washington DC: Institute for International Economics with the Twentieth Century Fund.

Diesendorf, Mark. 2002. "A Critique of the Australian Government's Greenhouse Policies." In *Climate Change in the South Pacific: Impacts and Responses in Australia, New Zealand, and Small Island State*, eds. Alexander Gillespie and William C.G. Burns. Dordrecht, Netherlands: Kluwer Academic Publishers, 79–93.

Doern, G. Bruce and Brian W. Tomlin. 1991. *Faith and Fear: The Free Trade Story*. Toronto: Stoddart.

—— 2002. "Seven Key Issues and Challenges: Canadian Energy Policy in the Sustainable Development Era." Carleton Research Unit on Innovation, Science, and the Environment (CRUISE) Conference on Canadian Energy Policy in the Sustainable Development Era. October 17.

Dokumentation zur Abrüstung und Sicherheit (Documentation on Disarmament and Security). 1996. Bonn: Siegler.

Dunlap, Riley E., George H. Gallup, and Alec M. Gallup. 2002. "Health of the Planet Survey: A George H. Memorial Survey." Princeton, NJ: Gallup International Institute.

Duchacek, Ivo. 1990. "Perforated Sovereignties: Towards a Typology of New Actors in International Relations." In *Federalism and International Relations*, eds. Hans J. Michelmann and Panayotis Soldatos. Oxford: Clarendon Press, 1–33.

Eckersley, Robyn. 2008. "The Environment." In *American Foreign Policy*, eds. Michael Cox and Douglas Stokes. Oxford: Oxford University Press, 42–71.

Eckstein, Harry. 1975. "Case Studies and Theory in Political Science." In *Handbook of Political Science*, eds. Fred Greenstein and Nelson Polsby. Reading, MA: Addison-Wesley, 79–138.

Ehrmann, Henry and Martin A. Schain. 1992. *Politics in France*, Fifth edition. New York: HarperCollins.

Eichenberg, Richard C. 1993. "Dual Track and Double Trouble: The Two-Level Politics of INF." In *Double Edged Diplomacy: International Bargaining and Domestic Politics*, eds. Peter B. Evans, Harold K. Jacobson, and Robert D. Putnam. Berkeley, CA: University of California Press, 45–76.

EKOS Research Associates Inc. 2003. *Canadian Attitudes Toward Climate Change: Spring 2003 Tracking Study. Final Report*. March.

Epstein, David and Sharyn O'Halloran. 1994. "Administrative Procedures, Information, and Agency Discretion." *American Journal of Political Science* 38(3): 697–722.

Evans, Peter B. 1993. "Building an Integrative Approach to International Domestic Politics: Reflections and Projections. In *International Bargaining and Domestic Politics*, eds. Peter B. Evans, Harold K. Jacobson, and Robert D. Putnam. Berkeley, CA: University of California Press, 397–430.

——Jacobson, Harold K., and Robert D. Putnam, eds. 1993. *Double-Edged Diplomacy: International Bargaining and Domestic Politics*. Berkeley, CA: University of California Press.

Faux, Jeff and Thea Lee. 1992. *The Effect of George Bush's NAFTA on American Workers: Ladder Up or Ladder Down*. Washington DC: Economic Policy Institute.

Fearon, James D. 1994. "Domestic Political Audiences and the Escalation of International Disputes." *American Political Science Review* 88(1): 577–92.

Federal News Service. 1993. "News Conference Concerning NAFTA with Various Anti NAFTA Groups." Federal News Service, Federal Information Systems Corporation (November 18).

Finnemore, Martha. 1996. "Norms, Culture, and World Politics: Insights from Sociology's Institutionalism." *International Organization* 50(2): 325–47.

——and Kathryn Sikkink. 1998. "International Norm Dynamics and Political Change." *International Organization* 52(4): 887–917.

Fiorina, Morris P. 1992. *Divided Government*. New York: Macmillan.

Fisher, Dana R. 2003. "Global and Domestic Actors Within the Global Climate Change Regime: Toward a Theory of the Global Environmental System." *International Journal of Sociology and Social Policy* 23(10): 5–30.

Foreign Broadcast Information Service [FBIS]. 1995. "President Chirac Holds News Conference in Paris." Paris France-2 Television Network. FBIS-WEU-95-136 (July 17): 14.

——1992. "Mitterrand Supports Referendum Despite Risks," in Paris Antenne-2 Television Network (in French)." FBIS-WEU-92-110 (June 8).

——1992. "Prime Minister on Maastricht Referendum." FBIS-WEU-932-109 (January 8).

——1993. "EC Might Impose Minimum Prices on Fresh Fish Imports." in Paris AFP 12:55 GMT. FBIS-WEU-93-036 (February 23).

——1993. "Protests Against Cheap Seafood Imports Turn Violent." FBIS-WEU-93-051 (March 17).

——1992. "Poll: 69% For." FBIS-WEU-92-108 (June 4).

Fox, Annette Baker. 1995. "Environment and Trade: the NAFTA Case." *Political Science Quarterly* 110(1): 49–68.

Friend, Julius W. 2001. *Unequal Partners: French-German Relations, 1989–2000*. The Washington Papers 180. Washington DC: Center for Strategic and International Studies.

Friman, H. Richard. 1993. "Side-Payments Versus Security Cards: Domestic Bargaining Tactics in International Economic Negotiations." *International Organization* 47(3): 387–410.

George, Alexander L. 1979. "Case Studies and Theory Development: The Method of Structured, Focused Comparison." In *Diplomacy: New Approaches in History, Theory, and Practice*, ed. Paul Gordon Lauren. New York: Free Press, 43–68.

——and Andrew Bennett. 2004. *Case Studies and Theory Development in the Social Sciences*. Cambridge, MA: MIT Press.

Glennon, Michael. 1991. "The Constitutional Power of the United States Senate to Condition Its Consent to Treaties." *Chicago-Kent Law Review* 67: 533–70.

Goldstein, Avery. 2000. *Deterrence and Security in the 21st Century: China, Britain, France, and the Enduring Legacy of the Nuclear Revolution.* Stanford, CA: Stanford University Press.

Gordon, Philip H. 1993. *A Certain Idea of France: French Security Policy and the Gaullist Legacy.* Princeton, NJ: Princeton University Press.

Graham, Thomas and Damien J. La Vera. 2002. "Nuclear Weapons: The Comprehensive Test Ban Treaty and National Missile Defense." In *Multilateralism and U.S. Foreign Policy: Ambivalent Engagement,* eds. Stewart Patrick and Shepard Forman. Boulder, CO: Lynne Rienner, 225–46.

Greenspon, Edward and Anthony Wilson-Smith. 1996. *Double Vision: The Inside Story of the Liberals in Power.* Toronto: Doubleday.

Grieco, Joseph. 2001. "Anarchy and the Limits of Cooperation: A Realist Critique of the Newest Liberal Institutionalism." *International Organization* 43(3): 485–507.

Gulbrandsen, Lars H. and Steinar Andresen. 2004. "NGO Influence in the Implementation of the Kyoto Protocol: Compliance, Flexibility Mechanisms, and Sinks." *Global Environmental Politics* 4(4): 54–75.

Gummer, John and Robert Moreland. 2006. "The European Union and Global Climate Change: A Review of Five National Programmes." Pew Center on Global Climate Change Report. June 2000. www.pewclimate.org/document.dfm?documentID=183 (accessed July 2, 2006).

Haigh, Nigel. 1996. "Climate Change Policies and Politics in the European Community." In *Politics of Climate Change: A European Perspective,* eds. Tim O'Riordan and Jill Jäger. London: Routledge, 155–85.

Hainsworth, Paul. 2006. "France Says No: The 29 May 2005 Referendum on the European Constitution." *Parliamentary Affairs* 59(1): 89–106.

Hamilton, Clive. 2001. *Running from the Storm: The Development of Climate Change Policy in Australia.* Sydney: University of New South Wales Press.

Hare, William. 2001. "Australia and Kyoto: In or Out?" *Forum: The University of New South Wales Law Journal* 24(2): 17–21.

Hart, Michael. 1990. *A North American Free Trade Agreement: The Strategic Implications for Canada.* Ottawa: Centre for Trade Policy and Law, Carleton University.

——Bill Dymond, and Colin Robertson. 1994. *Decision at Midnight: Inside the Canada-U.S. Free Trade Negotiations.* Vancouver: University of British Columbia Press.

Hatch, Michael T. 1986. *Politics and Nuclear Power: Energy Policy in Western Europe.* Lexington, KY: University Press of Kentucky.

——1995. "The Politics of Global Warming in Germany." *Environmental Politics* 4(3): 415–40.

Hayes, Graeme. 2002. *Environmental Protest and the State in France.* New York: Palgrave Macmillan.

Henehan, Marie T. 2000. *Foreign Policy and Congress: An International Relations Perspective.* Ann Arbor, MI: University of Michigan Press.

Henkin, Louis. 1995. "U.S. Ratification of Human Rights Conventions: The Ghost of Senator Bricker." *The American Journal of International Law* 89(2): 341–50.

Hermann, Margaret G. 1993. "Leaders and Foreign Policy Decision Making." In *Diplomacy, Force, and Leadership: Essays in Honor of Alexander L. George*, eds. Dan Caldwell and Timothy J. McKeown. Boulder, CO: Westview Press.

——Thomas Preston, Baghat Korany, and Timothy M. Shaw. 2001. "Who Leads Matters: The Effects of Powerful Individuals." *International Studies Review* 3(2): 83–132.

Heuser, Beatrice. 1998. *Nuclear Mentalities? Strategies and Beliefs in Britain, France, and the Federal Republic of Germany*. London: Macmillan.

Herzog, Dietrich. 1997. "Die Führungsgremien der Parteien: Funktionswandel und Strukturenwicklungen." In *Parteiendemokratie in Deutschland*, eds. Oscar W. Gabriel et al. Opladen: Westdeutscher Verlag, 301–22.

Hill, Robert. 2001. Speech Presented at the Equity and Global Climate Change Conference. Washington DC (April 17). www.pewclimate.org/events/hill.cfm (accessed March 8, 2007).

——2001. "International Climate Change Agreement: An Evolution." *Forum: The University of New South Wales Law Journal* 24(2).

Hopf, Ted. 1998. "The Promise of Constructivism in International Relations Theory." *International Security* 23(2): 171–200.

Hosli, Madeleine O. 1998. "The Formation of the European Economic and Monetary Union: Intergovernmental Negotiations and Two-Level Games." Paper Presented at the 39th Annual Convention of the International Studies Association. Minneapolis, MN (March 19).

Howarth, David J. 2001. *The French Road to European Monetary Union*. New York: Palgrave.

Huelshoff, Michel G., Andrei S. Markovits, and Simon Reich, eds. 1993. *From Bundesrepublik to Deutschland: German Politics After Unification*. Ann Arbor, MI: University of Michigan Press.

Hufbauer, Gary Clyde and Jeffrey J. Schott. 1993. *NAFTA: An Assessment*. Washington DC: Institute for International Economics.

Hug, Simon and Thomas Koenig. 2002. "In View of Ratification: Governmental Preferences and Domestic Constraints at the Amsterdam Intergovernmental Conference." *International Organization* 56(2): 447–76.

Hymans, Jacques E.C. 2006. *The Psychology of Nuclear Proliferation: Identity, Emotions, and Foreign Policy*. Cambridge: Cambridge University Press.

Jacobson, Harold K. 2002. "Climate Change, Unilateralism, Realism, and Two-Level Games." In *Multilateralism and U.S. Foreign Policy; Ambivalent Engagement*, eds. Shepard Forman and Stewart Patrick. Boulder, CO: Lynne Rienner, 424–36.

Jacobsson, Steffan and Volkmar Lauber. 1998. "Reaction of German Society and Politics to Social and Economic Crises Resulting from Conventional Energy Use Since the 1970s." *Energy Policy*. www.iff.ac.at/socec/backdoor/sose05-ring-sozoek/9_lauberLibDirReaktionderdtPolundGt.pdf (accessed July 12, 2006).

Jepperson, Ronald, Alexander Wendt, and Peter J. Katzenstein. 1996. "Norms, Identity and Culture in National Security." In *The Culture of National Security: Norms and Identity in World Politics*, ed., Peter J. Katzenstein. New York: Columbia University Press, 33–75.

Jesse, Neal G., Uk Heo, and Karl DeRouen, Jr. 2002. "A Nested Game Approach to Political and Economic Liberalization in Democratizing States: The Case of South Korea." *International Studies Quarterly* 46(3): 401–22.

Johnson, Jon R. 1994. *The North American Free Trade Agreement: A Comprehensive Guide*. Aurora, Ontario: Canada Law Book Co.

Johnson, Pierre Marc and Andre Beaulieu. 1996. *The Environment and NAFTA: Understanding and Implementing Continental Law*. Washington DC: Island Press.

Jones, Christopher D. 2001. "Rejection of the Comprehensive Nuclear Test Ban Treaty." In *Contemporary Cases in U.S. Foreign Policy Decisions: From Terrorism to Trade*, ed. Ralph G. Carter. Washington DC: Congressional Quarterly Press, 2002.

Jordan, Andrew. 1997. "Overcoming the Divide Between Comparative Politics and International Relations Approaches to the EC: What Role for 'Post-Decisional Politics'?" *West European Politics* 20(4): 43–70.

Kaltenthaler, Karl. 1998. *Germany and the Politics of Europe's Money*. Durham, NC: Duke University Press.

Kamp, Karl-Heinz. 1995. "Germany and the Future of Nuclear Weapons in Europe." *Security Dialogue* 26(3): 277–92.

Karp, Regina. 2005. "The New German Foreign Policy Consensus." *Washington Quarterly* 29(1): 61–82.

Keating, Paul. 2000. *Engagement: Australia Faces the Asia-Pacific*. Sydney: Pan Macmillan Australia.

Keck, Margaret and Kathryn Sikkink. 1998. *Activists Beyond Borders: Advocacy Networks in International Politics*. Ithaca, NY: Cornell University Press.

Keech, William R. and Kyoungsan Pak. 1995. "Partisanship, Institutions, and Change in American Trade Politics." *Journal of Politics* 57(4): 1130–42.

Kehoe, Timothy J. "Assessing the Economic Impact of North American Free Trade," in M. Delal Baer and Sidney Weintraub, eds., *The NAFTA Debate: Grappling with Unconventional Trade Issues* (Boulder, CO: Lynne Rienner, 1994), pp. 3–34.

Keller, John T.S. 1993. "Executive Power and Policy-Making Patterns in France: Gauging the Impact of Fifth Republic Institutions." *West European Politics* 16(4): 518–44.

—— and Martin A. Schain, eds. 1996. *Chirac's Challenge: Liberalization, Europeanization, and Malaise in France*. New York: St. Martin's Press.

—— —— 1996. "Presidents, Premiers, and Models of Democracy in France." In *Chirac's Challenge: Liberalization, Europeanization, and Malaise in France*, eds. John T.S. Keller and Martin A. Schain. New York: St. Martin's Press, 23–52.

Kennedy, Ellen. 1991. *The Bundesbank: Germany's Central Bank in the International Monetary System*. London: The Royal Institute of International Affairs.

Keraudren, Philippe and Nicolas Dubois. 1994. "France and the Ratification of the Maastricht Treaty." In *The Ratification of the Maastricht Treaty: Issues, Debates, and Future Implications*, eds. Finn Laursen and Sophie Vanhoonacker. Dordrecht: Martinus Nijhoff, 147–79.

Key, V.O. 1961. *Public Opinion and American Democracy*. New York: Alfred J. Knopf, Inc.

Koh, Harold. 1990. "The President Versus the Senate in Treaty Interpretation: What's All the Fuss About?" *Yale Journal of International Law* 15: 331–44.

Kohl, Helmut. 1992. *Stenographischer Bericht*. 2 December, Plenarprotokoll 12: 10824.

Kratochwil, Friedrich V. 1989. *Rules, Norms, and Decisions: On the Conditions of Practical and Legal Reasoning in International Relations and Domestic Affairs*. Cambridge: Cambridge University Press.

Krause, Joachim. 2001. "The Role of the Bundestag in German Foreign Policy." In *Germany's New Foreign Policy: Decision-Making in an Interdependent World*, eds. Wolf-Dieter Eberwein and Karl Kaiser. New York: Palgrave, 157–72.

Krepon, Michael and Dan Caldwell. 1991. *The Politics of Arms Control Treaty Ratification*. New York: St. Martin's Press.

Kriesler, Peter, ed. 1999. *The Australian Economy*, Third edition. St. Leonards, NSW: Allen & Unwin.

Küntzel, Mathias. 1995. *Bonn & the Bomb*. London: Pluto Press.

Labbé, Marie-Helene. 1996. "France." In *Nuclear Weapons After the Comprehensive Test Ban: Implications for Modernization and Proliferation*, ed. Eric Arnett. SIPRI: Oxford University Press, 31–40.

Lavoisier Group. 2001. Letter from Prime Minister John Howard to United States President George W. Bush. http://www.lavoisier.com.au/papers/articles/Howardletter.html (accessed July 4, 2007).

Levitt, Joseph. 1993. *Pearson and Canada's Role in Nuclear Disarmament and Arms Control Negotiations, 1945–1957*. Montreal: McGill-Queen's University Press.

Leonard, Elke. 1995. *Aus der Opposition an die Macht: Wie Rudolf Scharping Kanzler werden will*. Cologne: Bund Verlag.

Lijphart, Arend. 1971. "Comparative Politics and the Comparative Method." *American Political Science Review* 65(3): 682–93.

Lindberg, Leon N. and Stuart A. Scheingold. 1970. *Europe's Would-Be Polity: Patterns of Change in the European Community*. Englewood Cliffs, NJ: Prentice-Hall.

Lindsay, James. 1994. *Congress and the Politics of Foreign Policy*. Baltimore, MD: Johns Hopkins University Press.

Lipsey, Richard G. and Murray G. Smith. 1985. *Taking the Initiative: Canada's Trade Options in a Turbulent World*. Toronto: C.D. Howe Institute.

—— 1990. "Canada at the U.S.-Mexico Free Trade Dance: Wallflower or Partner?" *Commentary* 20. C.D. Howe Institute.

Malici, Akan. 2006. "Germans as Venutians: The Culture of German Foreign Policy Behavior." *Foreign Policy Analysis* 2(1): 37–62.

Mansfield, Edward D., Helen V. Milner, and B. Peter Rosendorff. 2002. "Why Democracies Cooperate More: Electoral Control and International Trade Agreements." *International Organization* 56(3): 477–513.

Martin, Lisa L. 2000. *Democratic Commitments: Legislatures and International Cooperation*. Princeton, NJ: Princeton University Press.

Mayer, Frederick W. 1992. "Managing Domestic Differences in International Negotiations: The Strategic Use of Internal Side-Payments." *International Organization* 46(4): 793–818.

——— 1998. *Interpreting NAFTA: The Science and Art of Political Analysis*. New York: Columbia University Press.

Mayhew, David R. 1991. *Divided We Govern: Party Control, Lawmaking, and Investigations, 1946–1990*. New Haven, CT: Yale University Press.

Mazzucelli, Colette. 1997. *France and Germany at Maastricht: Politics and Negotiations to Create the European Union*. New York: Garland Publishers.

McKibbin, Warwick J. and Peter J. Wilcoxen. 2002. *Climate Change Policy After Kyoto: Blueprint for a Realistic Approach*. Washington DC: Brookings Institution Press.

McLeay, Elizabeth and John Uhr. 2006. "The Australian and New Zealand Parliaments: Context, Response and Capacity." *Australian Journal of Political Science* 41(2): 257–72.

McLin, Jon B. 1967. *Canada's Changing Defense Policy, 1957–1963: The Problems of a Middle Power in Alliance*. Baltimore, MD: Johns Hopkins University Press.

Mendelsohn, Matthew and Robert Wolfe. 2001. "Probing the Aftermath of Seattle: Canadian Public Opinion on International Trade, 1980–2000." *International Journal* 66(2).

Michelmann, Hans J. and Panayotis Soldatos, eds. 1990. *Federalism and International Relations: The Role of Subnational Units*. Oxford: Clarendon Press.

Miller, J.D.B. 1974. "Australian Foreign Policy: Constraints and Opportunities." *International Affairs* 50(2): 229–41.

Milner, Helen V. 1993. "Maintaining International Commitments in Trade Policy." In *Do Institutions Matter? Government Capabilities in the United States and Abroad*, eds. R. Kent Weaver and Bert A. Rockman. Washington: Brookings Institution, 345–66.

——— 1997. *Interests, Institutions, and Information: Domestic Politics and International Relations*. Princeton, NJ: Princeton University Press.

——— and B. Peter Rosendorff. 1996. "Trade Negotiations, Information, and Domestic Politics: The Role of Domestic Groups." *Economics and Politics* 8(2): 145–89.

——— ——— 1997. "Democratic Politics and International Trade Negotiations: Elections and Divided Government as Constraints on Trade Liberalization." *Journal of Conflict Resolution* 41(1): 117–46.

Minchin, Nick. 2001. "Responding to Climate Change: Providing a Policy Framework for a Competitive Australia." *Forum: The University of New South Wales Law Journal* 2(2): 13–16.

Mogami, Toshiki. 1988. "The South Pacific Nuclear Free Zone: A Fettered Leap Forward." *Journal of Peace Research* 24(4): 411–30.

Moravcsik, Andrew. 1993. "Introduction: Integrating International and Domestic Theories of International Bargaining." In *Double Edged Diplomacy: International Bargaining and Domestic Politics*, eds. Peter B. Evans, Harold K. Jacobson, and Robert D. Putnam. Berkeley, CA: University of California Press, 3–42.

Mueller, Edda. 1990. "Umweltreperatur oder Umweltvorsorge? Bewaeltigung von Querschnittsaufgaben der Verwaltung am Beispiel des Umweltschutzes." *Zeitschift für Beamtenrecht* 38: 165–74.

Mueller, Harald, Alexander Kelle, Katja Frank, Sylvia Meier, and Annette Schaper. 1997. "The German Debate on Nuclear Weapons and Disarmament." *The Washington Quarterly* 20(3): 115–22.

Neustadt, Richard. 1990. *Presidential Power and the Modern Presidents*. New York: Free Press.

Newspoll Market Research. 2001. "Greenhouse Gas." Kyoto Protocol Study Prepared for Greenpeace Australia Pacific (6–8 April). www.geocities.com/jimgreen3/greenouse2.html (accessed March 11, 2007).

Niedermayer, Oskar and Richard Stoess, eds. 1993. *Stand und Perspektiven der Parteienforschung in Deutschland*. Opladen: Westdeutscher Verlag.

Nincic, Miroslav and Barbara Hinckley. 1991. "Foreign Policy and the Evaluation of Presidential Candidates." *Journal of Conflict Resolution* 35(1): 333–55.

Nossal, Kim Richard. 1997. *The Politics of Canadian Foreign Policy*, Third edition. Scarborough, Ontario: Prentice Hall Canada.

Oberthuer, Sebastian and Hermann E. Ott. 1999. *The Kyoto Protocol*. New York: Springer Verlag.

O'Brien, David M. 2003. "Presidential and Congressional Relations in Foreign Affairs: The Treaty-Making Power and the Rise of Executive Agreements." In *Congress and the Politics of Foreign Policy*, ed. Colton C. Campbell. Upper Saddle River, NJ: Prentice Hall, 70–89.

O'Connell, D.P. 1965. "The Evolution of Australia's International Personality." In *International Law in Australia*, ed. D.P. O'Connell. Sydney: Law Book Co, 1–33.

O'Halloran, Sharyn. 1994. *Politics, Process, and American Trade Policy*. Ann Arbor, MI: University of Michigan Press.

Opeskin, Brian and Donald Rothwell. 1997. *International Law and Australian Federalism*. Sydney: University of New South Wales Press.

Pahre, Robert and Paul A. Papayoanou. 1997. "Using Game Theory to Link Domestic and International Politics." *Journal of Conflict Resolution* 41(1): 4–11.

Palmer, Diego Ruiz. 1991. "French Strategic Options in the 1990s." Adelphi Paper 260. London: International Institute for Strategic Studies.

Papadakis, E. 2002. "Global Environmental Diplomacy: Australia's Stances on Global Warming." *Australian Journal of International Affairs* 56(2): 265–77.

Pernice, Ingolf. 2001. "The Role of National Parliaments in the European Union." Walter Hallstein-Institut für Europaisches Verfassungsrecht. Humbolt-Universtaet zu Berlin.WHI Paper 5/01 (July).

Peterson, Paul E., ed. 1994. *The President, the Congress, and the Making of Foreign Policy*. Norman, OK: University of Oklahoma Press, 1994.

Pielow, Johann-Christian. 2001. "Germany: Political Incentives Concerning the Implementation of the Kyoto Protocol." In *Kyoto: From Principles to Practice*, eds. Peter D. Cameron and Donald Zillman. The Hague: Kluwer Law International, 73–85.

Putnam, Robert D. 1988. "Diplomacy and Domestic Politics: The Logic of Two-Level Games." *International Organization* 42(3): 427–60.

—— and Nicholas Bayne. 1987. *Hanging Together.* Cambridge, MA: Harvard University Press.

Raunio, Tapio and Simon Hix. 2001. "Backbenchers Learn to Fight Back: European Integration and Parliamentary Government." *West European Politics* 23(2): 142–68.

Raustiala, Kal. 1997. "Domestic Institutions and International Regulatory Cooperation: Comparative Responses to the Convention on Biological Diversity." *World Politics* 49(4): 482–509.

—— and Anne-Marie Slaughter. 2002. "International Law, International Relations, and Compliance." In *Handbook of International Relations*, eds. Walter Carlsnaes, Thomas Risse, and Beth A. Simmons. Princeton, NJ: Princeton University Press.

Ravenhill, John. 1990. "Australia." In *Federalism and International Relations*, eds. Hans J. Michelmann and Panayotis Soldatos. Oxford: Clarendon Press, 76–123.

Reif, Linda C. 1998. "Environment Policy: The Rio Summit Five Years Later." In *Canada Among Nations 1998: Leadership and Dialogue*, eds. Fen Osler Hampson and Maureen Appel Molot. Toronto: Oxford University Press, 267–85.

"Report to the President, the Congress, and the United States Trade Representative on the U.S.-Australian Free Trade Agreement." 2004. Report by the Advisory Committee for Trade Policy and Negotiations (ACTPN) on the US-Australia Free Trade Agreement (March 12).

Reus-Smit, Christian. 2004. *The Politics of International Law.* Cambridge: Cambridge University Press.

Reynolds, Wayne. 1997. "Menzies and the Proposal for Atomic Weapons." In *Menzies in War and Peace*, ed. Frank Cain. St. Leonards, NSW: Allen & Unwin, 116–37.

—— 1998. "Rethinking the Joint Project: Australia's Bid for Nuclear Weapons 1945–1960." *Historical Journal* 41(3): 853–73.

Rhodes, Richard. 1986. *The Making of the Atomic Bomb.* New York: Simon & Schuster.

Riker, William H. 1962. *The Theory of Political Coalitions.* New Haven, CT: Yale University Press.

Risse-Kappen, Thomas. 1994. "Ideas Do Not Float Freely: Transnational Coalitions, Domestic Structures and the End of the Cold War." *International Organization* 48(2): 185–214.

—— 1996. "Exploring the Nature of the Beast: International Relations Theory and Comparative Policy Analysis Meet the European Union." *Journal of Common Market Studies* 34(1): 53–80.

Roy Morgan International. 2004. "Senate Should Pass Free Trade Agreement But Australia Divided." Finding #3756 (July 7). www.roymorgan.com/news/polls/2004/3756 (accessed May 3, 2007).

Rugman, Alan M. 1994. "North American Economic Integration and Canadian Sovereignty." In *The NAFTA Debate: Grappling with Unconventional Trade Issues*, eds. M. Delal Baer and Sidney Weintraub. Boulder, CO: Lynne Rienner Publishers, 97–116.

Saad, Lydia. 2002. "Poll Analyses—Americans Sharply Divided on Seriousness of Global Warming—Only one-third consider the problem grave." Gallup News Service (March 25). www.gallup.com/poll/releases/pr020419.asp (accessed September 3, 2002).

Sandholtz, Wayne. 1993. "Choosing Union: Monetary Politics and Maastricht." *International Organization* 47(1): 1–39.

Schreurs, Miranda A. and Elizabeth Economy. 1997. *The Internationalization of Environmental Protection*. Cambridge: Cambridge University Press.

Schubert, K. 1991. "France." In *Security With Nuclear Weapons: Different Perspectives on National Security*, ed. Regina Cowen Karp. Oxford: Oxford University Press, 162–88.

Schwartz, Stephen I. 2000. "Outmaneuvered, Outgunned, and Out of View." *The Bulletin of Atomic Scientists* 56(7): 41–9.

Schweib, Egon. 1964. "The Nuclear Test Ban Treaty and International Law." *The American Journal of International Law* 58(3): 642–70.

Seaborg, Glenn T. 1987. *Stemming the Tide*. Lexington, MA: Lexington Press.

Serre, Françoise de la and Christian Lequesne. 1993. "France and the European Union." In *The State of the European Community: The Maastricht Debates and Beyond*, eds. Alan W. Cafruny and Glenda G. Rosenthal. New York: Longman, 148–58.

Sherman, Richard. 2002. "Delegation, Ratification, and U.S. Trade Policy: Why Divided Government Causes Lower Tariffs." *Comparative Political Studies* 35(10): 1171–97.

Sigler, John H. and Dennis Goresky. 1974. "Public Opinion on United States-Canadian Relations." *International Organization* 28(4): 637–68.

Simmons, Beth A. and Daniel J. Hopkins. 2005. "The Constraining Power of International Treaties: Theory and Methods." *American Political Science Review* 99(4): 623–31.

Simpson, Erika. 2001. *NATO and the Bomb: Canadian Defenders Confront Critics*. Montreal: McGill-Queen's University Press.

Simpson, Jeffrey. 2001. *The Friendly Dictatorship*. Toronto: McClelland and Stewart, Ltd.

Siwert-Probst, Judith. 2001. "Traditional Institutions of Foreign Policy." In *Germany's New Foreign Policy: Decision-Making in an Interdependent World*, eds. Wolf-Dieter Eberwein and Karl Kaiser. New York: Palgrave, 19–37.

Smith, Dennis. 1988. *Diplomacy of Fear: Canada and the Cold War, 1941–1948*. Toronto: University of Toronto Press.

"Snowe Opposes Trade Agreement." Press Herald Online. http://snowe.senate.gov/articles/art062404_1.htm (accessed June 24, 2004).

Sokolsky, Joel J. 1989. "A Seat at the Table: Canada and its Alliances." In *Canadian Defense Policy: Challenges and Continuities*, Special Issue of *Armed Forces and Society* 16(1): 11–36.

Sperling, James. 1994. "German Foreign Policy after Unification: The End of Cheque Book Diplomacy?" *West European Politics* 17(1): 73–97.

Sprinz, Detlef and Tapani Vaahtoranta. 1994. "The Interest-Based Explanation of International Environmental Policy." *International Organization* 48(1): 77–106.

Stein, Eric. 1972. "Legal Restraints in Modern Arms Control Agreements." *The American Journal of International Law* 66(6): 255–89.

Stoler, Andrew L. 2003. "Australia-US Free Trade: Benefits and Costs of an Agreement." Paper Presented at the Conference on Free Trade Agreements and U.S. Trade Policy. Washington DC: Institute for International Economics (May 7).

Suter, Keith. 1995. "Paradise Lost." *Bulletin of the Atomic Scientists* 61(2): 13–14.

Taplin, Ross. 1994. "Greenhouse: An Overview of Policy and Practice." *Australian Journal of Environmental Management* 1(3): 142–55.

Trimble, Phillip and Alexander Koff. 1998. "All Fall Down: The Treaty Power in the Clinton Administration." *Berkeley Journal of International Law* 16(1): 55–70.

Trone, John. 2001. *Federal Constitutions and International Relations*. St. Lucia, Queensland: University of Queensland Press.

Tsebelis, George. 1990. *Nested Games: Rational Choice in Comparative Politics*. Berkeley, CA: University of California Press.

Twomey, Ann. 1997. "International Law and the Executive." In *International Law and Australian Federalism*, eds. Brian Opeskin and Don Rothwell. Melbourne: University of Melbourne Press, 69–76.

Uhr, John. 2006. "Bicameralism." In *The Oxford Handbook of Political Institutions*, eds. Rod A.W. Rhodes, Sarah A. Binder, and Bert A. Rockman. Oxford: Oxford University Press, 474–94.

Uleri, Pier Vincenzo and Michael Gallagher. 1996. *The Referendum Experience in Europe*. New York: St. Martin's Press.

Underdal, Arild. 1997. "Modeling the International Climate Change Negotiations: A Non-Technical Outline of Model Architecture." *CICERO Working Paper* 8.

——and Kenneth Hanf, eds. 2000. *International Environmental Agreements and Domestic Politics: The Case of Acid Rain*. Aldershot, UK: Ashgate Publishers.

United States Wheat Associates. 2004. "News & Policy: Wheat Letter" (February 19). www.uswheat.org/wheatLetter/doc/0C4D6AE43A107D1F852 (accessed March 8, 2007).

Valverde, Miguel. 1998. "Domestic Politics and the Formulation of Foreign Economic Policy: Negotiating NAFTA." Paper presented at the 39th Annual Meeting of the International Studies Association (March 20).

Vogler, John. 1999. "The European Union as an Actor in International Environmental Politics." *Environmental Politics* 8(3): 24–48.

Walker, William. 1998. "International Nuclear Relations After the Indian and Pakistani Test Explosions." *International Affairs* 74(3): 505–28.

Wallace, William. 2005. "European Union: A Treaty Too Far." *The World Today* (July).

Walsh, Jim. 1997. "Surprise Down Under: The Secret History of Australia's Nuclear Ambitions." *The Nonproliferation Review* 5(3): 1–20.

Waltz, Kenneth N. 1979. *Theory of International Politics*. Reading, MA: Addison-Wesley.

Warwick, Paul V. and James N. Druckman. 2001. "Portfolio Salience and the Proportionality of Payoffs in Coalition Governments." *British Journal of Political Science* 31(4): 627–49.

Waters, Sarah. 1998. "New Social Movements in France: The Rise of Civic Forms of Mobilisation." *West European Politics* 21(3): 170–86.

Waverman, Leonard. 1993. "The NAFTA Agreement: A Canadian Perspective." In *Assessing NAFTA: A Trinational Analysis*, eds. Steven Globerman and Michael Walker. Vancouver: British Columbia, Canada: The Fraser Institute, 32–59.

Weaver, R. Kent and Bert A. Rockman. 1993. "Assessing the Effects of Institutions," In *Do Institutions Matter? Government Capabilities in the United States and Abroad*, eds. R. Kent Weaver and Bert A. Rockman. Washington DC: Brookings Institution, 1–41.

———— 1993. "When and How Do Institutions Matter?" In *Do Institutions Matter? Government Capabilities in the United States and Abroad*, eds. R. Kent Weaver and Bert A. Rockman. Washington DC: Brookings Institution, 439–54.

Weidner, Helmut. 1989. "Die Umweltpolitiker konservativ-liberalen Regierung." *Aus Politik und Zeitgeschichte* (November 17): 16–28.

Weintraub, Sidney. 1993. "The North American Free Trade Agreement as Negotiated: A U.S. Perspective." In *Assessing NAFTA: A Trinational Analysis*, eds. Steven Globerman and Michael Walker. Vancouver: British Columbia, Canada: The Fraser Institute, 1–31.

Weiss, Linda, Elizabeth Thurbon, and John Mathews. 2004. *How to Kill a Country—Australia's Devastating Trade Deal with the United States*. Sydney: Allen & Unwin.

Wendt, Alexander. 1992. "Anarchy Is What States Make of It: The Social Construction of Power Politics." *International Organization* 46(2): 391–425.

———— 1994. "Collective Identity Formation and the International State System." *American Political Science Review* 88(2): 384–96.

Wilcox, Francis O. 1935. *The Ratification of International Conventions: A Study of the Relationship of the Ratification Process to the Development of International Legislation*. London: Allen & Unwin.

Wilkinson, David. 1992. "Maastricht and the Environment: The Implications for the EC's Environmental Policy of the Treaty on European Union." *Journal of Environmental Law* 4(2): 221–39.

Wittkopf, Eugene R. and James M. McCormick. 1998. "Congress, the President, and the End of the Cold War." *Journal of Conflict Resolution* 42(4): 440–66.

Wolff, Patricia M. 1996. Uncovering Determinants of International Environmental Cooperation: The Disjuncture Between Treaty Signing and Treaty Ratification. Master's Thesis. University of Oregon.

Wright, Vincent. 1989. *The Government and Politics of France*. New York: Holmes & Meier.

Yost, David S. 1994. "Nuclear Debates in France." *Survival* 36(4): 113–39.

Young, Oran. 1989. *International Cooperation: Building Regimes for Natural Resources and the Environment*. Ithaca, NY: Cornell University Press.

Zierler, Matthew. 2003. "Failing to Commit: The Politics of Treaty Nonratification." Ph.D. Dissertation. Madison, WI: The University of Wisconsin-Madison (unpublished).

Periodicals and Newswires

Agence France Presse
Australian Associated Press Newsfeed
Australian Financial Review
Boston Globe
British Broadcasting Corporation Monitoring
Bulletin of European Community
Calgary Herald
Canadian Press Newswire
Canberra Times
Channel News Asia
Christian Science Monitor
Congress Daily
Congressional Record
Daily Telegraph
Daily Telegraph (Australia)
Der Spiegel
Deutsche Presse Agentur
Deutschland Nachrichten
Die Welt
Dow Jones Newswire
Economist
Europe Energy
Europe Report
Financial Times
Focus
Frankfurter Allgemeine Zeitung
International Environment Reporter
International Herald Tribune
Issue Brief
La Tribune
Liberation
Los Angeles Times
Maclean's
Milwaukee Journal Sentinel
National Post
New York Times

Nuclear Proliferation News
Omaha World Herald
Power Economics
Quarterly Bulletin
San Diego Union-Tribune
St. Louis Post-Dispatch
Süddeutsche Zeitung
Sydney Morning Herald
Tasmanian Country Newswire
The Age
The Australian
The Guardian
The Independent
Times of London
Toronto Star
United Nations Press Release
Wall Street Journal
Washington Tariff and Trade Letter
Washington Times
Washington Post
Xinhua News Agency

Index

Ingram Content Group UK Ltd.
Milton Keynes UK
UKHW021020190623
423418UK00032B/237